The Bible and Mental Health

The Bible and Mental Health

Christopher C. H. Cook
and Isabelle Hamley

scm press

© The Editors and Contributors 2020

Published in 2020 by SCM Press
Editorial office
3rd Floor, Invicta House,
108–114 Golden Lane,
London EC1Y 0TG, UK
www.scmpress.co.uk

SCM Press is an imprint of Hymns Ancient & Modern Ltd
(a registered charity)

Hymns Ancient & Modern® is a registered trademark of
Hymns Ancient & Modern Ltd
13A Hellesdon Park Road, Norwich,
Norfolk NR6 5DR, UK

British Library Cataloguing in Publication data

A catalogue record for this book is available
from the British Library

978-0-334-05977-6

Typeset by Regent Typesetting
Printed and bound by
CPI Group (UK) Ltd

Contents

Author Biographies

Stephen C. Barton is an ordained theologian with a specialism in New Testament Studies. He was Tutor in Biblical Studies at Salisbury and Wells Theological College (1984–88), and Reader in New Testament in the Department of Theology and Religion, Durham University (1988–2010). Currently, he is an Honorary Research Fellow of Durham and Manchester Universities. His publications include *The Spirituality of the Gospels* (SPCK, 1992), *Discipleship and Family Ties in Mark and Matthew* (Cambridge University Press, 1994), *Invitation to the Bible* (SPCK, 1997), and *Life Together. Family, Sexuality and Community in the New Testament and Today* (T&T Clark, 2001).

Walter Brueggemann is William Marcellus McPheeters Professor Emeritus of Old Testament at Columbia Theological Seminary. He is a past president of the Society of Biblical Literature and an ordained minister in the United Church of Christ. He has recently published *Materiality as Resistance* (Westminster John Knox Press, 2020), *Money and Possessions* (Westminster John Knox Press, 2016), and *Gift and Task* (Westminster John Knox Press, 2017).

Jocelyn Bryan was until recently Academic Dean and Director of the Doctorate in Theology and Ministry Programme at Cranmer Hall, St John's College, Durham, where she teaches Pastoral and Practical Theology and Psychology and Christian Ministry. Her PhD is in psychology and she researches the interdisciplinary field of psychology, theology and ministry. Jocelyn has written *Human Being: Insights from Psychology and the Christian Faith* (SCM Press, 2016) and co-edited *Pastoral Challenges and Concerns* (Kevin Mayhew, 2018). She has also published on sexuality and reflections on pastoral issues and liturgies. She is editor of the online journal *Theology and Ministry*.

Joanna Collicutt is Karl Jaspers Lecturer in Psychology and Spirituality at Ripon College Cuddesdon and also teaches psychology of religion at Oxford University, where she is a supernumerary fellow of Harris Manchester College. She practised for many years as a clinical psychologist, initially working in the area of adult mental health before moving into neurological rehabilitation, and has had a longstanding interest in anxiety states and psychosis. After a period of studying theology, she was director of the MA programme in Psychology of Religion at Heythrop College, University of London for five years, and now works on the interface between psychology and faith, especially in the areas of biblical studies, liturgy and spirituality, on which she has published extensively.

Christopher Cook is Professor of Spirituality, Theology and Health, and Director of the Centre for Spirituality, Theology and Health, at Durham University. He is a Fellow of the Royal College of Psychiatrists, with research doctorates in medicine and theology. Ordained priest in 2001, he is an Honorary Chaplain for Tees, Esk & Wear Valleys NHS Foundation Trust. His books include *Spirituality, Theology and Mental Health* (SCM Press, 2013), *Spirituality and Narrative in Psychiatric Practice: Stories of Mind and Soul* (ed. with Andrew Powell and Andrew Sims, Royal College of Psychiatrists, 2016), *Hearing Voices, Demonic and Divine* (Routledge, 2018), and *Christians Hearing Voices* (Jessica Kingsley, 2020).

David Firth is Tutor in Old Testament at Trinity College, Bristol, and Research Associate of the University of the Free State. A Baptist minister, he and his wife have also served in Australia, Zimbabwe and South Africa. He is particularly interested in how the Old Testament contributes to our understanding of mission and ethics.

Jill Firth is a lecturer in Hebrew and Old Testament at Ridley College in Melbourne, Australia. She has ministered as a pastoral worker in rural and urban Australia, and cross-culturally in Groote Eylandt and Hong Kong. Jill is an Anglican priest and trained spiritual director and has been a canon of St Paul's Cathedral, Melbourne. She holds a PhD from the Australian College of Theology, and is preparing to publish her dissertation on Psalms 140 to 143. She is writing a commentary on Jeremiah.

Paula Gooder is a speaker and writer on the Bible, particularly the New Testament. She spent 12 years teaching in ministerial formation. Following this, she spent eight years as a speaker and writer on biblical studies, travelling the country seeking to communicate the best of biblical scholarship in as accessible a way as possible. She then worked for the Bible Society as Theologian in Residence and for the Birmingham Diocese as Director of Mission Learning and Development. Now she is Chancellor of St Paul's Cathedral in London. She is the author of many books, most recently *Phoebe: A Story* (Hodder & Stoughton, 2018).

Isabelle Hamley is chaplain to the Archbishop of Canterbury. She was a probation officer prior to ordination, and subsequently a parish priest in Edwalton. She taught Old Testament at St John's College, Nottingham. She is a prebendary of St Paul's Cathedral, and Visiting Research Fellow at King's College, London. She is a regular contributor on Radio 4's *Thought for the Day* and *Daily Service*. Her publications include *Unspeakable Things Unspoken: Otherness and Victimisation in Judges 19–21* (Pickwick Publications, 2019). Her research interests centre on questions of identity, otherness and violence in the Hebrew Bible.

Nick Ladd has been an Anglican minister for 37 years, during which time he has served in six parishes of very different social make-ups. For eight years he was Director of Ministry, Formation and Practical Theology at St John's College, Nottingham and has also spent time overseeing the training and support of curates for the Birmingham diocese. At present, he serves with his wife in a parish in Birmingham and works freelance, supporting churches in their missional development, teaching, researching, and offering spiritual accompaniment to clergy. He is completing a doctorate on Christian community formation and maturity.

Gordon McConville is Professor of Old Testament Theology at the University of Gloucestershire. Originally from Northern Ireland, he studied Modern Languages at Cambridge University, before moving to New College, Edinburgh for Theology, and finally to Queen's University, Belfast for doctoral study in the Old Testament, under Professor Gordon Wenham. He has taught at Trinity College, Bristol and Wycliffe Hall, Oxford, and has recently returned to Trinity as an adjunct faculty member. He has published numerous books and articles on aspects of the Old Testament, and is especially interested in its use in Christian theology and contemporary application.

John Swinton is Professor in Practical Theology and Pastoral Care and Chair in Divinity and Religious Studies at the University of Aberdeen. He has published widely within the area of mental health, dementia, disability theology and spirituality and healthcare. John is the author of a number of monographs including *Spirituality and Mental Health: Rediscovering a 'forgotten' dimension* (Jessica Kingsley, 2001) and *Finding Jesus in the Storm: The Spiritual Lives of Christians with Mental Health Challenges* (Eerdmans, 2020). In 2016 his book *Dementia: Living in the Memories* *of God* (SCM Press, 2016) won the Archbishop of Canterbury's Ramsey Prize for excellence in theological writing.

Megan Warner is Tutor in Old Testament at Northern College, Manchester. She is a Reader in the Church of England, a regular guest speaker at synods, festivals and other church gatherings around the UK and internationally and author and editor of several books, most recently *Re-Imagining Abraham: A Re-Assessment of the Influence of Deuteronomism in Genesis* (Brill, 2018), *Confronting Religious Violence: A Counter-Narrative* (with Richard A. Burridge and Jonathan Sacks; Baylor, 2018), *Tragedies and Christian Congregations: The Practical Theology of Trauma* (Routledge, 2020) and *Joseph: A Story of Resilience* (SPCK, 2020).

Nathan White is Associate Dean of the Graduate School for Army Chaplain Professional Development at Fort Jackson, South Carolina, the Executive Director of the Institute for Faith and Resilience, and a US Army Reserve Chaplain. He holds a PhD in theology from Durham University, UK. His research interests are in theological and scientific understandings of resilience and in theological ethics. His most recent work is *Biblical and Theological Visions of Resilience: Pastoral and Clinical Insights* (co-edited with Christopher C. H. Cook, Routledge, 2020). He has served in various forms of pastoral ministry around the world for 13 years.

Foreword by the Archbishop of Canterbury

The Church has not always been good either at talking about mental health or supporting those with mental health challenges, and yet when we turn to Scripture we find it awash with the entire range of human experience – yes, there is joy and succour in the great power of God, but there is also profound sorrow and depression. The reality of the suffering and pain that human beings experience is not avoided in Scripture, nor is it glossed over. It is accepted as a fact of life and a part of living as a human being.

Christians are not exempt from mental health issues. I have been open about my own struggles, and while I have received huge comfort from Scripture and the faith community, I am equally indebted to the mental health professionals with whom I have worked.

People who face mental health challenges do so in every aspect of their lives: in their faith, which often underpins the rest of their worldview, their work, their families and their identity. It has been the case in the past that the worlds of faith and mental health have often been polarized. The guilt that some in Christian communities have been made to feel when it is falsely assumed that mental health issues are a result of sin, and the erroneous belief that failure to be 'cured' means that one is somehow lacking in faith, have meant that many in the Church have suffered an extra and heavy burden unnecessarily.

And yet mental health and faith have much in common. As the editors identify, both address the question of what it means to live well and flourish in a world of suffering. Both explore questions of healing, values and personal value, purpose and relationship. The issue of mental health is one that requires a holistic approach on an individual basis, incorporating as appropriate psychiatric, medical and religious support. The pastoral and spiritual care of the Church cannot replace the expertise offered by mental health professionals, but the great gifts offered by spiritual and pastoral guidance shouldn't be underestimated as we seek to treat the whole person. Both are deeply valuable and should be complementary.

To that end, in 2019 we hosted a Mental Health Conference at Lambeth Palace, a marker on the journey to understand how Christians and churches can work alongside mental health professionals to support those with mental health issues appropriately and lovingly, as well as nurture hospitable communities where all are welcome and where speaking of mental health is a normal part of life together. This book is an example of the increasing collaboration in the relatively new but ever-expanding field of mental health and faith, where we have found that both have helped us have a deeper and richer understanding of our own tradition and expertise.

This book, to which many talented individuals have contributed, has both a theological and academic value while also offering deeply practical applications. I am delighted to be able to commend it both to church leaders and mental health practitioners who desire a greater understanding of their patients and how they might integrate their faith practically.

Scripture used carelessly, in any sense but most definitely in the context of mental health, can be and has been an opportunity to cause a tremendous amount of damage. As this book teases out the complexity and contextuality of Scripture, it offers a call that is for the whole Church. It is an opportunity to consider how Scripture can be used as a balm and an aide, for healing and understanding for those in times of distress and confusion.

Scripture acknowledges that we live in an imperfect world, rife with suffering and sorrow. But it sets our difficulties within the context of a God who offers love and acceptance (even when it doesn't feel that way). Its correct and wise use can offer those in the Church, as well as mental health practitioners, a resource with which to illustrate, question and discuss mental health and what it is to live a 'well' life.

I am deeply grateful to all those who have contributed to this book, and not least to the editors, the Reverend Prebendary Dr Isabelle Hamley and the Reverend Professor Chris Cook. I hope that it will spark dialogue, from discussions about mental health from the pulpit, conversations between fellow Christians, and between the worlds of faith and mental health care. My prayer is to see the Church as the frontline of places where those with mental health issues are welcomed, supported and loved, where communities are transformed and living in resurrection life, and where church leaders work with mental health professionals to help people to flourish and experience life in all its fullness. It is, as the editors identify, just a beginning, but it is an invitation to difficult conversations and complex questions, ones that will call us into relationship with different disciplines and different people, but that ultimately call us into a deeper relationship with God.

+ Justin Cantuar

Introduction

ISABELLE HAMLEY

CHRISTOPHER C. H. COOK

Life as a parish priest often found one of us (Isabelle Hamley) holding a cup of tea in one hand, and a Bible in the other – literally and metaphorically. In a myriad situations and encounters, I was trying to mediate between what Christians believe, or say they believe, and the bewilderment and complexity of daily life. At the bedside of the dying, in a secondary school following a student suicide, in the vicarage with a distressed parishioner, in church listening to the confession of someone struggling with a sex addiction, at two in the morning woken up by a member of our congregation with a severe personality disorder sobbing her heart out, in a café hosting a group for carers of those with dementia ...

Life as a psychiatrist found the other one of us (Christopher Cook) for many years unable to bring a Bible into the consulting room in which people of all faiths and none shared their struggles with mental health issues. At the same time, requests (usually outside of the professional context) for help from a Christian psychiatrist would present similar expectations of an ability to mediate between the complexities of daily struggles with mental ill health and a biblical worldview underlying Christian faith. The trauma of sexual abuse, compounded by unrealistic expectations of others to forgive; the suicidal despair of depressive disorder; the sense of failure in struggling with relapses to addictive behaviour; the bewilderment of demonic voices ...

Challenges with mental health weave in and out of every situation of life and, naturally, with every aspect of church life and Christian witness. Challenges to Christian faith similarly weave themselves in and out of mental health care. One might expect that faith would be a comforting element of life: providing meaning and comfort, and the assurance of a wider frame of reference for our experiences. And often that is true. Most Christians do turn to God when challenged by their own mental ill health, or that of their loved one. Yet, together with this natural turn towards God, there is also often a degree of puzzlement: Why do I feel this way? Can God take it away? *Should* Christians feel this way, or is it a sign of lack of faith or gratitude? Or even – is there anything that Christianity can possibly have to say about mental health? It is easy to polarize between a fusion of the two worlds (faith and health), as if to have faith should produce an automatic expression of happiness or, on the other hand, a complete dichotomy between the world of faith and that of emotions, as if Christianity had nothing much to say about mental health, or God was powerless or uninterested.

Different compartments of life

In many ways, this is not particularly surprising. We do not talk about mental health from the pulpit very often; nor do Lent courses or house-groups frequently focus on the topic. Mental health is often a topic that belongs almost exclusively to the realm of pastoral conversations. This lack of public focus, however, is surprising: the Bible itself has a great deal to say about emotions, and about the challenges and complexities of life in the world. Indeed, if we take the Psalter as an example of the public liturgy of a community of faith, we find that, alongside joy, praise and thanksgiving, a very large proportion of the psalms express extreme negative emotions: sorrow, grief, anger, the desire for revenge, doubt, dark and persistent negative feelings, even the desire for life to end. Yet if we look at the corpus of our public worship, whether it is liturgy or songs, we find mostly praise and thanksgiving, together with affirmations of faith. We seem to have lost our ability to acknowledge collectively the realities of our lives. And yet the Scriptures that undergird our liturgies, our songs, our preaching, teaching and faith as a whole are full to the brim of real life, with its ups and downs, its challenges, and with a vision of what healthy human communities may be, in ways always ready to surprise us. Whether we turn to the dark, pervading meaninglessness of Ecclesiastes, or we read of the struggles of people traumatized by exile and displacement, or the long struggle the Apostle Paul had with a 'thorn in his flesh', these texts are an invitation to conversation. In individual reading, in pastoral contexts, and in public worship, they can open up a space for honesty and exploration, and shape the life of a community of faith in such a way that to talk about mental health challenges is not stigmatized, or unusual, but simply part and parcel of the life of faith.

Conversely, within wider society questions of mental health are often considered to be primarily medical questions, and faith can be seen as irrelevant, or with suspicion, or even at times as a contributing factor. Questions of health and questions of spirituality are seen as belonging to two fundamentally different domains, whose underlying discourses and frames of reference differ markedly. As a result, it can become difficult for the two domains to interact, yielding a less than holistic approach to pastoral and medical care.

The compartmentalization of care between spiritual and mental (biopsychosocial) domains in clinical practice might seem very sensible. Patients talk to mental health professionals about medical things, and parishioners – or, simply, people in general – talk to clergy or chaplains about spiritual things (it is worth noting that at the outset, the very conceptualization of people into specific relational categories, patients vs parishioners, for instance, shapes subsequent discourse and categories of thought). However, those with mental health problems have often found this compartmentalization problematic. Faith easily gets labelled as a part of the illness by clinicians. Clergy do not always understand how mental disorders impact upon faith. It has also proven deeply problematic for research, because it is methodologically impossible to distinguish between the variables that are used by scientists to measure spirituality and those that are used to measure mental health.

For example, we might argue that spirituality is concerned with meaning and purpose in life. This may well be true, but in practice people who are depressed become negative about every aspect of life, including meaning and purpose. We therefore cannot separate out 'spirituality', as measured by meaning and purpose, and examine the influence of this upon depression. Similarly, inner peace, experiences of relationship with God, flourishing, and hope, all arguably very spiritual concerns, are directly dependent upon mental health. It is difficult to find meaning and purpose, peace or hope in the midst of a depressive disorder.

Mental well-being

A more recent phenomenon complicates the picture even further. Beyond medical discourse on mental (ill) health there is now an increasing movement of talk of well-being and flourishing, which connects with both medical models (by proactively seeking to foster positive health) and spiritual concerns (by painting a picture of what well-being and flourishing may look like or should be aspired to). Conversation about 'mental health' sometimes means conversation about mental *ill* health. At other times it means conversation about the normal emotional ups and downs of all human life. In yet other contexts it becomes a conversation about the *good* life. Should Christians, for example, expect a life lived well to be free from anxiety or depression?

Mental ill health, directly or indirectly, affects all of us. One in five people worldwide experience one of the more common mental disorders at some point in their lifetime; somewhere between 1 and 7 per cent of adults experience a major mental disorder; and half of all mental illnesses begin before the age of 14.[1] One-third of years lived with disability worldwide are due to mental illness,[2] making mental ill health by far the leading cause of disability. If we are fortunate enough not to experience mental illness ourselves, we all have friends, family and colleagues who do. Of course, people do not always seek help and do not always feel able to talk about such things even (or perhaps especially) within church or family. This difficulty with talking about the subject, combined with poor public knowledge about mental health issues and the significant stigma and prejudice with which they are associated, only adds to the suffering experienced by Christians and others struggling to make sense of what is happening to them and to those they love. The compartmentalization of medical and spiritual perspectives referred to above further complicates the problem. Where can the conversation be had that will enable Christians to make biblical sense of the challenges of mental ill health? And how can contemporary medical and scientific accounts of mental health illuminate (or obscure) our understanding of the faith passed down by Christian tradition?

The Bible and mental health

This book is an attempt to bring together these different discourses and different worlds, through the specific lens of the Christian Scriptures. Why through Scripture, though, rather than the wider Christian tradition? Partly because the Bible shapes Christian formal and informal liturgies: churches that use set liturgies find that these liturgies contain a high percentage of direct quotes and images from Scripture; non-liturgical churches equally quote Scripture in public worship and use its imagery in prayer and exhortation; traditional hymns and worship songs derive much of their content from biblical stories, words, concepts and affirmations of faith; Scripture is read in public worship, and often used as the basis for preaching and teaching. Whether explicitly or not, Scripture and how we use it shapes the way in which faith is expressed and lived in different contexts. The way in which Scripture is *used* is particularly important: emphasis on different texts, for instance, can create different contexts within which mental health is thought about differently. The full use of the psalms can enable a higher degree of emotional–spiritual literacy; an emphasis on the Gospels – and particularly on stories of healing – can easily create unrealistic expectations or feelings of guilt and inadequacy for chronic conditions, though at the other end of the spectrum rationalizing or dismissing concepts of healing altogether can remove sources of hope and turn God into an impotent bystander; heavy use of penitentiary texts can be hugely damaging to those struggling with misplaced guilt and low self-esteem, yet themes of forgiveness and acceptance, and stories of new beginnings (of which there are many in Scripture), can be tremendously liberating. Practices of communal reading, in whatever form, deeply shape the Christian imagination with pictures of what is aspired to, considered 'normal', possible or desirable, what induces shame or feelings of inadequacy, what language may be available to talk about struggles. The default use of Scripture in various contexts and in personal spirituality will inevitably shape responses to mental health challenges. Of course, our implicit use of Scripture is only part of the picture. Scripture is also used consciously and intentionally: in sermons, in teaching, in personal reading, in pastoral contexts. Here, Scripture can become a rich resource full of possibilities: a complex text, which mirrors the complexity of the contemporary world and human relationships, a text that weaves together personal, social, theological, spiritual, economic and political concerns, and provides multiple entry points to speak about mental ill health, well-being, and a vision of what it means to be fully human.

This book therefore is an invitation to explore the riches of Scripture and their interaction with the complex world of our emotions; to suggest how these riches can be harnessed by the community of faith in its reading, teaching, worship and conversations; to help connect the sometimes strange and alien world of Scripture with the questions the world of today asks about mental health and well-being. It is a book for pastors, teachers, vicars, chaplains, for all those involved in caring for others, whether professionally or in a volunteer capacity. It is for ordinary church members struggling with questions they would like to explore further. It is also, we hope, for mental health professionals who want to explore how their patients' faith interacts with and can shape their well-being. Although the book is not primarily intended as an academic text, we have also kept in mind an academic readership, and have sought not to avoid the critical questions posed for the interdisciplinary debate between biblical scholarship and the medical and social sciences. We have, however, attempted to ensure that the language employed is accessible to all and that no reader is excluded by lack of disciplinary, technical, vocabulary.

The academic world has only fairly recently awoken to the fruitfulness of bringing these two worlds together; in Biblical Studies, the use of psychological approaches in analysing the text and its stories has gained credibility,[3] though it is fair to say this is still a marginal interest. Many scholars are suspicious of reading anachronistic motifs into the text, or trying to psychoanalyse characters in a story, and the dialogue between disciplines therefore needs to include careful definition of terms and variant concepts.[4] In contrast, the more defined area of trauma studies has vastly shaped current scholarship on the Old Testament in particular.[5] Trauma, however, is only one area in studies of mental health and well-being, and therefore there are chapters in this book that explore a wider range of issues and questions, while being mindful of questions of culture, interpretation and vocabulary.

Within the world of the medical and social sciences, particularly psychiatry, psychology and psychotherapy, things are much more mixed. Psychiatry has tended to pathologize religious experience, and unhelpfully diagnose biblical figures.[6] On the other hand, there are now serious attempts to include scriptural material in religiously integrated forms of cognitive behavioural therapy, and research evaluations of these therapies show promise.[7] One of us (Christopher Cook) has sought to demonstrate that interdisciplinary engagement between Bible, theology and science can give us a richer and more complete understanding of conditions such as addiction, or religious experiences such as hearing voices (often labelled as auditory verbal hallucinations by mental health professionals).[8] The present volume continues these interdisciplinary conversations, and their application to pastoral and clinical practice.

Overview of the book

Bringing two disciplines together means that this book is intentionally multivocal, and reflects different starting points and methodologies. While every chapter will interrogate how Scripture can contribute to Christian discourse and practice in the area of mental health, some will start with the text of Scripture and seek to identify how the text speaks of mental health and well-being, and how this can either enrich or challenge contemporary understandings; others will start with psychological concepts or theory, and seek to identify how the biblical text may reflect or speak into the categories of analysis and understanding that we now use.

Part 1 of the book explores in some detail the gaps in discourse and conceptualization of humanity between today and the range of cultures reflected in Scripture. Jocelyn Bryan, in Chapter 1, opens with a reflection on meaning making and the role of stories: this is an invitation to consider both the nature of Scripture and how Scripture functions, and the nature of humanity as essentially organized around a narrative sense of personal and communal identity. Four chapters then follow, exploring how Scripture talks of human beings, of their emotions, of what it means to be fully human and healthy in a world that is never perfect. These chapters enable a complex picture to be painted of the difference between the biblical world and our own, so that we can be appropriately wary of simply projecting today's categories on to the text, and vice versa, but also identify areas of overlap and bridges between the text and contemporary psychological theory. In Chapter 2, Gordon McConville sets concepts of wholeness and illness within the Old Testament's realistic negotiation of real life and its brokenness, yet within a wider eschatological framework, with a clear challenge to ask ourselves what constitutes a theologically sound concept of human well-being. Joanna Collicut takes this further in her exploration in Chapter 3 of madness in the Gospels, and of how unstable the category of 'madness' is: it has porous boundaries, especially in interaction with the world of spirituality, given both madness and spirituality move beyond traditional concepts of rationality. In Chapters 4 and 5 Stephen Barton and Paula Gooder both analyse the theological anthropology that underlies the world of the New Testament, and the letters of Paul in particular. Barton focuses on Paul's understanding of life in Christ, and the shaping of Christian life and character in ways that interact with emotions and psychological health, while Gooder attends to Paul's focus on the mind.

Part 2 of the book zooms in on specific texts, and how these can be read and explored to bring out themes and questions of mental health and well-being. The majority of texts here are from the Old Testament, which reflects the nature of this part of Scripture as deeply embedded in human experience, with a high volume of storytelling, and the ubiquitous presence of lament in the psalms, the prophets and some of the narrative material. Beyond this, it also reflects the circumstances of the writing and gathering of Scripture. The Old Testament is a collection of texts shaped by pain and trauma: struggles for survival, war, slavery, exile and political oppression are ever present, and these texts weave together accounts of personal pain and trauma with the collective experience of Israel throughout history. The Old Testament, therefore, is both a story of trauma, and a theological and spiritual reflection on, and response to, trauma. It often seeks to find meaning in events themselves, and a wider eschatological framework of understanding. This search for meaning manifests itself not in pat answers or neat statements, but in a continuing struggle between the reality of life and the promises that Israel holds on to. The text is therefore at times ambiguous, at times inconclusive, and often multivocal, with different perspectives and views on how to understand and respond to the reality of psychological pain, individually and collectively. These various perspectives can be traced in the texts explored in this section: Isabelle Hamley looks in Chapter 6 at the interaction of individual and community in Job's experience of personal loss and grief; David G. Firth, in Chapter 7, examines the common problem of anxiety and its framing in the psalms; in the chapter that follows Brueggemann considers the importance of truth telling in the psalms and the importance of personal and communal lament in worship; and in Chapter 9 Jill Firth explores the impact of collective trauma in Jeremiah. Chris Cook then takes us into the New Testament with an analysis of the Sermon on the Mount and its vision for human well-being: a vision rooted in spiritual practices, with many connections to contemporary themes in mental health discussions (Chapter 10). This is followed by a case study of the Gerasene demoniac, a unique story of an encounter between Jesus and a man suffering from a major mental disorder (Chapter 11).

Part 3 moves us into more focused practical ground. John Swinton (Chapter 12) and Nick Ladd (Chapter 13) both use practical research to explore how the use of Scripture impacts and shapes the experience of church members with mental health difficulties. Swinton concentrates on questions of pastoral care and the complexity of reading Scripture when struggling with mental health, in order to challenge the Church to develop a 'mental health hermeneutic'. Ladd uses many years of experience as a church leader to reflect on how churches can be formed by their reading of Scripture into hospitable communities. In Chapter 14, Megan Warner sharpens the focus on communal habits and formation in the face of trauma with insights from the Tragedies and Congregations research project. Finally, Nathan White concludes (Chapter 15) with a consideration of how Scripture can reshape our notions of the nature and value of resilience.

Out of this wide range of approaches, concepts and texts, we find remarkable consistency in the themes that emerge, and can help guide readers throughout this collection: the call for truth telling and realism in conveying the experience of living with both hope and frailty; the need to move away from pat answers and a narrow use of the canon, to engaging fully with the depth, breadth and complexity of the scriptural witness; the significance of language, of story-telling and meaning-making; and finally, the overwhelming need to connect the public and private, the individual and the communal, which makes this book, and its recommendations, a book for the church, rather than just for individuals within it. When read as a whole, it is a plea to the Church to think consciously and explicitly about its use of Scripture, and about the people it comes into contact with, so that the fullness of Scripture can be brought to bear on the fullness of human experience.

Notes

1 The exact figures vary, depending upon survey methodology and which diagnostic groups are included. For helpful reviews, see P. E. Bebbington and S. McManus, 2020, 'Revisiting the One in Four: The Prevalence of Psychiatric Disorder in the Population of England 2000–2014', *British Journal of Psychiatry*, 216, pp. 55–7; and P. B. Jones, 2013, 'Adult Mental Health Disorders and Their Age at Onset', *British Journal of Psychiatry Supplements*, 54, pp. 5–10.

2 D. Vigo, G. Thornicroft and R. Atun, 2016, 'Estimating the True Global Burden of Mental Illness', *The Lancet Psychiatry*, 3, pp. 171–8.

3 W. G. Rollins, 1999, *Soul and Psyche: The Bible in Psychological Perspective*, Minneapolis, MN: Fortress Press; D. A. Kille, 1997, *Psychological Biblical Criticism: Genesis 3 as a Test Case*, New York: Graduate Theological Union; D. A. Kille and W. G. Rollins (eds), 2007, *Psychological Insight into the Bible: Texts and Readings*, Grand Rapids, MI: Eerdmans.

4 See W. J. Smith, 2004, 'Soul and Psyche: The Bible in Psychological Perspective', *HTS, Teologiese Studies*, 60 (1 and 2), pp. 431–40.

5 See E. Boase and C. G. Frechette (eds), 2016, *Bible Through the Lens of Trauma* (Semeia Studies), Atlanta, GA: SBL Press.

6 C. C. H. Cook, 2012, 'Psychiatry in Scripture: Sacred Texts and Psychopathology', *The Psychiatrist*, 36, pp. 225–9.

7 H. G. Koenig and colleagues, 2015, 'Religious Vs. Conventional Cognitive Behavioral Therapy for Major Depression in Persons with Chronic Medical Illness: A Pilot Randomized Trial', *Journal of Nervous and Mental Disease*, 203, pp. 243–51.

8 C. C. H. Cook, 2006, *Alcohol, Addiction and Christian Ethics*, Cambridge: Cambridge University Press; C. C. H. Cook, 2018, *Hearing Voices, Demonic and Divine: Scientific and Theological Perspectives*, London: Routledge.

PART I

Biblical Theology

Narrative, Meaning Making and Mental Health

JOCELYN BRYAN

This chapter reflects on the power of narrative to reveal meaning in life and how the narrative of Scripture has the power to meet the human need for meaning and transform a personal narrative from one of suffering to well-being.

The importance of stories to make sense of experience is undisputed. Psychology, psychiatry and theology have embraced the narrative turn. But for narratives to function and be meaningful they require interpretation; this applies as much to the narratives we share with others as it does to the Bible. Further, narratives are not created out of nothing, neither are they isolated. They influence one another, get absorbed into one another, contradict one another and compete with one another.

The role of narrative in personal identity and meaning making is significant for mental health.[1] The events of our life, our interpretation of them, and what we feel about them are stored in narrative form in memory. But the interpretation of the story of our past is shaped by what we hope for and imagine in the future. We engage in this process of narrative construction to give our lives a sense of unity, purpose and meaning.

This chapter examines personal narratives and their role in meaning making and relates this to mental health. It then draws on the narrative of the Bible to set up a constructive conversation as to how narratives from Scripture can be integrated into a personal narrative and meet the needs for meaning necessary to benefit mental health.

Living narratives: stories and experience

Stories can and do reveal insights concerning ourselves, others and the world. This is the case for the stories we tell about ourselves, the stories we listen to, and the stories we read. A significant amount of our time is spent interacting with stories. The stories we tell to others and the stories we listen to are the main substance of our conversations. In the exchange of stories, we reflect on and process our experiences to find meaning. The need for human beings to communicate and make sense of their experience in narrative form is widely acknowledged and has received considerable attention in academic psychology in recent years. By listening attentively to the stories of others and reflecting on our personal narrative, we gain deeper understanding and knowledge of the richness and complexity of human experience and how it may be interpreted and understood. This connection between human experience and narrative is summarized by Jerome Bruner as 'narrative imitates life and life imitates narratives'.[2] 'We are living narratives'.[3] Our stories are both enacted and created by us. We are the main protagonist in the plot of our lives and we connect the episodes and subplots of our story into an overarching narrative that is shaped by our beliefs and personal goals. In telling our story, we are using language to reconstruct our past, but the meaning we give to it is undoubtedly influenced by what we think the future may or may not hold for us. Stephen Crites makes an important connection between time, narrative and experience, claiming that experience is organized in narrative form because human consciousness is itself 'temporal'. Referring to Augustine and his reflections on experience and memory, Crites states:

> past, present and future cannot be three distinct realities or spheres of being that somehow coexist. Only the present exists, but it exists only in these tensed modalities. They are inseparably joined in the present itself. Only from the standpoint of the present experience could one speak of the past and future. The three modalities are correlative to one another in every moment of experience.[4]

The point is significant because it means that our experience of the present moment is contingent on both our past narrative *and* the future plot we anticipate. It is these narratives, held in memory, from which we make sense of our present experience and determine how we feel about it and our response to it. Hence, our responses to the present moments are not distinct from what has happened to us or from what we anticipate will happen. In other words, our narrative of the past and our imagined future narrative impact on our every moment.

But telling our story is not only about meaning making; these first person narratives forge our identity and our individual sense of selfhood. Hence, self-narrative discloses the self as the self sees itself and how our sense of self has evolved over time. In the act of telling our personal story we engage in identity construction describing who we are, how we

4

have become who we are, and possibly who we long to become. Polking-horne confirms this, claiming that we achieve our personal identities and self-concept through 'the use of the narrative configuration, and make our existence into a whole by understanding it as an expression of a single and unfolding story'.[5]

Our individual story may be a story experienced as ordered, planned and fulfilling or, conversely, it may be chaotic, dark and fearful. It might have episodes that are contrasting, including times when life was characterized by stability, ambitions being realized and good health, and other times when an unexpected illness or tragedy has driven the narrative into a time of disorientation and loss. These times of confusion and disruption in the narrative can have a significant impact on self-concept, identity and, consequently, mental health. They may cause us to struggle to make sense of what is happening and how to respond. We might even lose sense of who we are and our future becomes hopeless and fearful. When this happens, we can struggle to cope with the demands of everyday life and our coherent sense of self disintegrates and mental health problems occur. In such circumstances, evidence suggests that it is both important and difficult to revise and reconstruct the personal narrative to recover meaning, a sense of self and its contingent mental health.

The fact that we inhabit a social world is also important in our narrative. It means that although the content and plot of our personal narrative is unique, it is undoubtedly influenced by the narratives of those who make up the web of relationships that are part of it. The characters in these narratives will be part of our story's plot and elicit some of the emotions embedded within it. However, the web of narratives extends beyond our close social circle to include the story of our family, community, society, country and, for Christians, the story of God. And, like any web, changes or tension in one thread have an impact on the rest of the web. As living narratives enmeshed in a web of ever-changing narratives, each personal narrative incorporates to some extent these different narratives with their varying degrees of impact and significance on the overall content and trajectory of each personal story. Furthermore, how we interpret this complex interweaving of narratives in our personal narrative has considerable implications for mental health.

The Bible and narrative

Within the pages of the Bible, the truth about the nature of God, his relationship with both creation and human beings and his work of salvation in the life, death and resurrection of Jesus, is recorded in narrative form.

The numerous stories in the biblical text are set within an overarching narrative of God's act of creation, the fall, Yahweh and the people of Israel, the incarnation, the work of the Holy Spirit and the beginnings of the Church and the anticipation of a new creation with a new heaven and a new earth. Over the past two millennia, the transformative truth of the narrative of Scripture has been evidenced in human lives. The reality of the human condition and the loving participation of the creator in the world and in human lives captured in these ancients texts, has unleashed not only human imagination, but also the power of Scripture to heal and inspire lives in dramatic ways. We might conceive of this as a unification or integration of our personal narrative with God's unfolding narrative, and in this confluence of narratives the work of the Holy Spirit brings about transformation. Loughlin goes further and suggests that '[n]arrativist theology sets the scripture before us as a consuming text; or better, a text to consume in order that we might grow in the strength and shape of Christ'.[6] He suggests that by allowing the text to reside within us 'we are nourished by its word and enabled to perform its story'.[7]

In the rich narrative of the Bible a truth is proclaimed that affirms that all human beings are created and loved by God. This is the beginning of the narrative of every human life. The God who is outside of time and eternal, who has created all that is, reaches out to creation in love and gives every human being the identity of his child, who is created and loved by him. In the mystery of the incarnation, the story of God in time is radically manifest in Jesus, the Son of God, whose life events enacted in the history of the world offer us the possibility of a future that is free from the fear of death and gives the promise of everlasting life. This is the fundamental narrative of the Christian faith and it is a narrative that invites human beings to unite their story with the unfolding story of God.

In a reflection on story and the pastoral office, Jensen emphasizes the significance of story and the gospel narrative as one of promise.[8] He notes that it offers a future identified as the new creation and everlasting life with Jesus, which is not contingent on human achievement but on faith in Jesus as the crucified, risen Lord. This end point is the telos of the human story and is not generated by us, but is given to us in the sacred narrative of Scripture. It is a promise of a different present and a different future. Throughout the Gospels, the promise is witnessed to in the stories of the lives transformed by the ministry of Jesus. This is particularly evident in John's Gospel. Nathanael is told that he 'will see heaven opened and the angels of God ascending and descending upon the Son of Man' (John 1.51). The woman of Samaria is told that, 'The water that I will give will become in them a spring of water gushing up to eternal life' (John 4.14). After the feeding of the 5,000, Jesus promises that 'whoever comes to me will never be hungry and whoever believes in me will never be thirsty' (John 6.35).

The Gospels are stories of promise and of the transforming power of an encounter with Jesus in the present. The narratives witness to how his ministry changed who people were and who they became. In other words, the assumed trajectory of their personal narratives was altered dramatically as they saw themselves, their relationship with others, and their purpose in life in a new way. By believing in Jesus and who he was – namely, the Son of God – the narrative people lived by and by association their personal narrative – whether Jew, Samaritan, Levite or Roman – was challenged and reinterpreted. Jesus transformed personal identities by enabling people to revise their personal narrative and their understanding of the life they had led up to this point, and look to a new future centred on faith in him. He urged them to repent of their past and, through the power of God's forgiveness and grace, begin a new chapter in their story. In this way, Jesus enabled people to redeem the narrative of their past and offered them a different plot for their future narrative that was rooted in the hopeful promise of the good news of the gospel. In an encounter with Jesus, the three temporal modalities of human life – the past, present and future – are radically changed and the self, personal narrative and identity are re-envisioned through faith in him and his promise of salvation.

The integration of Scripture into personal narratives can bring about this radical change that is evidenced as a change in meaning and purpose in life, both of which have important implications for mental health. In what follows, the significance of the narrative of the Bible for mental health and human flourishing is explored by engaging Scripture in a conversation with narrative psychology, meaning making and psychological needs.

The role of meaning making

In his work as a psychiatrist, Victor Frankl traced several forms of neuroses in his patients to 'a failure to find meaning and a sense of responsibility in their existence'.[9] From his experience of being imprisoned in Nazi concentration camps in which most of his family died, Frankl identified his central thesis on searching for meaning, namely that 'to live is to suffer and to survive is to find meaning in the suffering'.[10] He argued that the will to meaning is part of our human nature and a significant motivation in human beings. Likewise, in a review of meaningfulness in life, Baumeister and Vohs[11] conclude that human beings have an innate need to search for meaning. In fact, Baumeister has gone so far as to conclude that meaning is something that we crave, implying that without it we become distressed.[12]

The meaning and purpose we ascribe to our lives is worked out primarily through our reflection on our past narrative. From the myriad of episodes that are held in our autobiographical memory we create a narrative identity that is internalized and evolves throughout our life span. Within this narrative, the memories of past events are blended with our perceived goals to give a coherent account of ourselves through time which affords us a sense of unity, purpose and meaning. Steger, reviewing the psychological research into the effect of meaning in life and having a sense of life purpose, concluded that those who believe their lives have meaning or purpose are happier, have greater overall well-being, life satisfaction, feel more engaged with their work, and report having greater control over their lives.[13] They are also less likely to suffer from anxiety and depression, workaholism, suicidal thoughts and substance abuse, and need less therapy. It appears that finding meaning and value in our lives is a primary goal in life and failing to obtain this is detrimental to mental health.

But what are the psychological factors that guide this narrative construction and its meaning? In a nuanced approach, Baumeister and Newman suggest that, 'constructing stories is just *one mode of, or one phase* [italics mine] in the process of making sense of one's experience'.[14] They argue that this drive to 'make sense of' or 'find meaning' in our experiences is too broad and vague a motivation and does not provide a complete explanation for the significance of storytelling. In their detailed analysis of the ways in which narrative is used in recalling experience, they conclude that 'making sense' is not the only motive at play in the ways in which we organize our experience in story form, but rather self-narratives are constructed to satisfy four needs for meaning, namely: purposiveness, justification, efficacy and self-worth.[15] Therefore, storytelling not only functions to fulfil our innate need to interpret events and find meaning, but it also functions in response to other needs for meaning necessary for psychological well-being. Baumeister and his colleagues claim that if one or more of these needs are not satisfied, then people 'show distress, emptiness and other indications that life lacks sufficient meaning'.[16] Furthermore, the argument that these four needs or motivations shape the narratives we tell about ourselves suggests that we interpret our experiences in ways that satisfy these needs, and if we are unable to do so we may experience mental health problems.

The process of constructing and interpreting our story to meet these needs involves applying our personal hermeneutical lens to the text of our experience. This lens has been created by drawing on narratives or scripts reinforced by significant others, culture, and our faith perspective, with the narratives it holds within its sacred texts and tradition. These narratives can significantly influence what we select as important in the content of our story and how it is construed in the light of the four needs identified by Baumeister.

Scripture and the four needs for meaning

Purpose

On the road to Emmaus, the two disciples were engrossed in exchanging their story of the recent events of Jesus' crucifixion and resurrection (Luke 24.13–15). In their subsequent conversation with the unrecognized Jesus after he had joined them on the road, they reveal that they were not only trying to make sense of what had happened in the previous days, but also their loss of purpose. The dramatic events of Holy Week had led to the loss of their master and the one they had decided to follow. They had hoped that he was the 'one to redeem Israel' (24.21) and their purpose was to be part of that. In the trauma of the crucifixion their meaning making and purpose were ruptured. On the road the two disciples, in their exchange of the narrative of the past week, struggled to regain meaning and purpose in their lives. The response of Jesus demonstrates the way in which the narrative of Scripture can make sense of the past and reorient someone to recover their sense of purpose. After reminding the two disciples that the prophets had declared that the story of the Messiah would involve suffering before entering his glory (24.26), Jesus goes on to interpret the events they have witnessed in Jerusalem through the lens of the narrative of the Old Testament. These stories have predetermined his story, identity and purpose. Hence, within this web of narratives the disciples begin to discern the meaning of their experience and start to recover their narrative identity and purpose.

Later in the resurrection narrative, Jesus appears to the disciples and again refers to the narrative of the Old Testament, the suffering of the Messiah, and his rising from the dead on the third day as foretold by the prophets. However, this time he makes the disciples aware of their involvement in this unfolding story of God when he tells them, 'You are witnesses of these things' (24.48). With their role of witnesses comes a sense of purpose; namely, to proclaim in his name the repentance and forgiveness of sins to all nations (24.47). Through interpreting the narrative of the present through the lens of the Old Testament narrative, Jesus has not only enabled the confused, fearful disciples to make sense of their story, but also enabled them to recover their mission and purpose. This is made even more explicit in the great commission at the end of Matthew's Gospel: 'Go therefore and make disciples of all nations, baptizing them in the name of the Father and of the Son and of the Holy Spirit' (Matt. 28.19).

Finding a purpose around which to organize our personal narrative is a formidable task and forms the central problem of identity.[17] The motivation to find a life purpose is therefore important for satisfying a need to have a coherent sense of who we are and that our lives are integrated into a coherent whole which has a trajectory that we can influence. Most of us organize our lives around several different purposes, such as achieving a stable source of income and success in our chosen career, finding a lifelong partner, owning a home and having a loving family. We interpret our experiences and ascribe meaning to them in relation to how they contribute or hinder us in achieving our main purposes which shape the narrative we embody.

The positive relationship between a belief that there is meaning and a purpose to life and mental health and life satisfaction is well documented.[18] The Gospel narratives tell the story of Jesus' life and ministry and claim that in this narrative God's loving purposes for the world have reached their revelatory climax. In his parables and instructive teaching, Jesus makes explicit that those who believe in him are to follow him and grow into the likeness of him. Their purpose is to live as obedient children of God, discerning his will and participating in his work of redemption in and for the world. God is the source of truth and meaning as shown to us in Jesus, 'the way, the truth and the life' (John 14.6). The narrative of Scripture is not before us to be read or listened to like other stories; rather, it is a story that we are called to perform. It is a story that takes its place deep within us and shapes our own story fed by the living word that satisfies our need for life purpose and identity. Hence, our imagined future is a product of the purpose and meaning of life given in Scripture and our interpretation of the story of our life so far. Gadamer conceived of this as a 'fusion of horizons'[19] and Ricoeur as 'refiguration'[20] in which the world presented to us in the text refigures the reader's or the listener's world.

Value and justification

Baumeister and Wilson claim that the moral dimension of our life story is of equal importance to purpose.[21] It seems that most of us want to construct a personal narrative that depicts us as a good person and we seek out evidence to justify this in the story we construct. The self-reflection involved in this process demands that we evaluate our actions and our underlying motives. However, this can give rise to unresolved guilt and shame and have a profoundly damaging effect on personal identity, and finding meaning and value in the life that we have lived.

Guilt and shame play a significant part in the stories of many people suffering with mental health issues. These moral emotions cause considerable distress. Living with mental illness can also be a contributing factor to feelings of guilt and shame. Clark advocates two therapeutic concepts in working with guilt and shame, namely acceptance and forgiveness.[22] He suggests that acceptance is an attitude that promotes the patient's self-acceptance. It involves listening and being with a person without judging them for what they may or may not have done. In mental health, forgiveness more often than not is focused on self-forgiveness rather than interpersonal forgiveness, and entails fostering an attitude of self-compassion. This can be a long and painful process, but it appears that this form of forgiveness is a transformational experience and plays a major part in psychological healing.[23]

Forgiveness is an important biblical concept and central to the narrative of God's relationship with human beings. The Bible begins with the story of creation and Adam and Eve. Early in the story, once Adam and Eve have eaten the forbidden fruit of the tree of knowledge, their disobedience to God characterizes their sinfulness. From this time onwards, human beings are deemed to be sinful and in need of forgiveness. But in order to receive divine forgiveness we must be willing to forgive, hence in the Lord's prayer we ask God to 'forgive us our trespasses as we forgive those who trespass against us'.

In the Gospel narratives, Jesus proclaims the forgiveness of sins. From the beginning of his ministry his message of repentance and forgiveness of sins heralds the coming of the kingdom of God. Jesus' ministry abounds with encounters and occasions when he declares the forgiveness of sins. The paralytic who was let down through the roof to Jesus is told 'Son, your sins are forgiven' (Mark 2.5). When the woman pours precious ointment on his feet in the house of Simon the Pharisee, Jesus declares, 'her sins, which were many, have been forgiven' (Luke 7.47). Forgiveness is emphasized in the Gospels as a necessary part of discipleship and Jesus both spoke and practised it. Even as he died on the cross he declared of his accusers, 'Father, forgive them; for they do not know what they are doing' (Luke 23.34). The forgiveness of sins is at the very centre of the good news of the kingdom of God. And it is not just a promise for the future age, it is available in the present. However, the journey towards forgiveness may be long and challenging. This is the case in forgiving others and in forgiving oneself. In both cases, there may be considerable guilt and a lack of self-acceptance that impacts on the need for value and justification and has negative consequences for mental health.

Part of the human condition is an acceptance of our limitations, and our capacity to hurt others and hurt ourselves. The significance of forgiveness and self-acceptance in meeting our need to have lived a good life is not to be underestimated. Unforgiveness is associated with a decrease in mental and physical health and economic, social and spiritual problems.[24] Psychologically, the act of forgiveness involves the replacement of the negative emotions of resentment, anger and bitterness with positive emotions that focus away from self towards the other and include empathy, compassion and love. Letting go of a long-harboured grudge is accompanied by a good feeling and a heavy burden being replaced by lightness.

Research in forgiveness has primarily focused on interpersonal forgiveness, with self-forgiveness receiving less attention, but this too has an impact on mental health. In a study of older people, asking for God's forgiveness was an important step in forgiving themselves, as was reading Bible stories that included characters who had sinned and were forgiven by God.[25] These stories enabled them to feel worthy of God's forgiveness and to forgive themselves. They moved from a state of experiencing something fundamentally wrong about their lives and feeling ill at ease with themselves and the world, to feeling at home in the world and reaching a point of self-acceptance. Hence, their re-evaluation of self in the light of the biblical narratives benefited their psychological well-being and improved their mental health.

At the heart of the miracle of forgiveness is a letting go and release from the interpretation of the self-narrative of the past to one based upon the biblical witnesses to God's grace and forgiveness supremely demonstrated in Jesus. Internal meanings are reset and our sense of self and relationships with others transformed. New meanings found in the Bible are woven into the personal narrative and self-acceptance; value and hope are restorative realities for mental health available through the power of God's forgiveness.

Efficacy

Efficacy refers to people's need for their life story and identity to demonstrate that they have made a positive contribution to the world and the positive outcomes are due to their own efforts and actions. In other words, a passive life is not evaluated as a satisfying life and presents challenges to mental health. Linked to efficacy is the need for some sense of control over our lives and our context.[26] In their work on motivation, Deci and Ryan claim that all human beings need to be competent, autonomous and in relationship with others.[27] Competence is related to efficacy in that it refers to a need to be effective in the world and negotiate successfully whatever challenges we face. Satisfying this need is seen as essential for our well-being and psychological growth.[28] Clearly, this need for efficacy and its relationship with mental health needs to be held in tension with what we understand it means to be a person who cannot exercise efficacy and control in the way that it is understood in the psychological literature.

In his work on dementia, Swinton draws attention to the countercultural narrative of Scripture that points to being 'dependent, embodied, relational and contingent, broken and deeply lost, and loved and profoundly purposeful'[29] rather than autonomous, independent, competent and successfully achieving personal goals. Personal narratives that tell a tale of perceived failures, betrayal and being at the mercy of circumstances and others carry considerable risk of mental health problems. A personal narrative dominated by helplessness often reveals many of the themes of depression, including meaninglessness with no motive towards the future, being trapped, abandoned and low self-worth. It challenges the very purpose and identity of a person and they struggle to know who they are and what, if any, meaning their life has had or will have in the future.

Incorporating the counter-cultural narrative of Scripture that Swinton articulates into one's personal narrative is particularly challenging in a world that rewards and affirms the individual, independence, economic contribution, celebratories and personal strivings and achievements. But the narrative of Scripture proclaims one very simple fact – namely, that all creation and all human beings are dependent on God for their very existence. God's gift of creation (Gen. 1.1) is the source of everything. Without God nothing would exist. Hence, the Bible from its first verses states that we are dependent beings. Nothing we achieve is due to us alone. Contingency is embedded in God's creation from the dynamics in the ecosystems to human functioning and survival.

Recognizing both our ultimate dependency on God and the systems of mutual dependency operating throughout creation releases us from the need for efficacy in its individualistic form. It offers us a radical interpretative lens through which everything is conceived as a gift, valued and loved by God. This foundational reality is echoed throughout the entire narrative of Scripture. Being valued and loved is a given. Nothing we do, whether we consider it as making a positive contribution or not, changes this fact. But it is not the case that what we do or don't do does not matter. The Bible does not affirm a passive life. On the contrary, 'faith ... without works is also dead' (James 2.26). The Gospels tell the story of Jesus who has come into the world 'to do the will of him who sent me and to complete his work' (John 4.34).[30] Discerning and being obedient to God is the primary goal of the Christian life. Jesus' call to 'follow me' demands that satisfaction in life is derived from following the commandments of God and submitting to his Lordship over all. God is in control and not human beings. Any positive contributions we make to the world are not for our personal satisfaction or self-glorification, but rather for the sake of the kingdom of God and in response to his love for us.

Hauerwas extends the giftedness of creation to draw attention to the way in which we construct our narrative and interpret the fundamental premises regarding who we are and our relationship with God.

> [W]e don't get to make our lives up. We get to receive our lives as gifts. The story that says we should have no story except the story we choose when we have no story, is a lie ... Christians are people who recognise that we have a Father who we can thank for our existence. Christian discipleship is about learning to receive our lives as gift without regret.[31]

The constructivist view of human personhood and identity strongly contests this. However, the transformative power of the Bible resides in the fact that God is the author of every story, and he calls us to live out our story by participating faithfully in his unfolding story. It is by participating in his work of loving redemption that we discover meaning and joy, not for our own sakes, but in loving response to the Creator who gave us the gift of life. Swinton warns of the perils of forgetting that God is our creator and seeing ourselves as creators.[32] He suggests that this leads to us believing that we are 'self-creating beings, whose task is to shape the world in our own image'. Adopting this stance overplays the need for competency and achievement – in other words, our efficacy – and may lead to feelings of failure and loss of control that are damaging to mental health.

Self-worth

The fourth need concerns self-worth or self-esteem. Studies confirm that low self-esteem plays a significant part in causing depression, alcohol abuse, teenage pregnancy, social anxiety and violence.[33] We need to feel that there is something to commend us, and that we are lovable. What others think about us, and what we think about ourselves, matters.

Within our personal narrative there are undoubtedly times when we have not achieved what we set out to achieve, when we have behaved in ways that we regret, when we have not been the person we aspire to be. All of these can have a negative impact on our self-worth.

Clearly, the need for self-worth is related to the other three needs already discussed. To be content with what you have achieved in life, have a sense of purpose, evaluate yourself as generally being a good person who has made a positive contribution to the world will all serve to maintain or raise self-worth. When these needs are not satisfied, then our feeling of self-worth is reduced and mental health problems are more likely to occur. There is now considerable evidence that those with low self-esteem are particularly vulnerable to depression.[34]

The narrative we tell about ourselves includes our attitude towards ourselves based on our life experiences, the way we have dealt with them, and what other people tell us about ourselves and how they have responded to us. People with high self-esteem have a personal theory that they are competent, and lovable, and those with low self-esteem believe that they are less competent or mediocre and are unattractive to others.[35] This leads to a self-bias in the interpretation of personal narratives and identity, and explains to some extent the vulnerability of those with low self-esteem to mental health problems.

The Bible tells a story that portrays human beings as sinful and in need of redemption and ends with the glorious vision of a new redeemed creation. The Christian Church upholds and embodies this story in the world. A central theme in the narrative is the sinful nature of humankind and God's response of love, forgiveness and grace demonstrated in the life, death and resurrection of Jesus. The simple message of the cross is that Jesus died to save us from our sins. But a feeling of unworthiness can not only lower self-esteem but be a significant barrier to receiving God's forgiveness. What's more, the goal of Christian discipleship as being Christ-like is one that can seem unattainable. This can develop into feelings of perpetual failure and unworthiness. It is also the case that the Church's liturgies of confession reinforce this feeling of wretchedness and unworthiness as sinners and the need for forgiveness. Hence, there is a complexity surrounding self-worth within the Bible and Christian tradition that requires careful handling. Embedded in human experience and evidenced in Scripture is a gap between the reality of who we are and who God longs for us to be, and for most of us a gap between who we are and who we aspire to be. This reality is present in Paul's letter to the Romans where he writes, 'For I do not do the good I want, but the evil I do not want is what I do' (Rom. 7.19). In dealing with this inner struggle, Paul turns to Jesus as the one who can rescue him from his negative spiral of self-condemnation. Through Jesus we have life in the Spirit which, as Paul proclaims, sets us free and gives us life and peace (Rom. 8.1–8).

The agony of self-condemnation and its impact on self-esteem dominates the narrative of the disciple Peter during Jesus' ministry. Peter was the one chosen by Jesus to be the rock on which he will build his church (Matt. 16.18–19). Yet he was the one who leaves the passion narrative as a liar, who denied Jesus three times. We can only imagine the agony and self-loathing he felt when the cock crowed for a second time and he broke down and wept (Mark 14.66—16.20). But Peter's story does not end in this place of low self-worth and self-condemnation. Redemption and restoration come through his relationship with Jesus. On the shore of the sea of Tiberius, the resurrected Jesus and Peter face each other. Peter has no doubt been tormented by his interpretation of his part in the narrative of Jesus, and following the crucifixion he has returned to his old identity and picked up his previous life as a fisherman. But the risen Jesus seeks him out and re-enters his story. They face each other on the lakeside and in that relational space Jesus challenges Peter three times with the question, 'Do you love me?' (John 21.15–19), mirroring the three denials. Since his denial of Jesus, Peter's imagined future narrative was most likely dominated by guilt, loss and failure. His shame and low self-worth were rooted in his failure to be faithful to his Lord, who he loved. But first Jesus reassures Peter that he has not rejected him and helps Peter begin the process of loving himself again. Then Jesus also shows Peter that he still has confidence in him by commanding him to 'feed my sheep'. Here, love, forgiveness, acceptance and trust in the other combine to transform Peter and restore his self-esteem.[36]

The love and acceptance of God for every human being is woven in Scripture. Being accepted and having a sense of belonging is significant for self-worth. Isolation, stigmatization, loneliness and rejection all lower self-esteem and are associated with mental health problems. They are echoed in the cries of the psalmist in the stories of desertion and persecution, and answered in the narrative of the faithfulness of God to his people and in the narrative of the cross. The spiritual struggle is often to accept and claim the truth of the narrative of God's forgiveness, acceptance and love and in that discover the bedrock of self-esteem.

Conclusion

The relationship between personal narrative, narrative identity and meaning making has received increasing attention in psychological research. Narrative identity is important to well-being, hence the construction and internalization of a life story is significant in mental health. But our lives are not lived in isolation from others. We are living narratives, embodying our own story and parts of other stories through their influence on our particular story. The biblical narrative of Scripture is a story that has the power to transform personal narratives and bears witness to the transformational work of the story of Jesus Christ in the early Church, and its continuation throughout history. It is a story to be lived out and performed.

This chapter has demonstrated that an understanding of personal narrative and the needs for meaning identified by Baumeister and Wilson[37] can provide insight into how the narrative of Scripture can influence mental health. The integration of Scripture into a personal narrative is the lifelong task of discipleship. However, within the Bible the source and purpose of human life is articulated. The story of God's relationship with creation in and beyond time orientates the human story and provides meaning even in the sufferings of the present as we wait for God's new creation. Our anticipation of the story that is to come and our part in it has a profound effect on our experience of the present and the plot of our personal narrative.

Critics of narrative psychology point to the authors of fiction as having the ability to create and control the events and characters in the story. In reality, we do not have this autonomy and we create our personal narrative out of whatever we are faced with. Many situations are difficult or too painful to tell or explain, they disrupt our narrative in ways that may destroy or contradict the story we have lived by, and cause our personal identity to disintegrate. In these times our mental health is vulnerable and our needs for meaning are not satisfied. All human experience holds meaning. The search for meaning is innate and necessary to our existence. But as 'suffering cries out for meaning',[38] within the narrative of Scripture, God's loving purposes for the world, his acceptance and love of each human being and his promise of salvation offer a truth that orientates and provides meaning to every living narrative.

Notes

1 J. J. Bauer, D. P. McAdams and J. L. Pals, 2008, 'Narrative Identity and Eudaimonic Well-Being', *Journal of Happiness Studies*, 9, pp. 81–104.

2 J. Bruner, 1987, 'Life as Narrative', *Social Research*, 54(1), pp. 11–32.

3 J. Bryan, 2016, *Human Being: Insights from Psychology and the Christian Faith*, London: SCM Press, p. 44. See also pp. 51–74 for an analysis of personal narrative, meaning making, and human flourishing.

4 S. Crites, 1971, 'The Narrative Quality of Experience', *The Journal of the American Academy of Religion*, 39, pp. 291–311, 301.

5 D. E. Polkinghorne, 1988, *Narrative Knowing and the Human Sciences*, Albany, NY: State University of New York Press, p. 150.

6 G. Loughlin, 1996, *Telling God's Story: Bible, Church and Narrative Theology*. Cambridge: Cambridge University Press, p. 139.

7 Loughlin, *Telling God's Story*, p. 139.

8 R. W. Jensen, 1977, 'Story and Promise in Pastoral Care', *Pastoral Psychology*, 26(2), pp. 113–23.

9 G. Allport, in the preface to V. E. Frankl, 2004, *Man's Search for Meaning: The Classic Tribute to Hope from the Holocaust*, London: Random House, p. 8.

10 Allport in Frankl, *Man's Search for Meaning*, p. 9.

11 R. F. Baumeister and K. D. Vohs, 2005, 'The Pursuit of Meaningfulness in Life', in C. R. Synder and S. J. Lopez (eds), *Handbook of Positive Psychology*, Oxford: Oxford University Press, pp. 608–18.

12 R. F. Baumeister, 1991, *Meanings of Life*, New York: Guilford Press, p. 359.

13 M. F. Steger, 2009, 'Meaning in Life', in C. R. Synder and S. J. Lopez (eds), *Handbook of Positive Psychology*, pp. 679–87.

14 R. F. Baumeister and L. S. Newman, 1994, 'How Stories Make Sense of Personal Experiences: Motives that Shape Autobiographical Narratives', *Personality and Social Psychology Bulletin*, 20(6), pp. 674–90.

15 Baumeister and colleagues use 'needs' as a synonym for 'motives' rather than something indispensable for life.

16 R. F. Baumeister and B. Wilson, 1996, 'Life Stories and the Four Needs for Meaning', *Psychological Enquiry*, 7, pp. 322–5.

17 Baumeister and Wilson, 'Life Stories', pp. 322–25.

18 M. F. Steger, 2012, 'Experiencing Meaning in Life: Optimal Functioning at the Nexus of Well-being, Psychopathology, and Spirituality', in P. T. P. Wong (ed.), *The Human Quest for Meaning: Theories, Research, and Application*, New York: Routledge, pp. 165–82.

19 H.-G. Gadamer, 1975, *Truth and Method*, London: Sheed & Ward.

20 P. Ricoeur, 1984, *Time and Narrative, Vol 1*, Chicago, IL: University of Chicago Press, p. 77.

21 Baumeister and Wilson, 'Life Stories', pp. 322–5.

22 A. Clark, 2012, 'Working with Guilt and Shame', *Advances in Psychiatric Treatment*, 18, pp. 137–43.

23 L. Bauer and colleagues, 1992, *Journal of Religion and Health*, 31(2), pp. 149–60.

24 L. L. Toussaint and E. L. Worthington, 2017, 'Forgiveness', *The Psychologist*, August 2017, pp. 29–33.

25 B. Ingersoll-Dayton and N. Krause, 2005, 'Self-forgiveness: A Component of Mental Health in Later Life', *Research on Aging*, 27(3), pp. 267–89.

26 Baumeister and Wilson, 'Life Stories', pp. 322–5.

27 E. L. Deci and R. M. Ryan, 2012, 'Motivation, Personality and Development within Embedded Social Contexts: An Overview of Self-determination Theory', in R. M. Ryan (ed.), *The Oxford Handbook of Human Motivation*, Oxford: Oxford University Press.

28 Deci and Ryan, 'Motivation, Personality', p. 87.

29 J. Swinton, 2012, *Dementia: Living in the Memories of God*, London: SCM Press, pp. 161–5.

30 Also see, for example, John 6.38, Mark 16.36 and Luke 22.42.

31 S. Hauerwas, 2008, in S. Hauerwas, J. Vanier and J. Swinton (eds), *Living Gently in a Violent World: The Prophetic Witness of Weakness*, Downers Grove, IL: InterVarsity Press Books, p. 93, quoted in Swinton, *Dementia*, p. 164.

32 Swinton, *Dementia*, p. 164.

33 M. H. Guindon, 2010, 'What is Self-esteem?', in M. H. Guindon (ed.), *Self-esteem Across the Lifespan*, New York & Hove: Routledge, p. 3.

34 U. Orth and R. W. Robins, 2013, 'Understanding the Link Between Low Self-Esteem and Depression', *Current Directions in Psychological Science*, 22(6), pp. 455–60.

35 T. C. Christensen, J. V. Wood and L. F. Barratt, 2003, 'Remembering Everyday Experience through the Prism of Self-esteem', *Personality and Social Psychology Bulletin*, 29(1), pp. 51–62.

36 See J. Bryan, 2016, *Human Being: Insights from Psychology and the Christian Faith*, London: SCM Press, pp. 222–4, for a more detailed analysis of this passage.

37 Baumeister and Wilson, 'Life Stories', pp. 322–5.

38 Baumeister and Wilson, 'Life Stories', pp. 322–5.

2

Wholeness and Illness:
A View from the Old Testament

GORDON MCCONVILLE

Introduction

A biblical approach to mental health, as to health generally, entails fundamental theological questions about the nature of the human being. Arguably, the entire scriptural witness is a response to such questions. That is to say, a biblical theology of humanity is inseparable from the Bible's portrayal of God and the world. It effects this portrayal in its many genres, including narrative, law, wisdom, myth, prophecy and gospel, all within a movement that culminates eschatologically in the glorification of Christ and his Church.

It follows that humanity is unfinished, imperfect. The question 'What are human beings that you regard them, or mortals that you think of them?' (Ps. 144.3) receives no single answer in the Old Testament, but in the text quoted the sequel is: 'They are like a breath; their days are like a passing shadow' (v. 4).[1] Human wholeness, therefore, has to be sought within this context of unwholeness, as the human is subject to illness, ageing and death. Death, indeed, is predicated close to the beginning of the biblical narrative in the story of Eden (Gen. 2—3), with its account of deep disturbance and loss. Ultimately, the biblical accounts testify to victory over death, because of the resurrection of Christ. In the Old Testament, however, this hope is at best inchoate, and its portrayal of the human experience largely confines it within the limits of mortal earthly existence. There is in its writings little reference back to the Eden story, but rather a many-faceted encounter with the realities of worldly existence.

For this reason, the Old Testament has resources for negotiating realistically with the hard edges of human experience. To the question whether it offers a fundamentally pessimistic or optimistic outlook on life, it has no single answer, but rather expresses a panorama of possibilities, with which readers can readily identify. It is not, therefore, a book of answers or winning formulae, but rather its potency lies in its capacity for engagement with the committed reader and reading communities. This, indeed, has been the function of Scripture throughout its history in the believing communities of Church and Synagogue. It has been a vehicle for them to know themselves in the presence of God. As such, it accompanies the human beings' honest recognition of their unfinished nature, and attends their spiritual commitment to formation and transformation. On this basis, Scripture becomes a rich resource for exploring the lineaments of human possibilities, for both good and ill.

Conditions of human wholeness

Granted these caveats, it is possible to identify some necessary conditions of human existence in the round, as an avenue into a biblical conception of health and malaise. There is no systematic description of what makes the human human; rather, a view of it may be derived from a range of biblical texts.

It is convenient, albeit not imperative, to begin with Genesis 1—3. These chapters put together elements in ordinary human existence that are regularly found in other parts of Scripture. The human is made, first, for relationship with God, who created them in his 'image' and 'likeness' (Gen. 1.26–27), and who seeks companionship with them (Gen. 3.8–9). They are made, second, for relationship with other humans, as is symbolized by their creation 'male and female' (Gen. 1.27), and consequently in marriage and in families. They relate, finally, to their created environment, animate and inanimate, as is entailed in the command to the first human pair to 'subdue the earth' and 'have dominion' over the other living creatures (Gen. 1.26, 28). Each of these elements is both established and troubled in the unfolding of Genesis 1—3. And they are present variously in the complex human portrayal that runs through Scripture.

The human relationship with God is manifest in narratives of encounter, as in Abraham's welcome of the LORD in the guise of three mysterious visitors (Gen. 18.1–2), in Jacob's dream at Bethel (Gen. 28.10–17), and his wrestling with the angel at the Jabbok river (Gen. 32.24–32). It is manifest also in the making of covenants, especially the Sinai covenant, whose terms and laws are outlined in Exodus 20—23 and in Leviticus and Deuteronomy. And it is seen in the practices of worship, in tabernacle and temple, and in other sacred localities in Israel. The biblical evidence for it includes the book of Psalms, which has proved an indispensable staple of worship and spirituality throughout the Christian centuries. But it is found too in narratives of prayer and pilgrimage, and indeed in the recurring story of the LORD's contest for the heart of Israel over against the attractive claims of other gods. The relationship between God and humans is complicated by human waywardness, in which people are repeatedly confronted in the severest terms by the prophets. Yet everywhere the possibility of harmony between God and humans is presupposed, and held out as the ultimate reality.

Relationships between people provide much of the texture of Scripture. They are often malignant. Cain's murder of his brother Abel (Gen. 4.1–16) sets down a marker early in the story of the primeval world, and has echoes everywhere, from the hatred of the sons of Jacob for their brother Joseph (Gen. 37), to the centuries-long fraternal enmity between Jacob-Israel and Esau-Edom (Amos 1.11–12; Obadiah), stories of abuse and adultery (2 Sam. 11, 13; Judg. 19), and the endless warring of nations bidding in turn for supremacy. Yet this litany is balanced by the real potential for good relating, in a love story such as Isaac and Rebekah's (Gen. 24), in the moving self-effacement of Esau at the return of the brother who had stolen his inheritance (Gen. 33), in the erotic love poems of the Song of Songs, in the faithful friendship of David and Jonathan (1 Sam. 20), and in the images of an inclusive 'Zion', to which nations come in pilgrimage to learn the teaching (tôrâ) of the LORD (Isa. 2.2–4).

The human relationship with the earth is also an essential part of the story. In Genesis the first humans are given responsibility for maintaining the garden which is their life-giving environment. It has been rightly noted that the idea of the Garden of Eden, in the ancient Near Eastern context, is far from a modern Western idea of a garden.[2] Rather, it denotes order as opposed to wildness, a suitable milieu for human growth and development, every kind of constructive undertaking, and indeed the creation of culture. While the human beings were expelled from their idyllic habitat (Gen. 3), the story nevertheless affirms our irrevocable relationship with the earth and everything in it. This is the reason why the LORD promises his chosen people not only that they will become numerous, but that they will flourish in a land he will give them – the pervasive theme of Deuteronomy. In one of that book's great climaxes, a section known formally as 'blessings and curses' (Deut. 28), the dual possibilities of great human happiness and great human distress are spelled out, largely in terms of the possession or non-possession of fruitful land. And the narrative-history of Israel follows suit, in a repeating counterpoint of the enjoyment and the forfeiture of land (as in the books of Judges and Kings). In this case too, however, the outlook is not all bleak, for the Old Testament is liberally seasoned with images of human enjoyment of bounty. Once again, the Song of Songs is a case in point, as is the book of Ruth, and numerous prophetic evocations of prosperity and well-being (such as Amos 9.11–15).

These elements in human flourishing do not come piecemeal, but are typically intertwined. The three fundamental relationships we have identified have the capacity to be healthful, and especially so when they are integrated together. Such integration can simply occur in ordinary life, as illustrated again by the book of Ruth. In the psalms too, there are glimpses of the flourishing life, in which the human agents exercise responsibility for the world around them and the people in it (e.g. Ps. 112.2–5, 9). Integration is particularly marked in the sphere of worship, as in the great pilgrimage feasts, when Israelites decide together to make journeys from their many places to one place, there to seek the face of the LORD. These harmonies come to expression in a number of psalms (e.g. Pss. 84 and 122), and their natural mode is one of joy (Deut. 16.13–15).

Aspects of human wholeness

We may now enquire further into what constitutes a healthy human being. The Old Testament has rich resources for an anthropology. Robert Gordis's *The Book of God and Man*[3] is actually about Job, but the title could serve for the whole Old Testament. We need not try to decide whether the Old Testament is centrally about God or about humanity. Suffice to say that every page is part of its portrayal of the great human adventure. No single genre can contain this portrayal. Narratives stage comedy and tragedy. Wisdom depicts a sense of beauty and order, as well as puzzlement over disorder. Songs of worship express the most intense emotions in praise, thanksgiving and lamentation. And the 'poetics' of all this literature enables the exploration of these deep things in the most exquisite and suggestive language. The Old Testament's unrivalled aesthetic achievement, in its entirety, is made to serve its articulation of what it is to be human. Our apprehension of its portrayal of the human experience, therefore, depends on the reader's, or reading community's, sensitive engagement with texts.

It follows that the Old Testament's depiction will resist any analytical reduction. However, it employs certain language concerning the human being that helps to build up a picture of what it means to speak of health.

The Old Testament writers use a variety of terms when they talk about themselves as persons.[4] In Psalm 103.1–5, the psalmist addresses himself as his 'soul' (*nepeš*), in a way that shows awareness of his inner self. In this passage (v. 1) it stands in parallel with the phrase 'all that is within me', which, though imprecise, also suggests inwardness. Yet equally these phrases apparently seek to express a totality of the human being. Indeed, the use of language for the human self resists any idea of compartmentalization. The term *nepeš* itself can bear various meanings, including physical ones, such as 'throat' (Ps. 105.18; Jon. 2.6), and the person simply as an individual,[5] as well as denoting the person's innermost or essential being. The range of meanings suggests that the idea of their essential being is not separable from their physical being, so that it can be hard to decide in some contexts whether to translate with a physical term or with the familiar 'soul'.[6]

The same holds true for the important term *lēb* or *lēbāb*, which is most often translated into English as 'heart', but can sometimes be rendered 'mind'. For example, in Deuteronomy 29.4 [29.3], some standard translations take *lēb* as 'mind' (the NRSV and the NIV), no doubt because in the context the term is associated with understanding. Others, however, like the ESV, translate it 'heart', perhaps under the influence of the common understanding of the term (there *lēbāb*) in Deuteronomy 6.5. The same dilemma was also known to the translators of LXX and the authors of the New Testament.[7] These instances suggest that the Hebrew writers were working with a kind of unitary understanding of the human that modern readers may not immediately recognize.

The point can be pursued across a wider field of expressions for the human being. The key term *rûaḥ*, 'spirit', is not some segment of the human make-up separate from the 'heart/mind' or 'soul'. Rather, in the Old Testament's usage, it can often overlap with these. It also plays a distinctive role in characterizing individual human beings. The psalmist who prays, 'Create in me a clean heart (*lēb*), O God' goes on to plead, 'put a new and right spirit (*rûaḥ nākôn*) within me' (Ps. 51.10 [12], 12[14]). 'Within me' is strictly 'in my midst', an undetermined concept implying that the person has a centre which is not encompassed by any one term.[8] It follows that the range of vocabulary for the human being is a function of the Old Testament writers' efforts to express the complexity of the whole person. It also belongs to its depiction of the human potential for relating to God. God's covenant people are to love him 'with all your heart/mind, with all your soul and with all your strength' (Deut. 6.5). And when the human 'spirit' is rightly disposed, it shows a likeness to the 'spirit' of God, hence the psalmist's prayer: 'Do not take your holy spirit (*rûaḥ qodšĕkā*) from me' (Ps. 51.11[13]).

The unity of the person is crucially important for the present topic. At issue is what might be meant by the 'mind' in the Old Testament perspective. The point has been addressed directly by Michael Carasik, who has argued that in Deuteronomy may be found 'the first coherent attempt to understand the mind'.[9] He argues that, both in Deuteronomy's emphasis on learning, knowledge and memory, and in other Old Testament writings, there was a 'psychology of knowledge', by which he means that, for the biblical writers, there was a state of awareness, or inner attitude, distinct from intention and action, though related to these.[10]

Carasik concedes, however, that there is in Deuteronomy an integration of the intellectual and the emotional in what he calls 'psychological commands'.[11] Deuteronomy's rhetoric is highly rational, in the sense that it regularly offers reasons for its commands: Israel is to serve Yahweh because he liberated them from bondage to another master in Egypt (Deut. 5.15); they are to keep the commandments because Yahweh disciplines them as a father disciplines his son (8.5); they are to love the 'stranger' (gēr) because they were themselves 'strangers in Egypt' (Deut. 10.19; 15.15).

Yet this reasoning rhetoric is also emotive, the classic text being, once again, the command to 'love' Yahweh. As Yahweh is 'one' (6.4), so his people are to love him with their whole being (6.5). The same exhortation reappears in 11.13, in a passage (11.13–23) that echoes the language of Deuteronomy 6.4–9. And so the whole section between the Decalogue (in chapter 5) and the law code (chapters 12—26) is framed by the call to 'love Yahweh'. This exploration of a biblical view of the mind, therefore, supports the contention that while the 'mind' is an unavoidable concept when we think about what it is to be human, it cannot be isolated from other essential aspects of the human constitution.

This point has some relevance to modern ways of thinking. The philosopher Mary Midgley has cautioned against what she sees as the residual attachment in public intellectual discourse to 'Descartes' violent separation of mind from body'.[12] She sees opposing dangers in materialism, in which only the body is real and the mind is not, and a kind of idealism that elevates the mind over the body to the point at which the body becomes a mere hindrance.[13] Both of these are 'reductions' of the human that fail to understand its complexity. She particularly warns against a Cartesian concept of the self as an abstraction from the embodied person, 'a kind of disembodied ghost'.[14] The myth of the intellect alone as the supreme human function she finds in certain modern scientific thought. Against all such reductive dualisms she argues against segmenting the human person. In common with Carasik (though in a different idiom), she argues for the unity of intellect and emotion.[15] Her argument for a conception of the human as a fusion of its various faculties and properties chimes with the biblical view I have been outlining, though Midgley herself argues from entirely different premises.

Human wholeness and worship

I have suggested so far that the conditions for human wholeness consist in relationships, between human persons, between humans and the non-human creation, and between humans and God. I have argued too that the individual is a complex unity. We go on now to consider how these two perspectives relate.

The book of Psalms offers avenues into an enquiry about both health and the disturbance of health. Claus Westermann's template of praise and lament[16] provides a key, as does Walter Brueggemann's model sequence of orientation, disorientation, and re-orientation.[17] In the psalmist's praise, they celebrate harmonies in the spheres we have identified. Praise may be broadly defined to include thanksgiving, and every kind of expression that affirms the goodness of God's ways in creation and salvation. That being so, praise can embrace petition.

The psalmist's address to God establishes the human–divine relationship as primary. This address can take different forms. Often it is direct, as in the opening of Psalm 30: 'I will extol you, O LORD.' This opening gives way to an appeal to others to join in praise (v. 4), affirmations about what the LORD has done in answer to prayer (vv. 5–10), and finally a return to direct address, with the accent on thanksgiving for restoration (vv. 11–12).

This divine–human relationship has a context in a world in which the parts interact for the benefit of all. Psalm 104 is the leading instance of this, with its affirmation of a harmonious creation, in which 'springs gush forth in the valleys' to quench the thirst of the wild beasts (vv. 10–11), the trees are homes for the birds, and the mountains for the wild goats (vv. 16–18). All creatures look to God, who gives them 'their food in due season' (v. 27). Human beings too are part of this construal of the world. Psalm 72 is a prayer for the king, in which his just rule is a correlative of prosperity and peace (vv. 5–7, 16). The harmonies in the created order are thus brought into the political and social realm, with its stipulation of justice and righteousness, and its protection of the vulnerable (v. 2). In Psalm 72's poetic imagination, these human goods are interwoven with the elements in nature, hence the prayer that 'the mountains [should] yield prosperity for the people, and the hills, in righteousness' (v. 3); and that the king himself should 'be like rain that falls on the mown grass, like showers that water the earth' (v. 6). This poetic evocation of deep harmonies in the world is matched by the beautiful climax of Psalm 85:

Steadfast love and faithfulness will meet;
  Righteousness and peace will kiss each other.

Faithfulness will spring up from the ground,
And righteousness will look down from the sky. (Ps. 85.10–11)

In these lines, first, virtues in human relating are given flesh in the social actions of meeting and kissing (v. 10); and, second, the same virtues[18] suggest the fruitfulness of the earth, and rain dropping from the sky (v. 11). These moral and social virtues do not only characterize human beings in harmony, but also belong to God.

The context in which all these relationships are supremely expressed is worship. The psalms look pervasively towards Zion, 'the joy of the whole earth' (Ps. 48.1), as the place of encounter with Yahweh, God of Israel. Zion was the place chosen by God, in which he installed his 'son', the king (Ps. 2.6–7). Zion is not merely a symbol or concept; it has a physical reality and actual location: 'We heard of it in Ephrathah, we found it in the fields of Jaar' (Ps. 132.6). It is contrasted with the 'mountain of Bashan' (Ps. 68.15–16), a reference to a mountain farther north that was a sanctuary of Baal. The LORD 'marched' to Zion from Sinai in order to take up his abode there (68.7–8, 17–18[8–9, 18–19]). His reign in Zion establishes his possession of the land of Israel, the land inhabited by his people in its many localities, in which they had their life and being. Most importantly, they regularly gather together in their localities in order to travel in pilgrimage to the holy place. The singer of Psalm 122 rejoices at the prospect of pilgrimage (122.1). He would not go alone: 'Let *us* go ... To it the tribes go up' (vv. 1, 4). His prayer for the peace of Jerusalem is made in part 'for the sake of my relatives and friends' (v. 8). The heart of the life of Israel is exposed in images of co-journeying through the localities of the land, with all the challenges of difficult terrain, and bringing it to life in the course of their travel and its goal (Ps. 84.5–7[6–8]). The God who made covenant with Israel and gave them land exerts his benevolent rule over it all by virtue of his dwelling in Zion. Here is the harmonious triangle: God and people; people and people; people and land.

In the midst of these fundamental interrelationships the voice of the individual is ever present, the prayers being uttered by one who speaks as 'I'. For the reader, this projected person is the universal entry-point to the psalms' world of human experience. The psalmist speaks in all the complexity of his/her inner being, sometimes signalled by a kind of inner dialogue, in which the self calls on the self to seek and praise God:

Bless the LORD, O my soul (*napšî / nepeš*). (Ps. 103.1)

'Come,' my heart (*libbî / lēb*) says, 'seek his face!'
Your face, LORD, do I seek. (Ps. 27.8)

For the pilgrim, the desire for God takes shape in the journey, requiring the investment of body and soul:

> My soul (*napšî / nepeš*) longs, indeed it faints for the courts of the
>   LORD;
> My heart (*libbî / lēb*) and my flesh (*bǝsārî / bāsār*) sing for joy
> to the living God. (Ps. 84.2[3])

To the elements of the inner life is added the psalmist's very flesh. It is their whole being that yearns for the coming encounter with God.

The life of the person encountered in the psalms is deep and only partly known to himself. The LORD's searching knowledge of the psalmist 'is too wonderful for me; it is so high that I cannot attain it' (Ps. 139.1, 6). This person is perpetually on the way to self-knowledge and fulfilment, which is the hoped-for goal of his standing in the presence of God.

Breakdown

As the praying person is perpetually 'on the way', it is not surprising that the journey can lead through dry places and deep darkness (Ps. 23.4; 84.6a[7a]). In the psalms, praise and thanksgiving are interwoven with the realities of illness, fragility and the presence of death. This is why many of the psalms are designated formally as 'laments' – that is, prayers in which the psalmist gives expression before God to feelings of distress and dislocation. These experiences are not exceptional, but part and parcel of human existence. In a representative example (Ps. 13), the psalmist bemoans the loss of God's presence, exacerbated by the fear of being shamed by triumphant enemies. Typically, these psalms return to praise. The act of protest at the grievous experience is also a prayer of petition, so that, against the grain, the psalmist posits again his trust in God's 'steadfast love', and declares his resolve once more to rejoice and praise (Ps. 13.5–6[6–7]).

In this psalm of dislocation and recovery (or 'disorientation' and 'reorientation' in Brueggemann's terms) it is noteworthy that the language is emotive, as in the psalms of praise that we have observed. The cries 'How long!' express anguish and impatience. The pain is 'in my soul' and sorrow 'in my heart' (v. 2). In this experience of dislocation, the primary relationships are fractured. The face of God is hidden; and the human relating is one of enmity (v. 4[5]). The psalmist is in lonely darkness ('Give light to my eyes') and feels the imminent threat of death (v. 3[4]).

These notes abound in the laments. The famous Psalm 22, adopted by the dying Jesus, opens with a poignant cry of God-forsakenness (vv. 1–3[2–4]). The psalmist, his body broken (vv. 14–18[15–19]), feels barely human (v. 6[7]) and knows the scorn and contempt of others (vv. 7–8[8–9]). Even more intensely, Psalm 88 depicts a shocking sense of forsakenness, in which the psalmist is thrust by God in his anger into deep, dark subterranean regions (vv. 3–7[4–8]): his companions desert him, consigning him to tormenting loneliness; terror and death stare him in the face; and the final line, with its triple abandonment by 'friend', 'neighbour' and 'companions', evokes the most devastating separation from every source of love and compassion, divine or human, and from the light itself (v. 18[19]).

If Psalm 88 depicts a near-total alienation, it need not be a final word. The laments more typically lead back from darkness to light. In Psalm 18, the subject is in the toils of death and feels a downward pull into the earth (vv. 4–5[5–6]). Here, however, God, commanding the forces of nature (vv. 7–15[8–16]), reaches down to haul the sufferer out of 'mighty waters', in order to deliver him into a 'broad place'. The primary relationships, to God, to other humans, and to the earth, intermingle here. Delivered by God from 'mighty waters', the psalmist is at the same time delivered from enemies (vv. 16–18[17–19]). The elements in the dire threat to his life reappear in the recovery. In response to the inner distress, 'the LORD, my God, lights up my darkness' (v. 28[29]); oppressed by enemies, he in turn overcomes them, and attains a position of rule (vv. 34–48[35–49]). Suffocating in the depths of the earth, he is brought out into a 'broad place', and has the physical strength to 'leap over a wall' (v. 29[30]), with all the light agility of a deer (v. 33[34]). And, finally, he is able to praise again the God in whom he can trust (vv. 49–50[50–51]).

Recovery

Given this portrayal of human existence, we may ask what can be learned from it about wellness and illness. May the psalms' brilliant, variegated picture of the person be read simply as a record of ordinary, 'unfinished', life in a fallen world? Among their evocations of deep disturbance, can one identify any that have moved beyond common experience into the realm of the pathological?

Such questions demand more than the psalms themselves can answer. There is no special language for mental illness in them. Their sense of the unity of the person, physical and non-physical, together with their lack of modern scientific categories, probably makes the search for evidence of mental illness fruitless. Yet this is only half an answer. As the psalms' genius is to reach deeply into the hearts and minds of those who read and use them, it is only readers who can give a verdict on the point.[19]

Nevertheless, if our survey has rightly identified the elements of a flourishing human life, it follows that these are also the elements in which unhealthiness may be marked. These elements are relationship to God, to other people, and to the non-human world. We remarked also that issues of health and unhealth may be played out in the spheres of worship and memory.

Psalm 42–43[20] illustrates the point. The psalmist's low mood is communicated to the reader by the repeated self-address: 'Why are you cast down, O my soul, and why are you disquieted within me?' (42.5, 11[6, 12]; 43.5). The psalmist utters his deep inner disturbance against a back-cloth of memory. He 'thirsts' for the presence of God (vv. 1–3[2–4]) as one who has in the past known the sweetness of that presence. Enwrapped with its memory is the memory of going to worship in company with others: not only going with them, but leading them, a throng and multi-tude, in an atmosphere of noisy rejoicing. The present disturbance of soul consists in these losses and the memory of them. He is now as one in mourning, beset by enemies who seek to shame him, and seriously damaged, 'as with a deadly wound in my body' (v. 10[11]). The loss of communion with God has ramifications for every part of his life.

Crucially, the memory of worship plays a healing part. It is in calling to mind his past existence as a co-worshipper that the psalmist understands the reality of who he is, and thus his true destiny. The repeated rhetorical question to himself, 'Why are you cast down ...?', is each time answered by the exhortation, again to himself: 'Hope in God, for I shall again praise him, my help and my God'. Curiously, this anticipation of praise is itself an act of praise. It also re-locates the psalmist in a relationship with God, which is more than a statement of intent, but a re-appropriation: '*my* help and *my* God'. Memory of the past becomes a pointer to the future. Here is a soul who knows that he is subject to great weakness, yet also that he is perpetually 'on the way', and that the destination is renewed fellowship with God and other human beings. It is a realization that is made in the act of worship.

Recovery is also a recovery into the living, active world. For a king, this might mean victory over enemies and restoration to rule (Ps. 18.43–48[44–49]); for one who confesses sin,[21] a return to 'teaching transgres-sors' (51.13[15]). For an ordinary person, perhaps a shepherd, it may mean walking and working in safe and pleasant places (Ps. 23.1–3), or the enjoyment of good hospitality in a protected environment (23.5).[22] The metaphors of negotiating terrain in Psalm 23 suggest a life of prac-tical adaptation to the external world. Such is the quiet assumption of a number of psalms. For example, Psalm 37, in terms reminiscent of wisdom literature, contrasts the modes of life of the righteous and the wicked, in which the righteous 'inherit the land' as a corollary of their right living (37.11, 21–22, 29), are generous with the fruit of their labours (v. 26), and do better with little than the wicked do in their abundance (v. 16; cf. Prov. 16.8). These are images of people who know how to relate to the external world, human and non-human together, in the exercise of their responsibilities as members of a community and stewards of the earth, and who flourish as a result.

Conclusion

Wholeness in Old Testament perspective is not perfection, nor does it consist in some ideal state of well-being. Rather, in biblical modelling, it inhabits the space between reality and the hoped-for perfection of all things.[23] Wholeness is a practice in which human fragility is fully self-aware, but finds a context in belonging and love, in the 'social body', in shared memory, and in the community's affirmations of the faith.

In seeking a biblical view of wholeness, it is not enough to analyse its elements, as in the foregoing. As indicated at the outset, the development of a biblical view is a matter of practice, involving the committed reader and reading community. The use of Scripture, therefore, in line with our observations about the unity of the person, is moral as well as intellectual, a matter of will as well as 'heart'. One corollary of this in the Church's life is the need to deploy in its practice the full range of biblical language, as argued by Brent Strawn,[24] who highlights discrepancies between the Old Testament's language of worship and some contemporary use of it in hymn and lectionary, the latter showing a tendency, he argues, to elide or diminish expressions of loss, oppression, fear, and fragility. To begin to lay hold on the kind of wholeness of which the Old Testament offers hope is to face honestly the problem of brokenness that is its consistent premise.

Notes

1 The terms for the human being are 'ādām and ben 'ĕnôš, traditionally 'man' and 'son of man'. The psalmist's question occurs also in Ps. 8.4[5] and Job 7.17. Where verse-numbering differs between English versions and the Hebrew Bible, the English numbering is adopted, with the Hebrew following in [...], as in the reference just given.

2 C. Bartholomew, 2011, *Where Mortals Dwell: A Christian View of Place for Today*, Grand Rapids, MI: Baker Academic.

3 R. Gordis, 1965, *The Book of God and Man: A Study of Job*, Chicago, IL: Chicago University Press.

4 The following passage draws somewhat on my 2016 *Being Human in God's World*, Grand Rapids, MI: Baker Academic, pp. 47–59.

5 See Gen. 46.15–27, several times, not always translated; Num. 31.28.

6 A case in point is Ps. 63.5[6], where *nepeš* is taken by *HALOT* as 'throat', but the NRSV has: 'My *soul* is satisfied as with a rich feast'.

7 Deut. 6.5 LXX[A] has *ex holēs tēs kardias sou*, but LXX [B] has *dianoias*. Both Matt. 22.37 and Mark 12.29–30 have forms of *kardia*, but also *dianoia* instead of 'might'. Luke 10.27 adds *dianoia* after 'strength'. Other texts where *lēb* or *lēbāb* is taken as 'mind' include: Num. 16.28 (KJV; NRSV paraphrases to 'of my own accord'); 24.13 (KJV; NRSV has 'will'). In Neh. 4.6 (3.38); Ps. 31.12 (13); Isa. 46.8; 65.17, NRSV has 'mind', in agreement with KJV.

8 It is similar to 'all that is within me' in Ps. 103.1.

9 M. Carasik, 2006, *Theologies of the Mind in Biblical Israel*, Studies in Biblical Literature 85; New York: Peter Lang, p. 215.

10 Carasik, *Theologies of the Mind*, pp. 75–80, cf. p. 47.

11 Carasik, *Theologies of the Mind*, pp. 199–201.

12 M. M. Midgley, 2004, *The Myths We Live By*, London and New York: Routledge, p. 57.

13 Midgley, *Myths*, p. 54. The latter misconception she attributes to David Hume. She notes certain modern scientific fantasies in which humanity evolves away from its current style of embodiment, and perhaps takes form, as Freeman Dyson has it, 'in an interstellar black cloud … or in a sentient computer' (*Myths*, pp. 142–3).

14 Midgley, *Myths*, p. 99.

15 'The division between mind and body, conceived as essentially one between reason and feeling, is not necessary. There is no set of perforations down the middle of a human person directing us to tear at this point' (Midgley, *Myths*), p. 144.

16 C. Westermann, 1981, *Praise and Lament in the Psalms*, Edinburgh: T&T Clark.

17 W. Brueggemann, 1980, 'Psalms and the Life of Faith: a Suggested Typology of Function', *Journal for the Study of the Old Testament*, 17, pp. 3–32.

18 Faithfulness and righteousness may be said, because of the parallelism, to stand for the more expanded list in v. 10.

19 In thinking about this topic I have been influenced by Sharon Hastings' 2020 book, *Wrestling With My Thoughts*, Nottingham: IVP. The author, a qualified doctor, gives an account of her experience of severe mental illness, which reveals unflinchingly the darkness and terrors of it in ways that resonate with the language of the psalms, which she liberally cites. I am grateful to Sharon for allowing me to see her work in stages of its development. Sharon is my niece.

20 These two appear to constitute a single psalm, because of formal continuities between them.

21 According to the superscription, the one who confesses is David, but in the body of the psalm the one who utters the confession could be anybody.

22 The 'shepherd' in the psalm is, of course, the LORD. However, the imagery is evidently drawn from the life of someone, like a human shepherd, who is obliged to

find a way through terrain both hospitable and inhospitable. The heading 'A Psalm of David' no doubt trades on the idea of a king as shepherd. But the life-setting appears to be more humble.

23 Jesus' 'Beatitudes' are another example of this (Matt. 5.3–10). The term 'blessed' there (*makarioi*) is close to the cry 'Happy is the one', in, for example, Ps. 1.1 (*'ašrê hā'îš*).

24 B. Strawn, 2017, *The Old Testament is Dying: A Diagnosis and Recommended Treatment*, Grand Rapids, MI: Baker Academic.

3

Jesus and Madness

JOANNA COLLICUTT

Either this man was, and is, the Son of God, or else a madman or some-thing worse.[1]

This oft-quoted phrase of C. S. Lewis rests on the unquestioned assumption that 'madness'[2] and the divine are mutually exclusive. The assumption gains plausibility from two more fundamental theses, the first appealing to the modernist mindset of Lewis's time, and the second of more contemporary concern. The first thesis is that *madness* represents irrationality whereas God is rational. The second thesis is that *madness* represents ill health whereas God is healthy.

In this chapter I interrogate aspects of these assumptions, paying par-ticular attention to the treatment of the *madness* of Jesus of Nazareth, both in the biblical texts themselves and their later reception. I go on to consider the theological and pastoral implications (both risks and benefits) of uncoupling madness from the concept of irrationality and ill health in order to develop the scandalous idea of a *mad* God incarnate.

Resisting the rush to premature explanation: the odd, the weird and the strange

In one of the foundational but often overlooked texts of modern psychi-atry, *Allgemeine Psychopathologie* first published in 1913, the polymath Karl Jaspers drew a key distinction between 'understanding' and 'explan-ation'.[3] He advocated understanding, by which he meant detailed empathetic description of anomalous human experience, as the first task of the psychiatrist.[4] Explanation of this experience as a 'symptom' of something else (whether this be a psychiatric illness like 'depression', a psychological process like 'reaction to trauma', or a biological observ-able fact such as 'reduced levels of brain serotonin') comes second, for it can only take place once the experience is understood in its own right.

Jaspers held that the phenomenon of *madness* has inherent structure and meaning (it can be understood, not just explained), and thus a kind of rationality.

I try to communicate and promote this philosophy to my students in my mental health teaching. We begin by considering a series of case studies in which it would be all too easy to rush to diagnosis. Instead I ask the students to resist this by tuning into their feelings of 'This person is (being) a bit odd' and to reflect on the conditions under which 'a bit odd' becomes 'really weird' and even 'deeply strange'. These terms are chosen resolutely to avoid technical or explanatory language, to illustrate that experience and behaviour seem to vary along one or more continua, and to emphasize that encountering human case studies like these involves interpersonal intuition as much as objective judgement. We go on through group discussion to draw out issues of meaning, relationality, vulnerability, distress, and life-span context. In my experience the students' first instinct is to say things like, 'She's got OCD', but having intentionally set that aside, they can readily enter a more phenomenological mode of engaging with the material.

It soon becomes evident that charting a path through anomalous experience is not as straightforward as deciding whether an individual has crossed a line from 'normal' to 'abnormal' and then reaching for a diagnostic manual to confirm which variety of abnormality s/he is displaying.

Madness and religion

This talk of varieties brings to mind William James's Gifford lectures of 1901–2, published under the title *The Varieties of Religious Experience*, and highlights the apparent connection between *madness* and religiosity, especially its ecstatic forms, which has been noted from earliest times (see for example, 1 Sam. 10; Jer. 29.26). As it happens, I lifted the taxonomy of 'odd→weird→strange' from a drinks party conversation in which it was being applied not to psychiatric patients but to churchgoers. James himself writes:

> In delusional insanity … we may have … a sort of religious mysticism turned upside down. The same sense of ineffable importance in the smallest events, the same texts and words coming with new meanings, the same voices and visions and leadings and missions … It is evident that from the point of view of their psychological mechanisms, the classic mysticism and these lower mysticisms spring from the same mental level.[5]

James is arguing that there is phenomenological overlap, if not identity, between *madness* and what he calls 'religious mysticism', and it raises the question of how and why one might draw a distinction between them,[6] and also other related conditions, such as being under the influence of psychedelic drugs.[7] This is an aspect of the broader task of imposing some sort of order on anomalous behaviours, a task not limited to the 'developed' West:

> there is no culture in which men and women remain oblivious to erratic, disturbed, threatening or bizarre behaviour in their midst, whatever the culturally defined context of that behaviour.[8]

The medical anthropologist Cecil Helman has argued that communities approach the challenge by invoking two dimensions, one relating to the nature of the behaviour displayed, and one relating to the norms of the community. These are used to delineate four conceptual zones, which determine the way the behaviour is recognized, labelled, explained, and 'treated' by the community. Figure 1 is a modified version of his model.[9]

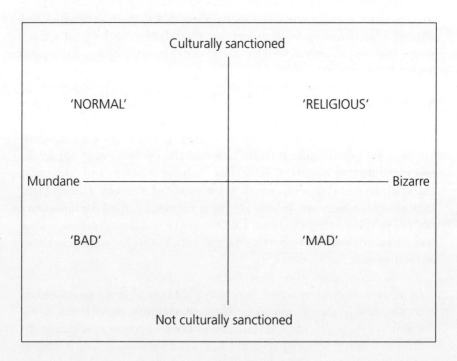

Figure 1

Helman emphasizes that these zones are fluid both between cultures and within the same culture over generations. He uses the example of alcohol consumption, which may be framed as 'enjoying a drink' (normal); a religious practice, as in the wine of Communion; a sign of moral degeneracy; or a (mental) health issue. A similar analysis could be applied to self-imposed food restriction, which may be framed as going on a diet (normal); religious fasting; being overly picky; or having an eating disorder.[10] Later generations may look critically at the attributions of previous generations or contemporary but socially and geographically distant cultures; the case of same-sex relationships is an obvious example that is currently relevant for the Anglican Communion.

According to this scheme, the classification of bizarre behaviour as religious rather than *mad* rests on the degree to which its form and the circumstances under which it occurs are sanctioned by the community and seen as having a rationale and purpose in line with its worldview. For example, trance in an official shaman during a recognized ritual would be seen as religious, but an ordinary villager entering altered states of consciousness (ASCs) unpredictably would be seen as *mad*. The role of a shaman is to predict and control events that are important for community survival, but unpredictable and uncontrollable by the usual methods of skill and common sense.[11] Shamans may indeed show very bizarre behaviour, especially while undergoing ASCs, but this occurs in a controlled context, with an intelligible rationale that is itself all about control. Paul draws the distinction between this and *madness* in his instructions on speaking in tongues in 1 Corinthians. People who speak in tongues that do not disclose knowledge beneficial to the community look as if they are *mainomai* (out of their minds) (1 Cor. 14.23).

Not all unsanctioned behaviour is classified as *mad*; it may be seen as simply immoral. The distinction rests on its strangeness, together with the level of social awareness shown by the individual concerned; for example, the behaviour of a man who murders his partner and hides her body would be seen as bad, but that of a man who murders his partner and shares his bed with her remains for many months is more likely to be seen as *mad*.

This distinction between *mad* and bad is written into the British judiciary system, and is the focus for complex and contentious arguments (a recent example is the case of Sally Challen whose conviction of murdering her abusive husband was quashed by the High Court in February 2019 on the grounds that she was suffering from PTSD at the time). But the boundaries are blurred, and things become even more complex when behaviour that is not sanctioned by the dominant culture nevertheless has religious content or religious rationale ('bad religion' or '*mad* religion'), as in the murder of Private Lee Rigby in 2013 by Islamist extremists Michael Adebolajo and Michael Adebowale. Their trial was nearly hijacked by the public statements of Russell Brand in a newspaper article entitled 'Blame this on madness ... not Muslims'[12] in which he attempted to remove Islam from the discourse altogether by arguing that the crime was simply a symptom of a particularly pernicious form of mental illness. In the event, Adebowale was convicted but subsequently diagnosed with a form of psychosis complicated by drug use, whose course was intertwined with his religion (the psychosis was in remission during his period as a Muslim when the killing took place, but re-emerged when he reverted to his cradle Christianity).

A particularly interesting case that straddles the *mad*/bad/religious zones is that of Franz Jägerstätter (1907–43), an Austrian peasant who was executed by the Nazis in Berlin for refusing to fight for the Third Reich. He had experienced a religious awakening in 1936, and thereafter adopted a profound, if not obsessive, Roman Catholic faith. Jägerstätter felt called by Christ to passive resistance to the Nazis, and persisted in this stance despite attempts to dissuade him by the local police, his parish priest, and the Bishop of Linz – the latter arguing that Jägerstätter was neglecting the higher call of Christ to provide for his wife and three small daughters. Jägerstätter's community also felt that his behaviour was reckless and might endanger the whole village. When his defence lawyer pointed out that millions of Catholics, including priests and seminarians, were engaged in combat for the Third Reich, Jägerstätter responded, 'They have not been given the grace.'[13] Even the Nazis were reluctant to execute him; at his court martial he was offered a guarantee that he would not be called to bear arms as long as he agreed to serve. He refused, was condemned, and beheaded some weeks later.

Gordon Zahn's careful study of the relevant documents, and his interviews with many of the key witnesses in visits to Jägerstätter's home village of St Radegund in the 1960s, revealed a mix of attitudes to him: solidarity, grief, compassion, and exasperation. There was nevertheless an almost unanimous opinion held by the community who had known him since childhood that he had always been '*g'spinnt*' ('touched in the head', p. 141 in Zahn), and that his religious awakening had pushed him over the edge to total derangement. That is, he started off odd, became weird, and ended up self-destructively strange, a view apparently shared by the senior officers at his court martial. The Roman Catholic Church has taken a different view; Jägerstätter was beatified in 2007, the ceremony taking place in Linz Cathedral, the seat of the Bishop who had argued against his proposed course of action on theological grounds 64 years earlier.

The genuine ambiguities in the story of Franz Jägerstätter lead quite naturally into a question that I routinely put to my students: 'Where might Jesus of Nazareth sit in Helman's model?' There is little doubt that he exhibited challenging and anomalous behaviour that went beyond the odd: 'It is not historically impossible that Jesus was weird and ... the view that he plotted his own redemptive death makes him strange in any century.'[14]

As this section has indicated, the elegance of Helman's model comes at the cost of a degree of over-simplification. Nevertheless, it has the capacity to form a useful hermeneutic framework to draw out processes at work in the biblical text and in its later reception. The exercise of trying to 'place' Jesus for oneself can also form the basis of some important theological reflection, with the potential to support a hospitable understanding of the odd, weird and strange in both ourselves and others.

The Gospel accounts of Jesus' behaviour

The madness of Jesus

As the reference to Paul in the previous section indicates, first-century Near Eastern culture drew a conceptual distinction between ecstatic states that represent encounter with the divine and just being 'out of one's mind'. This has been described as 'divine' versus 'clinical *madness*';[15] however, in this chapter I will avoid the medical connotations of 'clinical' and instead use the terms 'divine *madness*' and 'simple *madness*'. In Mark's Gospel Jesus' family seek to restrain (perhaps protect) him apparently because they assume he is the latter; he was said to be *exestē* (Mark 3.21). It is not clear from the Greek exactly who was saying this (it could have been his family or other people). The tense suggests a time-limited state rather than a stable condition; that is, Jesus is said to be having an episode of weirdness rather than to be inherently a weird person. Nevertheless, Mark fills out the picture by recording that this was troubling to at least some of his family circle rather than a source of pride or awe (Mark 3.31–32 may be a continuation of this theme).

Paul uses the same word – *exestēmen*, perhaps ironically, to describe his and Timothy's mental state in a passage on zeal amid affliction in the Corinthian correspondence. Crucially he asserts that the form of the behaviour is of little consequence in itself compared with its telos: 'if we are beside ourselves, it is for God; if we are in our right mind, it is for you' (2 Cor. 5.13).

Neither of these verses posits a specific explanation for being 'beside oneself', but the opening section of Mark's Gospel can be read as broadly explanatory. It begins with an assertion that this is an account of 'good news'. The choice of the word *euangelion* positions Jesus' kingdom programme as a subversion of the good news of the *Pax Romana* of the Emperor Augustus, and is intricately connected with the concept of *shālôm* from the Hebrew Bible, something that we might understand as holistic well-being. At characteristic fast pace the narrative recounts a series of incidents in which Jesus is shown to have astonishing authority. Some of these are in areas of conventional religious practice (Mark 1.21–22), others are in the moral arena (2.5–12), some involve healing, and finally in chapter 4 he is shown to have authority over the forces of nature. Descriptions of Jesus' behaviour in all these contexts vary from an almost casual mundanity (2.5; 4.39), through feelings of compassion (6.34), to being marked by a degree of charisma that pulled in vast crowds (1.33, 37, 43; 2.2; 3.7, 20), with an observation of clairvoyance (2.8) along the way.

It is perhaps not surprising that following his baptism, during which he is said to have had a mystical or visionary experience, and the subsequent testing in the wilderness that implies undergoing one or more ASCs, the first healing encounter is with a demoniac. Jesus successfully commands a demon to come out of a man, and this is immediately interpreted as an external mark of authority that validates the experientially authoritative nature of his teaching (1.27). This connection between casting out demons and teaching authority is repeated in 3.15, and it alerts the reader to the fact that the word 'authority' is linguistically connected with 'authenticity': truth-telling is set in opposition to the demonic.

For Mark, everything Jesus does, whether 'beside himself or in his right mind', points to his authority and to the good news that he proclaims; it is divine rather than simple *madness*. Yet Mark shows himself aware that other interpretations of Jesus' behaviour are to be had, and presumably were doing the rounds both in Jesus' community and in Mark's own context 30 years later; for within the narrative he offers perspectives from the religious authorities, the family, the crowds, and Jesus himself. A related and important point is that Jesus' behaviour only becomes of interest because of the interplay between it and those who encounter him. This is not an account of someone being weird in the privacy of his own room but on the public stage;[16] it is not so much that Jesus *is* weird but that a weirdness emerges in particular sorts of interactions with others. This is perhaps most clear in Jesus' encounters with demoniacs.

Madness and demons

As has often been noted,[17] reconstructing the thought-world within which Jesus practised his ministry is a hazardous exercise; the documents available are limited, and from only very roughly similar time and place, and even these are susceptible to multiple readings and over-readings. The Gospels, written towards the end of the first century and in the diaspora with its more Hellenized ethos, are already works of interpretation of the original historical events that occurred 30 or more years previously in rural Galilee. Mark has a particular interest in and perspective on demons.[18] Luke takes a more naturalistic approach, reminding us that *madness* was not always attributed to demons in the ancient world, especially by the educated elite:[19] 'While [Paul] was making this defence, Festus exclaimed, "You are out of your mind, Paul! Too much learning is driving you insane!"' (Acts 26.24).

Here the assumed cause of Paul's *madness* (*mania*) is presented as quite mundane: a psychological phenomenon we would all recognize – information overload. In fact, Luke does not use the language of demons at all in Acts (referring to the exorcisms in Acts 16 and 19 in terms of '(evil) spirits'). Nevertheless, he uses it freely in his Gospel. A possible reason for this is that demon vocabulary came unnaturally to him, but as a meticulous historian he showed respect for his source Jesus material (including Mark) by retaining this vocabulary in his Gospel.

In an earlier study I explored demon language in the New Testament:

> The gospels use the phrase 'having a demon' or 'demonized one' (participles of the verb *daimonizomai*), together with the phrase 'having an unclean or evil spirit' to describe certain distressing conditions. (People in the New Testament are never described as being 'possessed by' demons or spirits – they 'have' them in rather the way we might have a cold.) ... These all conform to a pattern: there is some sort of behavioural disability or disturbance, and there is no obvious physical cause.[20]

At its most basic, demon vocabulary is used as a fairly vague idiom. Today we use words like 'bug' or 'virus' in this way; while these terms can denote a complex technical explanation, their casual everyday usage is more descriptive than explanatory. It may be objected that people today do not think of viruses and other popular disease concepts as intentional malign agents, but a moment's thought will confirm that we often speak as if they are.[21] This is not surprising in light of research in cognitive science of religion indicating the natural human capacity for invoking invisible agents as a kind of folk explanation for things that are hard to predict and control.[22] We need to remember that it is in just such areas of life that shamans come into their own.

The New Testament does of course use demon vocabulary in a more specific way to denote people who behave and speak as if they are totally controlled by unseen agents, and whose normal identity appears to have been supplanted by another – that is, people who are not simply lacking some ability (Matt. 9.32), but who are subject to certain forms of ASC. Again, this vocabulary, while more specific in its reference, may nevertheless be used purely descriptively – rather as we might say 'He's psychotic' without specifying which of the many underlying health conditions this behaviour pattern might signify, or indeed without indicating whether we bought into a medical model of psychosis at all.

This is the most that can be said with any certainty about New Testament accounts of demonized individuals, for the references to these phenomena do not go beyond description to explanation.[23] In summary, the people involved were experiencing a range of conditions that were troubling to themselves and/or their community in various ways; a subset of these, conditions involving ASCs, fall most easily into Helman's *mad* zone.

It is possible to make sense of such phenomena from a number of perspectives, pre-modern, modern or postmodern. Clearly, there was a popular understanding in Jesus' culture that malign invisible agents were at work. (The degree to which this might connect with the various angelologies and demonologies in the literature surviving from the Second Temple period[24] is unknown.) Something bad was thought to be driving the affected individuals *mad*. Again, this is not so far from present-day accounts of psychosis and dissociative disorders that implicate the malign agents of community and familial pressures, childhood abuse, and trauma experiences as major causal factors.[25] Whereas the ancient world conceived of these agents as personal, granting them conscious intentionality and supernatural powers,[26] the modern world post-Freud posits the operation of impersonal natural biological and intrapsychic processes, and the postmodern world post-Foucault posits impersonal natural power dynamics working via socio-linguistic construction. But all agree that people are demonized by the largely invisible operation of malign forces.

From mad to bad

At one point in John's Gospel Jesus is described by his opponents as both having a demon and being insane (*mainomai*) (John 10.20), the two being used interchangeably in the style of a Hebrew parallelism. Here the issue is not that Jesus is in an ASC but that he is talking grandiose nonsense, or expressing what we might describe as thought disorder together with what sounds very like suicidal ideation. Earlier (7.20) the crowds have used demon vocabulary to communicate that Jesus is exhibiting what we would call paranoid delusions. Yet the text makes it clear that this is an issue of debate (10.19, 21), a debate that circles through chapters 7 to 10. If Jesus is exhibiting simple *madness*, then how could he have healed the man born blind (in chapter 9)? Surely this would point to divine *madness*? If so, then Jesus would sit firmly in the 'religious' zone of Helman's model; but in order to place him here, some connection with the religious tradition must be made – hence the introduction of Abraham in chapter 8. This is then blown completely out of the water by Jesus' enigmatic words, 'Before Abraham was, I am' (8.58). This is such an existentially disorienting statement that it is perhaps not surprising that 'they picked up stones to throw at him' (8.59; 10.31).

All the Gospels in their different ways describe a similar process: Jesus' behaviour and message are anomalous; various hypotheses are advanced to explain it, but there is a relentless move by the authorities towards placing him in the 'bad' quadrant of Helman's model; this is effected by the introduction of a narrative that moves beyond dismissing his *madness* in terms of having a demon – 'He's a nutter, so you don't need to take anything he says seriously' – to explaining it in cosmic moral terms – 'He's evil' or 'He is the Satan'. In the synoptic Gospels this finds its expression in 'The Beelzebul controversy' (Matt. 10.25; 12.24–29; Mark 3.22–30; Luke 11.15–22) in which Jesus' special connection with demonized people who so often recognized him[27] is attributed to his sharing their condition – 'it takes one to know one' – and his apparent authority over evil and unclean spirits comes from the fact that he is the Lord of evil and uncleanness.

This elision of *madness* with moral ambivalence is particularly clear in Mark 3 where the Beelzebul controversy follows on immediately from the incident when Jesus' family attempt to seize him. It is a common move in our own time, often via the notion of 'pathology', an ostensibly morally neutral medical term that nevertheless has moral overtones. Louise Lawrence[28] observes this move in psychological interpretations of biblical characters such as Ezekiel, whose message is largely discredited in the process. In our own time the elision of mystical experiences with temporal lobe epilepsy has been used to support arguments that not only reduce such experiences to brain processes,[29] but declare them to be sick and 'thus' morally harmful.[30]

Jesus' response to the Beelzebul charge is to pronounce it an unforgivable category error (Matt. 12.31–32 and parallels). While it might be excusable to wonder if Jesus is simply *mad* rather than divinely *mad* when first encountering him (doing the Son of Man an injustice), it is quite another matter cynically to place his behaviour in the 'bad' zone when faced with all the evidence (the sin against the Holy Spirit). The Evangelists present this move as cynical precisely because it is an intentional step towards the goal of removing Jesus by Roman judicial execution. To be fair, this goal appears to have been helped along by Jesus' violent actions in the Temple (Matt. 21.12–13 and parallels), equally interpretable as *mad* or bad, but certainly not normal or religious.

In his 2007 article 'The Madness of King Jesus', Justin Meggitt addresses the issue of the apparent reluctance of Pilate to execute Jesus for sedition and, more importantly, the fact that, in an otherwise inexplicable departure from the usual practice, none of his disciples were arrested and executed.[31] He presents a persuasive argument that the Roman authorities believed Jesus to be neither a political insurgent nor a mystic or prophet, but someone, in today's terminology, with a mental health condition or a learning disability or both (a striking parallel with the case of Jägerstätter). While such individuals were often simply chastised (for example by flogging) and released, Meggitt argues that Jesus' behaviour and attitude may have been just troublesome enough to get him executed. His movement was a bizarre personality cult, not a political force, and so his followers were not pursued.

Meggitt draws heavily on the accounts of the mocking of Jesus (as a lunatic) by the Roman guard (Mark 15.16–20 and parallels, which include jeering at his reputed clairvoyance in Matthew and Luke's accounts). These find close parallels with Philo's account of the treatment of the 'madman' Carabas in 'Against Flaccus'. The parallels with Josephus' account of Jesus ben Ananias appear even closer:

> there was one Jesus the son of Ananus, a plebian and husbandman, who ... began on a sudden to cry aloud, 'A voice from the east, a voice from the west, a voice from the four winds, a voice against Jerusalem and the holy house, a voice against the bridegrooms and the brides, a voice against the whole people!' This was his cry, as he went about by day and by night, in all the lanes of the city (302) ... Hereupon, as our rulers supposing, as the case proved to be, that this was a sort of divine fury in the man, brought him to the Roman procurator; (304) where he was whipped until his bones were laid bare; yet did he not make

any supplication for himself, nor shed any tears, but turning his voice to the most lamentable tone possible, at every stroke of the whip his answer was, 'Woe, woe to Jerusalem!' (305) And when Albinus (for he was then our procurator) asked him who he was, and whence he came, and why he uttered such words; he made no manner of reply to what he said, but still did not leave off his melancholy ditty, till Albinus took him to be a madman, and dismissed him (306).[32]

Conclusions from New Testament evidence

The Gospels agree that Jesus was thought to be *mad*, and they present a fierce debate within the Jewish culture of his time as to whether this was simple or divine *madness*. The fact that this debate is presented quite openly suggests that the issue was well-known as an independent tradition.[33] Invoking a hermeneutic of suspicion, it may be that the biblical record of Jesus' weirdness is the 'tip of an iceberg, intimating what is submerged'.[34] Meggitt's historical argument that the Roman authorities took it for granted that Jesus was *mad* (probably simply *mad*, but for their purposes the type of *madness* is largely irrelevant), adds weight to the hypothesis that weirdness and strangeness were recognized aspects of his personality, interconnected with his ministry of proclamation and healing, and a key aspect of his ultimate mission.

The Church

Just as the Gospels depict the Jewish religious authorities as seeking to move Jesus from the *mad* to the bad zone in Helman's model, the Church has sought to move him to the religious zone. The beginnings of this can be seen in the pages of the New Testament itself. A first move is to establish that Jesus was not bad. This is most characteristic of Luke, whose writings can in part be framed as an exercise in political apologetics: 'When the centurion saw what had taken place, he praised God and said, "Certainly this man was innocent"' (Luke 23.47).

Alongside this theme, and dominating it, is the move to (re-)connect Jesus with the inherited religious tradition. This is evident throughout the New Testament, in which Jesus is repeatedly and systematically presented as the fulfilment of prophecy. This is not without its challenges – for example, that his home town was Nazareth (John 1.46) and that he was not descended from a priestly line (Heb. 7.3, 15–16). The most serious difficulty is the scandalous manner of his death, described by Paul as a 'stumbling block' to devout Jews (1 Cor. 1.23), including himself (Gal. 3.13).[35]

In an article that explored the rise of the early Church through the lens of the psychological concept of post-traumatic growth,[36] I argued that the Emmaus Road story can be viewed as a summary narrative depicting the process of struggling with this stumbling block (Luke 24.20–21). I argued that it is 'both a simple story about three people on one particular day and a sophisticated microcosmic account of the presumably more gradual birth of the early Church' as it got to grips with reconciling the traumatic and deeply strange death of Jesus with the inherited religious tradition.[37] This centres on the phrase 'Was it not necessary that the Messiah should suffer these things...' (v. 26). I suggested that the active connection of disorienting events with existing but re-worked cultural assumptions and personal beliefs ('beginning with Moses and all the prophets', v. 27) represents positive, indeed transformative, trauma processing. But in the context of this chapter it could equally be described as a way of moving Jesus out of the *mad* zone towards that of institutional religion. The episode even ends with a reference to a formal cultic practice – the 'breaking of the bread' (v. 35).

While premodern culture had little difficulty in accommodating divine *madness*, tolerating a blurred boundary between *madness* and religiosity, the rise of modern psychiatry has rendered this problematic. Following on from the Enlightenment, public discourse has located *madness* firmly in the mind of the individual, conceiving it as a kind of sickness – a 'mental health' issue. It is not considered appropriate or enlightened to describe people with psychosis simply as 'strange'; it is more usual to describe them as 'very unwell'. This is the dominant discourse in our society, and there are no doubt significant advantages to understanding *madness* in this way; it is nevertheless controversial. This is most evident in, but not limited to, the areas of diagnostics, where the charge is the meaningless medicalization of human distress;[38] medication, where the charge is that drugs do not provide a cure but only supress 'symptoms' and often bring significant unwanted effects;[39] and conceptual foundations, where the evidence-base for the whole notion of psychiatric disease entities is questioned.[40]

There is also a theological problem. If the public imagination equates all *madness* with sickness, the idea of divine *madness* no longer has a place. Having established that Jesus was not bad, he can only be rationally religious or mentally ill (Lewis's alternatives set out at the beginning of this chapter). The idea of a constitutionally sick Jesus cannot be accommodated within traditional Christian theology that conceives of God as the source of all health and well-being, though it has precedents in liberation theology approaches to disability.[41] It also creates a big problem for Christian apologetics. Yet the evidence for Jesus' weirdness remains, and Christian interpreters in the age of psychiatry have to find a way around it.

In her book *Bible and Bedlam*, Louise Lawrence explores the way that this has been done, identifying something she refers to as 'ideological gatekeeping' of the *madness* of Jesus (and also Paul).[42] Perhaps the earliest example of this is Albert Schweitzer's push-back against the psychiatric biographies of Jesus that were doing the rounds at the beginning of the twentieth century.[43] Schweitzer, writing as both biblical scholar and medical man, emphasized the eschatological content and context of Jesus' teaching partly as an attempt to open up a space between rational religiosity and mental illness that can accommodate at least some of Jesus' apparent eccentricities.

Lawrence identifies and criticizes several other tropes that also seem to fulfil this function in the subsequent literature: Jesus as creative genius (productive *madness*); Jesus as psychiatrist (empathetic *madness*); Jesus as resilient hero (*madness* conquered); Jesus the wounded healer (therapeutic *madness*); Jesus as representative of all human experience (*madness* normalized). She sees these as to varying extents expressions of sanism,[44] because, by drawing limits around or providing meaning and purpose to Jesus' own *madness*, they 'other' people whose *madness* cannot be re-framed in these benign sorts of way. Sanitized *madness* is no longer *madness* or, to use Pauline terms, an unproblematized cross is no longer the cross.

Divine folly: really dead and simply *mad*

In a famous passage in 1 Corinthians, Paul speaks boldly of the 'foolishness' (*mōria*) of the cross, not modifying it with terms like 'apparent', and even going so far as to speak of the 'foolishness of God' (1 Cor. 1.25). This inversion of the usual ways of talking about the divine is strongly connected with his language of boasting and shame:

> May I never boast of anything except the cross of our Lord Jesus Christ. (Gal. 6.14a)

> For I am not ashamed of the gospel. (Rom. 1.16a)

> But God chose what is foolish in the world to shame the wise; God chose what is weak in the world to shame the strong. (1 Cor. 1.27)

There is also a subtle link with Paul's assertions that Christ became a 'curse' (see Gal. 3.10) and was made sin (2 Cor. 5.21).

These theological statements connect well with Meggitt's historical reconstructions of the nature of the mocking of Jesus by the Roman authorities and also with the Gospel accounts of his humiliation on the cross. Here the debate about whether he is divinely *mad* or simply *mad* continues, as passers-by taunt him to save himself and wonder whether Elijah will come to save him (Matt. 27.42 and parallels; Matt. 27.49). Public mocking and baiting has been the lot of the *mad* throughout history; the treatment of mental hospital patients as theatrical spectacles even has a central place in the genesis of modern psychiatry through the practice of Jean-Martin Charcot (1825-93).[45]

There is a horrible irony in this, because exposure to public shaming is one of the core themes at the heart of the psychic distress experienced by people seeking help from mental health professionals. Anxiety at being uncovered, out in the open, and stared at is part of our evolutionary heritage,[46] and is the focus for several phobias and forms of psychosis. The 'depressive cognitive triad'[47] holds the world to be meaningless, the future hopeless, and crucially the self to be worthless (and thus an object of shame). Human self-worth is a socially negotiated quality, and it is closely tied to a sense of belonging to and abiding by the cultural and moral norms of one's family and tribe.[48] The emotion of shame is a signal that something more fundamental – belonging – is in jeopardy.

The deepest, most primal human fears are those of being abandoned by our primary caregivers and cast out from our social group; of losing control of our everyday existence; and of being unable to master chaos by making meaning. They signify physical and existential annihilation. All 'mental health conditions' are variations on these themes, differing simply in terms of which theme is foregrounded; the balance between undergoing the feared experience and defending against it; and the sorts of psychic defences that are employed.

In the crucifixion of Jesus all these primal fears are realized. The cross is death unsanitized by tropes such as 'military hero' or 'political martyr' (Phil. 2.8b). Instead, Jesus is rejected by his own and handed over to a jurisdiction that is outside of his own nation (Rom. 4.25); he is executed 'outside the camp' (Heb. 13.11–12) and undergoes a profane death (Deut. 21.23); he is deserted by his friends (Mark 14.27); he utters a cry of parental abandonment (Mark 15.24). As has already been noted, he is naked and exposed to the critical and shaming public gaze (Phil. 2.8a, where the word *etapeinōsen* literally means 'made ashamed'); he is passive, with no control over his fate;[49] he is in a place that is devoid of meaning. And then he dies.

Martin Luther made the important point that Jesus' undergoing a particularly unpleasant form of dying is only part of the message of the cross. It is easy to pass over the fact that he was really dead at the end of it. He did not have a brief nap before awakening refreshed on Easter Sunday – a kind of pseudo-death. Instead, Luther writes:

> He descended into the depths of all depths, under the law, under the devil, death, sin and hell; and that, I think, is verily the last and lowest depth. (*Sermon* on Ephesians 4.8–10)

This descent has been characterized psychologically by Anthony Harvey as into:

> that primordial experience of utter darkness and defencelessness ... [to] ... the beasts and demons deep down in our psyche [that] are relics of a past that goes far back through our history into geological time.[50]

Harvey is writing about Holy Saturday, the day when Jesus was not dying or rising but just dead, as a lens through which to interpret the ministry of Donald McNeile (1930–2015). McNeile was an Anglican priest who, together with his wife, ran a therapeutic community for over 35 years for young people with severe drug-resistant psychosis. Harvey's article draws close links between this extremely costly ministry and 'carrying in the body the death of Jesus' (2 Cor. 4.10). This ministry only began to make sense to McNeile himself in the light of the reality of Jesus' death, understood as a descent into an even deeper *madness*. (It's telling, as noted on p. 39, that only a few verses after explicitly aligning himself with Jesus' death (*nekrōsis*) here Paul also implicitly aligns himself with Jesus' madness (*exestēmen*).)

In a similar way Lawrence would hold that ministry by, to, and with *mad* people only begins to make sense if Jesus is understood to be simply *mad*. She pursues this idea through a report of a contextual Bible study group made up of members of the local Hearing Voices Network (pp. 140–5). The chosen text was Mark's Gospel. The readings that emerged were enlightening, if subversive, in relation to the text and often positive for the reader(s), but more importantly the whole exercise was one of 'repositioning individuals not as objects of pathology, but rather phenomenologically as vehicles of seeing' (p. 149).

Here we are back with phenomenology – the quest to understand rather than explain. To understand the rationality of Jesus' *madness* – what Paul calls God's wise foolishness (1 Cor. 1.25) – one must, as far as is possible, inhabit it. In this we may find that *mad* people, *mad* ways of thinking, and *mad* times in life can be unexpectedly helpful. Certainly, the tendencies to explain, to sanitize, to label, to medicalize, to theologize, to achieve closure need to be suspended, at least for a time. Provisionality, unknowing, irresolution and genuine mystery have to be tolerated, and simple attentive looking cultivated.

Conclusions

What are the implications of this for the life of people living with what are generally referred to as mental health conditions in our churches? Any conclusions we reach in this will be tentative ones, with cautions. I would suggest four conclusions, together with two cautions:

1 We need to face and embrace more fully the challenges posed by the *madness* of Jesus in our theological thinking and teaching.
2 While it is important to respect medical approaches, and certainly unethical to challenge medical treatment regimes in individual cases, it is also advisable to sit lightly to this framework, especially in relation to the vocabulary of 'healing', and to be open to additional perspectives. For example, a diagnosis of schizophrenia does not in itself invalidate a person's wisdom nor should it silence his or her prophetic voice in the community.
3 Church communities can be hospitable places that offer access to therapeutic practices such as Christian meditation and faith-based programmes for living well with these conditions (for example, 'Living Grace' groups).[51]
4 Systematic theological reflection on the invisible systemic agents ('natural demons') that combine to lead people into dark psychic places should be a key activity of the churches, informing preaching, teaching and social action.
5 Romanticizing or sentimentalizing mental suffering is to be avoided at all costs.
6 A focus on discernment is crucial: where does a refusal to pathologize aspects of people's *madness* imprison rather than liberate them, especially in a faith context?[52] As noted in the earlier part of this chapter, this is a perennial issue, usually settled with hindsight in the light of the ultimate fruits of the *madness* in question (Matt. 7.20; Phil. 1.9–11). But there are also present-based frameworks that can be employed.[53]

It is surely no accident that Mark's Gospel, in which Jesus is so affect-laden, frank and at the same time secretive and human, and in which he

cries from the cross in despair – the Gospel in which he is simply *mad*
and that ends while he is still, in the minds of his followers, really dead,
and with the word 'afraid' – has been used so productively with people
living with *madness*. The traditional symbol for this Gospel is the lion, an
image taken up by Lewis to depict Christ in the Narnia books, in which
he writes of him in terms much more in tune with this chapter than the
opening quotation:

> He'll be coming and going ... one day you'll see him and another you
> won't. He doesn't like being tied down ... He's wild, you know. Not
> like a *tame* lion.[54]

Notes

1 C. S. Lewis, 1952, *Mere Christianity*, London: Collins, p. 54.

2 Throughout this chapter the words 'mad' and 'madness' are italicized to indicate that these are used primarily as descriptive summary statements, leaving open what these may represent but connecting most closely with the use of these terms in Mad Studies (see R. Ingram, 2016, 'Doing Mad Studies: Making (non)sense Together', *Intersectionalities: A Global Journal of Social Work Analysis, Research, Polity, and Practice*, 5, pp. 11–17).

3 K. Jaspers, 1997 (trans. J. Hoenig and M. Hamilton), *General Psychopathology*, Baltimore, MD: Johns Hopkins University Press, p. 461.

4 G. Stranghellini and T. Fuchs, 2013, *One Century of Karl Jaspers' General Psychopathology*, Oxford: Oxford University Press, p. xviii.

5 W. James, 1902, *The Varieties of Religious Experience*, New York: Longmans, Green & Co., p. 426.

6 K. M. Loewenthal and C. A. Lewis, 2011, 'Mental Health, Religion and Culture', *The Psychologist*, 24, pp. 256–9.

7 R. Griffiths and colleagues, 2006, 'Psilocybin Can Occasion Mystical-type Experiences Having Substantial and Sustained Personal Meaning and Spiritual Significance', *Psychopharmacology*, 187, pp. 268–83.

8 G. Foster and B. Anderson, 1978, *Medical Anthropology*, Chichester: Wiley, p. 81.

9 C. Helman, 2007, *Culture, Health and Illness*, London: Hodder Arnold, p. 246.

10 See W. Bell, 1987, *Holy Anorexia*, Chicago, IL: University of Chicago Press, for a historical analysis.

11 M. Singh, 2018, 'The Cultural Evolution of Shamanism', *Behavioral & Brain Sciences*, 41, pp. 1–62.

12 R. Brand, 2013, 'Blame this on Madness ... not Muslims', *The Sun*, 25 May.

13 G. Zahn, 1986, *In Solitary Witness: The Life and Death of Franz Jägerstätter*, Springfield, IL: Templegate, p. 86.

14 E. P. Sanders, 1985, *Jesus and Judaism*, London: SCM Press, p. 333.

15 S. Kyaga, 2015, *Creativity and Mental Illness: The Mad Genius in Question*,

London: Palgrave McMillan, p. 21; see also Y. Ustinova, 2018, *Divine Mania: Alteration of Consciousness in Ancient Greece*, London: Routledge.

16 A. Witmer, 2012, *Jesus, the Galilean Exorcist: His Exorcisms in Social and Political Context*, London: T&T Clark, p. 205.

17 For example, J. Meggitt, 2004, 'Sources: Use, Abuse and Neglect', in E. Adams and D. Horrell (eds), *Christianity at Corinth: The Scholarly Quest for the Corinthian Church*, Louisville, KY: Westminster/John Knox Press, pp. 241–53.

18 C. Myers, 1988, *Binding the Strong Man: A Political Reading of Mark's Story of Jesus*, Maryknoll, NY: Orbis Books.

19 W. Harris, 2013, *Mental Disorders in the Classical World*, Leiden: Brill.

20 J. Collicutt, 2009, *Jesus and the Gospel Women*, London: SPCK, p. 101.

21 See, for example, in the 'Cancer, we're coming to get you' Race for Life campaign of 2013. www.youtube.com/watch?v=GWJEmMDQXoA.

22 For example, J. Barrett, 2004, *Why Would Anyone Believe in God?*, Walnut Creek, CA: AltaMira Press.

23 The one exception may be the woman with the curved spine in Luke 13 who is said to have been 'bound by Satan' though she is not described as demonized, and there are arguments against this (J. Wilkinson, 1998, *The Bible and Healing*, Grand Rapids, MI: Eerdmans).

24 Found, for example, in the Dead Sea Scrolls, 1 Enoch, Jubilees.

25 For example, D. Freeman and D. Fowler, 2009, 'Routes to Psychotic Symptoms: Trauma, Anxiety and Psychosis-like Experiences', *Psychiatric Research*, 169, pp. 107–12; for a discussion in relation to the Gospel accounts, see S. Davies, 1995, *Jesus the Healer: Possession, Trance and the Origins of Christianity*, New York: Continuum, chapter 6.

26 But see Horsely (R. Horsely, 2014, *Jesus and Magic: Freeing the Gospel Stories from Modern Misconceptions*, Eugene, OR: Wipf and Stock, p. 8) for the important point that the strict division between 'natural' and 'supernatural' is a post-Enlightenment phenomenon.

27 This in contrast to the religious authorities who are presented as wilfully blind to his identity (e.g. John 9.39–41).

28 L. Lawrence, 2018, *Bible and Bedlam: Madness, Sanism, and New Testament Interpretation*, London: T&T Clark, pp. 34–9.

29 M. Persinger and F. Healey, 2002, 'Experimental Facilitation of the Sensed Presence: Possible Intercalation Between the Hemispheres Induced by Complex Magnetic Fields', *The Journal of Nervous and Mental Disease*, 190(8), pp. 533–41.

30 R. Dawkins, 2006, *The God Delusion*, London: Transworld.

31 J. Meggitt, 2007, 'The Madness of King Jesus: Why Was Jesus Put to Death, but His Followers Were Not?', *Journal for the Study of the New Testament*, 29, pp. 379–413.

32 Josephus, 'The Wars of the Jews', Book 6, Chapter 6, trans. W. Whiston.

33 E. P. Sanders, 1993, *The Historical Figure of Jesus*, Harmondsworth: Penguin, p. 153.

34 E. Schüssler Fiorenza, 1983, *In Memory of Her: A Feminist Theological Reconstruction of Christian Origins*, London: SCM Press, p. 32.

35 G. Theissen, 1983 (trans. J. P. Galvin), *Psychological Aspects of Pauline Theology*, Edinburgh: T&T Clark, p. 311.

36 This is the phenomenon of unexpected transformative psychosocial gains made in the aftermath of trauma (R. Tedeschi and L. Calhoun, 1995, *Trauma and*

Transformation: Growing in the Aftermath of Suffering, Thousand Oaks, CA: Sage).

37 J. Collicutt, 2006, 'Posttraumatic Growth and the Origins of Early Christianity', *Mental Health, Religion & Culture*, 9, p. 300.

38 K. Allsopp, J. Read, R. Corcoran, and P. Kinderman, 2019, 'Heterogeneity in Psychiatric Diagnostic Classification', *Psychiatry Research*, 279, pp. 15–22.

39 See R. Bentall, 2010, *Doctoring the Mind: Why Psychiatric Treatments Fail*, London: Penguin.

40 For example, R. Bentall, 2004, *Madness Explained: Psychosis and Human Nature*, London: Penguin.

41 For example, N. Eisland, 1994, *The Disabled God: Towards a Liberatory Theology of Disability*, Nashville, TN: Abingdon Press.

42 Lawrence, *Bible and Bedlam*, p. 5.

43 A. Schweitzer, 1913 [1948], *The Psychiatric Study of Jesus* (trans. C. J. Joy), Boston, MA: Beacon Press.

44 Sanism (like racism, sexism, ageism, etc.) is defined as prejudice against people diagnosed with or perceived as having a mental health condition.

45 For a full account, see A. Hustvedt, 2012, *Medical Muses: Hysteria in Nineteenth Century Paris*, London: Bloomsbury.

46 I. Marks, 1987, *Fears, Phobias, and Rituals: Panic, Anxiety, and their Disorders*, Oxford: Oxford University Press.

47 A. T. Beck, 1976, *Cognitive Therapy and the Emotional Disorders*, New York: International Universities Press.

48 G. McDonald, J. Saltzman and M. Leary, 2003, 'Social Approval and Trait Self-esteem', *Journal of Research in Personality*, 27, pp. 23–40.

49 W. Vanstone, 1982, *The Stature of Waiting*, London: Darton, Longman & Todd.

50 A. Harvey, 2012, 'Schizophrenia in Young People and the *nekrōsis* of Christ', *Theology*, 115, pp. 97, 95.

51 E. Rogers and M. Stanford, 2015, 'A Church-based, Peer-led Group Intervention for Mental Illness', *Mental Health, Religion & Culture*, 18, pp. 470–81.

52 H. Hanevik and colleagues, 2017, 'Religiousness in First-episode Psychosis', *Archive for the Psychology of Religion*, 39, pp. 139–64.

53 K. I. Pargament and colleagues, 1998, 'Patterns of Positive and Negative Religious Coping with Major Life Stressors', *Journal for the Scientific Study of Religion*, 37, pp. 710–24.

54 C. S. Lewis, 1959, *The Lion, the Witch and the Wardrobe*, Harmondworth: Puffin, pp. 165–6.

4

Paul and Mental Health

STEPHEN C. BARTON

Introduction

It may be thought anachronistic to offer a study of Paul in relation to what we think of today as 'mental health', given that the disciplines of psychology, psychiatry, psychotherapy and neuroscience are developments of modernity, notwithstanding their sophisticated precursors.[1] Certainly, anyone who has read theologian Kathryn Greene-McCreight's meditation on mental illness will be wary of straightforward appeals to Paul as a fount of wisdom on clinical depression or bipolar disorder.[2] Nevertheless, there is a growing literature pursuing a dialogue between theology, spirituality and mental health,[3] as also between biblical interpretation and psychology.[4]

Two provisos are in order at the outset. First, there is the matter of ambiguity and complexity. According to the World Health Organization, mental health may be defined as 'a state of well-being in which the individual realizes his or her own abilities, can cope with the normal stresses of life, can work productively and fruitfully, and is able to make a contribution to his or her community'.[5] Given the capacious and multi-dimensional quality of such a definition, it is not surprising that determinations of mental health are a complex matter of objective and subjective judgement concerning which there is a range of views not only across the relevant professional communities, but also across cultures.

Second, the relation between faith and mental health is complex also. As Fraser Watts puts the matter:

> For religiously committed people, well-being is never the overarching objective. Saint Ignatius of Loyola makes this point well when he says that, for the Christian, events are evaluated, not in terms of whether people like them or not, but in terms of whether or not they bring them close to God ... So, for the Christian, well-being is not the immediate objective, though in the long run a consistent policy of seeking closeness to God may be good for our well-being.[6]

54

Third, writing on mental health often gravitates quickly to matters of mental *illness or disorder* and thence to the various therapies deemed appropriate. However, this is not my concern here – not least since, if we ignore the portrait of Paul as a miracle-worker in Acts, the evidence for Paul as a practitioner of healing is remarkably opaque.

Notwithstanding these provisos, and on the assumption that religious traditions play an important role in the human business of *making sense of things*, what I hope to show is that the letters of Paul are rich in reflection on the self and on both what threatens, and what is conducive, to personal and interpersonal well-being. That this is a reasonable proposal is so for the following reasons.

First, Paul's life and thought were shaped by traditions in Judaism and the wider Greco-Roman world which were expressive of serious attention to the life of the mind and the attainment of happiness, and which, in the modern period, continue to inspire sophisticated moral and psychological reflection.[7] Second, Paul's calling as an apostle of Christ, operating within and across multiple legal frameworks, disciplinary regimes, social networks and cultural arenas, inevitably made for occasions of conflict, personal crisis and threats to life: all of which helps to explain why his letters are so personally *witness-bearing* in character, offering a unique window into his understanding of the self and its dynamics.[8]

Paul's apocalyptic worldview and the self at risk

Central to our investigation is Paul's theological anthropology, his understanding of what it means to be human within the loving sovereignty of God. As the last generation of scholarship has shown, Pauline anthropology (and his theology as a whole) is indebted, at least in part, to a christological and pneumatological reshaping of the worldview of *Jewish apocalyptic*, itself a religious – even mystical – mode of scriptural interpretation and practice.[9] An appreciation of Paul's apocalyptic worldview is essential for a nuanced, historically grounded reading of Paul in relation to mental health. At the risk of over-simplification, this worldview has a number of aspects.

First, the *cosmological*. In the context of a fundamental belief in the oneness of God and God's sovereignty over all, Paul's worldview displays a form of dualism. Creation as a whole, and humankind in particular, are caught in a cosmic battle between the forces of light and the forces of darkness, between God and Satan (cf. 2 Cor. 6.14b–15). The idea is common in Second Temple Judaism, especially in the texts from Qumran (cf. *Community Rule* 3.13—4.26). In Paul, it is evident in his references to 'Satan', 'the tempter', 'the god of this age', 'the rulers of this age', 'the principalities and powers', and 'Sin' as a power in its own right.[10] Paul's language is robust, reflecting biblical holy war traditions and the language of the moral philosophers.[11] The Thessalonians, as people who 'belong to the day', are to 'be sober, and put on the breastplate of faith and love, and for a helmet the hope of salvation' (1 Thess. 5.8). The Corinthians are exhorted to 'Keep alert, stand firm in your faith, be courageous, be strong' (1 Cor. 16.13; cf. 2 Cor. 10.3–6). The believers in Rome are assured that 'The God of peace will shortly crush Satan under your feet' (Rom. 16.20a). Such warrior language continues in the Pauline tradition, famously in Ephesians 6.11: 'Put on the whole armour of God, so that you may be able to stand against the wiles of the devil.' Language like this testifies to the *felt reality* of the dynamics of cosmic war and its attendant fears and anxieties for Paul and his contemporaries.

Bound up inextricably with the cosmological aspect is the *anthropological*. In a context of cosmic war, played out in the lives of nations and peoples, the human situation is perilous. The peril is exacerbated by what was held to be a *disposition of the heart towards evil* going back to the Garden of Eden and its sequel, the Flood.[12] Indicative is the statement in Genesis 6.5 (cf. also 8.21): 'The LORD saw that the wickedness of humankind was great in the earth, and that every inclination of the thoughts of their hearts was only evil continually.' This represents a *pessimistic* anthropology (cf. Rom. 1.18—3.20; 8.5–8). The cosmic battle is felt as an existential reality within every individual human being, each of whom is understood as predisposed towards evil – indeed, as *enslaved* by sin.[13] Paul essentially shares this anthropology. As he says in Romans 7:

> For I know that nothing good dwells within me, that is, in my flesh. I can will what is right, but I cannot do it. For I do not do the good I want, but the evil I do not want is what I do. Now if I do what I do not want, it is no longer I that do it, but sin that dwells within me ... Wretched man that I am! Who will rescue me from this body of death? (Rom. 7.18–19, 24; cf. also Gal. 5.16–17)

In this light, human existence is indeed perilous, with that aspect of the self characterized as 'the flesh', *vulnerable to invasion and enslavement*. What is necessary in response is the activation of human agency: in Judaism, by way of Torah-obedience and Torah-mysticism; in the moral tradition more widely, by the practice of 'self-mastery' (*enkrateia*).[14]

To this context of cosmic warfare with its anthropological corollary of fear of demonic occupation and enslavement to evil inclinations, a third aspect needs to be added – which is really an extension of the second. We might call this the *socio-political*. The 'principalities and powers' were understood as cosmic realities, certainly, but they were held to act at the terrestrial level through the agency of empires, governments, social orders, armies and ruler cults. In this sphere, the central socio-political dynamic was the sustained competition for domination and its attendant glory, access to which was bound up inevitably with competitors' birth, wealth, status, gender, ethnicity, age and personal prowess. Ultimately, domination was achieved through violence or the threat of violence. Strategies for survival, both individual and corporate, were diverse and numerous. They included withdrawal into the desert to train in sanctity for end-time holy war, as at Qumran; accommodation to foreign domination, as in the case of the ruling Judean elite and the Temple authorities; critical co-existence and the intensification of personal and domestic Torah-piety as practised by the Pharisaic party; prophetic, visionary activity, seeking the moral and spiritual renewal of the people, such as that associated with John the Baptist and Jesus; and militant opposition through revolutionary action often associated with messianism of one kind or another. In so far as Saul/Paul was a member of the Pharisaic party, it is reasonable to assume that the core of his sense of self arises out of his self-professed 'zeal' for God manifest in his zeal for his ancestral traditions (cf. Gal. 1.13–14; Phil. 3.6; Acts 22.3–4) to the point even of participating in the judicial killing of his opponents in the Christ-cult (cf. Acts 23.9–11).

But Paul's apocalyptic worldview and intense Torah-piety – indeed, his very life – were turned upside-down by a personally cataclysmic disruption, a heavenly invasion in the form of a vision-revelation of the risen Christ (Gal. 1.12). As he recounts the event: 'But when God, who had set me apart before I was born and called me through his grace, was pleased to reveal his Son to [literally 'in'] me, so that I might proclaim him among the Gentiles, I did not confer with any human being ...' (Gal. 1.15–16). That God had raised Jesus Christ, the crucified, from the dead and exalted him to divine sonship, *and* that the Risen Christ had appeared to the persecutor himself (not to judge but to call!), impelled a transformation in Paul's understanding of reality – of God, time, space, value and the self.

Concerning *God*, it meant a revolution in Paul's sense of the boundless scope of divine freedom, grace and mercy, and a radical reappraisal of divine wisdom as (in human terms) 'foolishness', the folly of the cross. Concerning *time*, it meant the beginning of the age of the eschatological Spirit, and the death-throes of Satan and the powers of evil. Concerning *space*, it meant the presence of God in the lordship of Christ over all things and the revelation of the new creation embodied in the gatherings of believers, united even in their diversity. In respect of *value*, it meant an end to the attribution of 'glory' on the basis of 'boasting' in human achievement, with its destructive religious and social corollaries of separation and division, and its displacement by value acquired extrinsically as gift from God (or Christ or the Spirit).[15] In respect of the *self*, it meant a new sense of identity both at the individual and social levels – expressed variously as being the privileged recipient of an eschatological 'mystery', as being found 'in Christ', as belonging to Christ, as having died with Christ, as being a member of the body of Christ, and as having the honoured status of a citizen of heaven.

It would be a mistake, however, to think that, in the light of the revelation of Christ and the empowering gift of the eschatological Spirit, Paul regarded the self as at risk no longer. On the contrary, Paul gives every indication that he believes that the cosmic battle of the end-time has *intensified*, and that he and his fellow-believers are caught up in the 'birth-pains' (cf. Gal. 4.19; Rom. 8.22–23) of the coming kingdom of God.

Without an account of Paul's worldview and call/conversion such as the above, it would not be possible to engage Paul's anthropology – not least his understanding of the life of mind and heart – with historically informed imaginative seriousness. That, in turn, would vitiate any attempt to appropriate Pauline insights for how we think and practise what we call 'mental health' today.

Paul apostle of weakness and the de-centred self

I have spoken of the self 'at risk' within the framework of Paul's inherited worldview. This may give the impression that what is important for Paul and his world is the salvation and preservation of the self – for example, through appropriate defensive action and strategies of empowerment. In a word, through human agency, individual and corporate. This is true as far as it goes, and finds expression, *inter alia*, in the pattern of indicative and imperative so characteristic of the structure of Paul's letters – as in Romans: in the light of the grace of God revealed in the gospel (Rom. 1—11), *so live* (Rom. 12—15)!

Even more important, however, and what is the truly remarkable aspect of Paul's anthropology, is that the self, its preservation and empowerment, is *christologically de-centred*. Indicative is what Paul says to the Galatians: 'I have been crucified with Christ; and *it is no longer I who live, but it is Christ who lives in me*. And the life I now live in the flesh I live by faith in the Son of God, who loved me and gave himself for me' (Gal. 2.19b–20). Such a de-centring – made possible by *divine agency* in the self-giving of the Son of God and the transforming work of the Spirit – has profound existential consequences. The taken-for-granted, culturally approved practices of self-identification and self-affirmation – the 'boasting' that marks out the 'I' – has been *put to death*, by co-crucifixion with Christ, in favour of an eschatological identity or 'new creation' (cf. Gal. 6.14–15).

In this new creation – and so characteristic of the dislocating and disruptive creativity of apocalyptic epistemologies – a way towards a revolution in values and ways of seeing is opened up. The crucifixion and resurrection of the Son of God, as the victory of God over the powers of sin and death, heralds the demise, not only of death, but of cultures and values that are death-dealing. This gains startling clarity in Paul's Corinthian correspondence. Here, Paul's target is highly prized notions of 'wisdom' and 'knowledge' which serve both to bolster a socially conservative hierarchy of persons and values, and to keep in place a competitive and divisive culture of 'boasting' and self-display. Paul's response is to problematize and reinterpret Corinthian wisdom in the light of the paradoxical wisdom of God revealed in the cross. Indeed, God's wisdom is 'foolishness', and this (argues Paul) is displayed in three ways: in the inglorious crucifixion of God's Messiah (1 Cor. 1.18–25); in the humble identity of (most of) those called (1 Cor. 1.26–31); and in the weakness of Paul's person and preaching (1 Cor. 2.1–5). The subversive impact of Paul's apocalyptic gospel on the cultural value ascribed honour and shame is particularly striking:

> God chose what is foolish in the world to shame the wise; God chose what is weak in the world to shame the strong; God chose what is low and despised in the world, things that are not, to reduce to nothing things that are, so that no one might boast in the presence of God. (1 Cor. 1.27–29)

The antinomy of weakness and strength is explored most intensively, however, in 2 Corinthians,[16] where Paul is again on the defensive and his apostolic identity is in question. Accused of being 'weak', and therefore unworthy of honour as an apostle, Paul, with considerable rhetorical daring, turns the cultural currency of honour and shame on its head. He glories in his weakness! He boasts, but as a 'fool' (cf. 2 Cor. 11.16–21; also 1 Cor. 4.10)! And what his boasting displays is a sense of personal identity utterly *reconfigured* in terms of conformity to the (strong!) weakness of God revealed in the cross of Christ: so much so that his life now consists in his being given over to vulnerability, humiliation and death for Christ's sake (cf. 2 Cor. 11.23ff.).

Even mystical experiences of 'visions and revelations of the Lord', including a heavenly journey into Paradise, are inflected with weakness:

> [A] thorn was given me in the flesh, a messenger of Satan to torment me, to keep me from being too elated. Three times I appealed to the Lord about this, that it would leave me, but he said to me, 'My grace is sufficient for you, for power is made perfect in weakness.' So I will boast all the more gladly of my weaknesses, so that the power of Christ may dwell in me ... for whenever I am weak, then I am strong. (2 Cor. 12.7–10)

In sum, texts from Galatians draw attention to Paul's christological de-centring of self, and texts from 1 and 2 Corinthians show Paul problematizing and reinterpreting cultural norms of personal worth, such that values associated with wisdom and folly, honour and shame, strength and weakness, perfection and imperfection are *recalibrated* according to the measure of Christ crucified. In such texts we are witnessing a revolution in the notion of what it means to be human.

But we can go further. In problematizing cultural norms of identity definition and personal worth in the light of the crucifixion and resurrection of the Son of God, the revolution in the notion of what it means to be human is also a *de-stabilizing* and a *liberation*. Personal identity and worth become radically *open*, determined now by the individual's orientation to the eschatological future and the life of heaven – determined, that is, by the grace of God transforming the individual through the agency of Christ and the Spirit.

Paul as psychagogue

Against the backdrop of this eschatological christocentric anthropology, it is possible to identify aspects of Paul's apocalyptic theology and apostolic practice that are 'good to think with' in relation to the self, its identity and well-being. This is not an artificial exercise because it can hardly be doubted that Paul comes across as (what the ancients would have recognized as) a psychagogue, a 'leader of souls', identifying sacrificially with his communities and passionately engaged in their moral and spiritual formation.[17] Indicative is the following:

> I am hard pressed between the two [i.e. between living and dying]: my desire is to depart and be with Christ, for that is far better; but to remain in the flesh is more necessary for you. Since I am convinced of this, I

know that I will remain and continue with all of you *for your progress and joy in faith*. (Phil. 1.23–25)

Among the many aspects of Paul's psychagogic activity on behalf of his churches, the following have a particular resonance in relation to our theme.

Paul, epistemology and the oneness of God

In Pauline Christianity, the truth about reality matters. There is a cognitive aspect to personal integrity and to feeling at home in the world – even if only relatively so! Gaining a sense of *attunement* with the fundamental order of things makes for a positive sense of self. It is significant therefore that, in a culture where competition for personal allegiance to one god or another was strong – a competition conducive at the existential level to anxiety, rivalry and violence (cf. Acts 16.16–40) – Paul engages in a kind of reality-check: not 'many gods', but one!

> Indeed, even though there may be so-called gods in heaven or on earth – as in fact there are many gods and many lords – yet for us there is one God, the Father, from whom are all things and for whom we exist, and one Lord, Jesus Christ, through whom are all things and through whom we exist. It is not everyone, however, who has this knowledge. (1 Cor. 8.5–7a)

Here, in the knowledge of the *one God* who is the beginning and end of all things, and in the knowledge of the *one Lord*, Jesus Christ, who is the agent of creation and salvation, are grounds for a sense of the coherence of reality and the security of personal existence in time and space. Arguably, such a sense of the divine economy – with God as 'Father' and Jesus as 'Lord' – is an important factor in positive Christian identity formation and in the confident negotiation of everyday matters of life and death.

Knowledge of the one God and of God as one – a *complex* oneness, christologically shaped and pneumatologically revealed – is an important factor also in facing *suffering*. For Paul, as the famous 'hardship' catalogues make clear,[18] true knowledge of God, Christ and the Spirit makes possible the *re-narration* of weakness, shame and suffering as not a liability, but an asset, since those are moments when the eschatological creation-resurrection power of God is revealed. Drawing specific attention to the critical epistemological aspect, Susan Garrett, commenting on Paul's acknowledgement of 'treasure in clay jars' in 2 Corinthians 4.1–12, says this:

> The perishing look to the cross and see humiliation rather than Christ's glory, which must be divinely revealed. They look to Paul and see only a devastated and decomposing 'outer nature' (4:16). In their state of blindness, they see only the visible and transient; hence they regard Paul's afflicted condition as a disgrace. *Paul, by contrast, is the recipient of divine knowledge: knowledge of things unseen and eternal* (4:6, 18). Paul explains the contrast between his knowledge and his opponents' ignorance as the consequences of differences in alliance: Paul is allied with God and Christ, whereas those who reject Paul are allied with the god of this age.[19]

Rightly does Garrett describe Paul as 'the recipient of divine knowledge'. The source and subject of this knowledge is the Creator God attested first in Scripture and now, eschatologically, in Christ: 'For it is the God who said, "Let light shine out of darkness," who has shone in our hearts to give the light of the knowledge of the glory of God in the face of Jesus Christ' (2 Cor. 4.6).

Paul and the individual

Within that framework of divine knowledge, a second feature of Pauline psychagogy is a clear sense that individuals matter. While there can be no doubt that Paul's letters are written to communities and that the well-being of the believing community is a prime focus, it must not be overlooked that the concerns he expresses often have to do with individuals and, indeed, with the important process of *individuation*.[20] As Paul himself has a clear sense of his own identity as an individual called by Christ (cf. Gal. 1.15–16; Phil. 3.7–11), so too does he have a sense of the importance of the appropriate recognition of each one among the groups he is addressing. This is because, in the light of the 'new creation' brought about by the revelation of God in Christ through the Spirit, former patterns of identity, including what we might call 'group think' (conformist and oppressive as it tends to be), no longer hold in the ways they once did, and new patterns and options oriented towards the eschatological future are opening up.

Noteworthy, first, is the place given to *personal agency*. For example, in relation to salvation: '[I]f you [sing.] confess with your lips that Jesus is Lord and believe in your heart that God raised him from the dead, you [sing.] will be saved' (Rom. 10.9).[21] For Paul, complementary to the sovereign action of God in Christ is the graced faith-response of the individual given expression in outward testimony ('lips') and inward conviction ('heart'). Nor does personal agency end with the initial faith-confession. It continues in the practices (moral and ritual) of mind and body that constitute the Christian *habitus* (cf. Rom. 12.1—15.13).

Second, in relation to the Church, even when Paul seeks to encourage communal solidarity, he endeavours not to do so at the expense of the individual and individual difference. On the contrary, understood and experienced as a pneumatic community, gifts are given by the Spirit in an individuating way: '*To each* is given the manifestation of the Spirit for the common good … All these [gifts] are activated by one and the same Spirit, who allots *to each one individually* just as the Spirit chooses' (1 Cor. 12.7–11; cf. Rom. 12.3).

Third, attention to the individual is evident in relation to the moral life. Here, Paul teaches other-regarding love on the grounds that each brother or sister is of inestimable value – each person is one 'for whom Christ died' (1 Cor. 8.11). He calls also for respect for individual moral conscience (1 Cor. 8.12; cf. Rom. 14.1–4). Furthermore, he makes space for the free judgement of the individual, especially in matters of relative indifference (1 Cor. 10.29; cf. 6.12; 10.23). All in all, we may say that one of the ways in which Paul builds group solidarity is by encouraging individual responsibility (cf. Gal. 6.4–5; Rom. 14.12, 22) and by making possible the empowerment of each individual member.

Finally, that individuals matter is reflected also in the long list of names of both men and women in the greetings and commendations with which Paul concludes his letters. Exemplary is the list at the end of the Letter to the Romans (Rom. 16.1–23), a list with strong hints of personal knowledge of, and affection towards, individuals on Paul's part. To such lists may be added the effort to which Paul goes on behalf of particular individuals, the slave Onesimus being a case in point (Philemon 8–21).[22]

Paul and the self-in-relation

But if individuals matter for Paul, as they surely do, this is not to say that Paul is an advocate of the individualism that we think of as a characteristic of modernity, and that many today find so challenging to identity-formation and personal happiness. On the contrary, for Paul, the individual self is a *self-in-relation*. Paul's perspective on the person is what Susan Grove Eastman has called a 'second-person perspective', according to which the 'I' is constituted by its relation to a 'Thou'. She says:

'There is no freestanding "self" in Paul's cosmos, nor is there a neutral environment within which human beings may act out their personal lives. Rather, Paul's anthropology is participatory all the way down.'[23] Thus, in line with Paul's apocalyptic epistemology outlined earlier, believers are selves previously constituted by their relation of slavery to sin and death (cosmic powers both external and internal to the self) but now constituted by their relation to God, Christ and the Spirit in a new time, a new space, and a new people.

Impressive in this context is Paul's deployment of powerful identity-creating and identity-sustaining *metaphors of belonging*, especially drawn from the field of kinship and family. One such is the metaphor of *adoption*.[24] This is expressive of belonging to God in the privileged relation of a son or daughter, a corollary of which is the gift of the Spirit, who enables the invocation of God as 'Abba! Father!' (Gal. 4.4–5). It is also expressive of a graced belonging that perdures. As Paul says elsewhere: 'When we cry, "Abba! Father!" it is that very Spirit bearing witness with our spirit that we are children of God, and if children, then heirs, heirs of God and joint heirs with Christ' (Rom. 8.15b–17a). Here is a metaphor – that of family-related inheritance – potent with *hope*. Expressive of participation in the life of God and the people of God, it speaks in a quite transformative way into situations of status-loss, rejection by kith and kin, social isolation and anonymity, related no doubt to the consequences of religious conversion.

Another metaphor of belonging – again, family-related – is *siblingship*.[25] Thus, according to Romans 8.29, Jesus, as God's Son, is the 'firstborn within a large family [literally among many brothers]'. Put simply, within the semantic domain of kinship, God is the heavenly Father, Jesus is the divine Son and God's 'firstborn' (with its eschatological connotations), and believers are – through Jesus' divine sonship – children of God and siblings of Jesus. Such connections confer identity and status. In both theological and social terms, such 'family' connections are *salvific*. Furthermore, there is a moral corollary. As children of God and siblings of Jesus and one another in God's eschatological family, believers are to practise *philadelphia*, 'brotherly [and sisterly] love' (1 Thess. 4.9–12; Rom. 12.9–13). Along with identity and status, therefore, there is mutual responsibility arising out of the bonds of family affection. Especially noteworthy is Paul's deployment of siblingship language to encourage the 'strong' in the Christian fellowship to care for the 'weak' (1 Cor. 8; Rom. 14), an ethic provocative in its time and a foundation for a new humanity.

We would be remiss, however, if we omitted mention of one other important metaphor pertinent to the self-in-relation, that of *believers as a body* – specifically, 'the body of Christ' (cf. 1 Cor. 12; Rom. 12.3–8). This is an organic metaphor, well known in contemporary political rhetoric,[26] which, in its existential appeal and symbolic richness, allows Paul to convey what is essential to the well-being of the community and its members. First, it expresses the relation that is fundamental: the self and the believing community are 'the body *of Christ*'. This is a relation both existential and eschatological since it is a matter of belonging to Christ crucified *and risen* and is therefore a relation that involves ongoing conversion and transformation. Second, as an image of one body with many members, it speaks of *unity and diversity*, and especially of *diversity in unity*. As an image of unity, it serves as a vital impediment on the social plane to rivalry, division and faction. As an image of diversity in unity, it expresses the pneumatic, individuating character of the community with gifts (*charismata*) given by the Spirit 'to each one individually *just as the Spirit chooses*' (1 Cor. 12.11b). Third, as an image where some body parts are normally reckoned of a higher order or of greater worth than others, the body is a metaphor of *ordering and valuation*. But since *this* body is the body of the crucified and risen Christ, and since it is the sphere of the gift-bestowing activity of the Spirit, conventional patterns of social and political order, and conventional ways of ascribing value or worth, are open to – indeed, *demand* – reconfiguration and revaluation. Notably, what we see in Paul is a radical and creative reconfiguration of hierarchy, and a revaluation of worth, in favour of those of low status, the poor, the bearers of shame, 'the weak':

> The eye cannot say to the hand, 'I have no need of you', nor again the head to the feet, 'I have no need of you.' On the contrary, the members of the body that seem to be weaker are indispensable ... *But God has so arranged the body, giving the greater honour to the inferior member,* that there may be no dissension within the body, but the members may have the same care for one another. If one member suffers, all suffer together with it; if one member is honoured, all rejoice together with it. (1 Cor. 12.21–26)

What such a statement represents is a reimagination of the self and society in the light of the revelation of the grace of God in the crucified Christ (cf. 2 Cor. 8.9). In this reimagining, honour is accorded the weak in a society that would let the weak go to the wall. At the same time, life circumstances that might, in the wider society, become for the individual a situation of alienation, become in the body of Christ an opportunity for solidarity: what Paul goes on to articulate as the 'more excellent way' of love (1 Cor. 13).

In the matter of love, we must pause. Although several leading scholars have wanted to play down the significance of love in Paul's moral teaching,[27] its pertinence to our present theme is too great to let it pass. For love is the moral corollary of the metaphors of belonging just discussed. It is the complex of feeling, thought and practice that sustains the self-in-relation. It is a virtue – or *spectrum* of virtues identified by a considerable lexicon of different words and concepts[28] – the practice of which is constitutive of *the ethos and relational matrix* within which the individual and the community are enabled by the Spirit to grow and flourish in unity. As Paul says, in counteracting the debilitating factionalism in the Corinthian house-churches, 'Knowledge puffs up, but love [*agapē*] builds up' (1 Cor. 8.1b). Indeed, that the inculcation of the other-regarding ethic of love is the purpose of the letter as a whole is indicated by the concluding admonition in chapter 16: 'Let all that you do be done in love' (v. 14).

Pre-eminent, of course, is Paul's appeal to love in 1 Corinthians 12.31b—13.13. Here, we note the following. First, love is presented as the 'more excellent *way*'. As such it is a whole pattern of devotion and way of life (cf. 4.17; also Acts 24.14, 22), and by no means the fleeting feeling or self-gratifying sensation it has become in modernity. Second, to a degree that distinguishes it from other gifts and virtues (even faith and hope), love is *the* eschatological reality. That is why it has the primacy that it does: 'Love never ends' (13.8a). It is also why the measure of love is applied to all else.

If we consider in what this love consists, we note (in 13.4–7) that it is characterized both negatively ('love is not ...') and positively ('love is ...'). The negative characteristics are feelings and behaviours conducive of the degradation of the self-in-relation: jealousy, boasting, arrogance, self-promotion, anger, and so on. Conversely, the positive characteristics are feelings and behaviours conducive of the well-being of the self-in-relation: patience, kindness and joy in the truth, a list capped off with a rhetorical flourish celebrating the kind of love that knows no limits (13.7). It is hard to think of any christologically grounded virtue more conducive to the well-being of the self-in-relation than the virtue of love so understood.

Paul and the emotions

In introducing Paul earlier as a psychagogue, I mentioned his passionate engagement with the moral and spiritual formation of his children in the faith. In 2 Corinthians 11.28–29, Paul talks about his 'anxiety' for the churches and his being 'indignant' on behalf of the vulnerable; and in Philippians 1.25, he speaks of his goal for the churches of Philippi as 'your progress *and joy* in faith'. Such expressions of the emotions open a door onto another important contribution of Pauline faith to what might be thought to constitute mental health: namely, the formation of a constructive *culture of the emotions* shaped by relation to Christ and the Spirit.

To sharpen our interpretation, insights from the social sciences are helpful.[29] From a social-scientific point of view, emotions are a kind of local knowledge, a kind of bodily cognition, shaped over time by cultural norms, social relations, interpersonal interactions and 'feeling rules'. As such, emotions are *learnt*: and, if learnt, open to change. As we shall see, emotions like grief and joy, among others, all come within the orbit of Paul's psychagogy as he seeks to nurture individuals and communities in the life of the new creation.

Take grief (*lupē, penthos*).[30] This is an emotion with a wide semantic range and valence on which Paul offers advice more than once.[31] Regarding grief as a response to the loss in death of believers in the Thessalonian church, Paul says this: 'But we do not want you to be uninformed, brothers and sisters, about those who have died, so that you may not grieve as others do who have no hope' (1 Thess. 4.13–18). Here, at a point of individual and communal crisis and vulnerability, Paul invites what we may call a *conversion of the emotions*. Grief, along with associated rituals of mourning, is made the subject of a kind of discipline: *the eschatological discipline of hope*. Now, that grief, as a social (as well as individual) emotion, was subject to culturally accepted rules and conventions of various kinds will have been taken for granted, as it was a common theme of philosophical psychagogy.[32] Against that background, Paul appears to offer guidance of a recognizably Stoic kind. The Thessalonian believers are to exercise maximum constraint. What is striking, however, is that the rationale Paul offers is not Stoic detachment but eschatological hope in line with his christologically shaped apocalyptic worldview: 'For since we believe that Jesus died and rose again, even so, through Jesus, God will bring with him those who have died … Therefore encourage one another with these words' (1 Thess. 4.14–18).

In the face of death, the personal and social bonds that have been stretched to breaking-point are renewed and reimagined by means of *a compelling narrative* which reshapes reality by bringing the future into the present and heaven to earth. What it achieves is *a reincorporation of the dead with the living* in a cosmic christological drama that embraces time, space and persons under the sovereign protection of the One identified in the letter's final benediction as 'the God of peace' (1 Thess. 5.23).

As a second example, this time of a positive emotion, take *joy* (*chara*), focusing on its use in Philippians. We find here one of the greatest concentrations of 'joy' language in the Pauline corpus. Given that the letter is written from the generally appalling conditions of a first-century prison (cf. Phil. 1.13), it would be natural to expect expressions of fear and anxiety. Instead, Philippians displays repeated and profound expressions of joy (cf. 1.18, 25; 2.2, 17, 18, 28, 29; 3.1; 4.1, 4, 10). Overall, what Paul as psychagogue offers the Philippians is *a pedagogy in joy*. In general, it may be said that joy here reflects an experience of uplifting spiritual and material partnership (*koinōnia*) in an inhospitable social environment set against the vivid, felt horizon of participation in the life of heaven. The experience of partnership is one of joy because Paul and the Philippians know that *their story is part of a larger story*: the story of salvation, as yet unfinished, but whose ending – because it is the story of God, Christ and the Spirit – is sure.

To take just one instance: Paul's *apologia* in 1.12–26. Here Paul proceeds to give an account of his current situation as a prisoner. He does so because, in an agonistic cultural context, his imprisonment renders him vulnerable by giving his competitors the advantage (cf. 1.15–17). Be that as it may, what is notable is that Paul is able to interpret his circumstances in terms of a hermeneutic of joy. He rejoices in the fact that his imprisonment has so emboldened the Church – presumably by his personal example of courage – that it has had the beneficial consequence of advancing the gospel (1.14). Whether it is his friends or his rivals who are so engaged, one thing is important for Paul: 'Christ is proclaimed; and in that I rejoice' (1.18). It is as if Paul can rise above his circumstances of shame and suffering because his sights are set, not on personal advantage in a competition for glory, but on the fulfilment that comes in service of his risen Lord. A word for that fulfilment is 'joy'.

Strikingly, Paul appears to have a penchant for (so to speak) *double* joy, for joy piled upon joy – hence, 'in that I rejoice. Yes, and I shall rejoice' (1.18b–19a; cf. 4.4). Paul then goes on to rejoice in the assurance that his imprisonment for the sake of Christ will bring the benefit of eschatological vindication (1.19). Invoking the pivotal social values of honour and shame, Paul expresses his confidence that, whether his incarceration ends in life or death, he himself 'will not be at all ashamed' and, more importantly, Christ 'will be honoured' (1.20). Here is precisely the kind of profound joy that social anthropologist Mary Douglas speaks of: that which arises from living in, and being willing to die for, what she calls 'the sacred order'.[33] Put in Pauline terms, what fulfils Paul, what gives him joy, is that complex of allegiance, belief and practice summed up in three things: the name of Christ, partnership in the gospel, and participation in the life of heaven both now and at the day of resurrection (cf. 3.11, 14, 20–21).

In the light of Philippians, it is reasonable to make the following claims about joy. First, as both a gift (cf. Gal. 5.22) and a discipline, joy is a significant cognitive-evaluative feature of early Christian self-definition. It is the expression of the believer's sense of alignment with – even possession by – Christ and the Spirit. It is the believer's *condition* (cf. Rom. 14.7). Second, joy is an experience of individual and communal *revitalization*, an experience so profound that it makes possible the transcendence in hope of suffering, grief, shame and all that is death-dealing – even death itself. Third, precisely because it has that elative quality, joy opens the way for *new ways of classifying the world* and therefore new ways of being in the world. It expands *the felt realm of the possible*. That joy is thus a key ingredient of (what we call) mental health is hard to deny.

Paul's psychagogic shaping of a habitus 'in Christ'

I turn to one final aspect of Paul's psychagogy relevant to our theme: Paul's attention to practices generative of what we have learnt from Pierre Bourdieu to call a *habitus*, what he defines as: 'a system of lasting, transposable dispositions which, integrating past experiences, functions at every moment as a matrix of perceptions, appreciations, and actions and makes possible the achievement of infinitely diversified tasks'.[34]

Particularly important in forming and sustaining these dispositions are *practices of the body*:

> [N]othing seems more ineffable, more incommunicable, more inimitable, and, therefore, more precious, than the values given body, *made body* by the transubstantiation achieved by the hidden persuasion of an implicit pedagogy, capable of instilling a whole cosmology, an ethic, a metaphysic, a political philosophy through injunctions as insignificant as 'stand up straight' or 'don't hold your knife in your left hand'.[35]

Among Pauline practices of the body, the following are exemplary. First, *baptism* (cf. 1 Cor. 6.11; 12.13; Gal. 3.26–28; Rom. 6.3–11; Col. 2.12).[36] As a rite of initiation involving a symbolic purification by bodily immersion in water, baptism marks a transition from one socio-symbolic world to another. It marks a new beginning dense with meaning: participation with Christ in his death and resurrection; entry into new life in the Spirit; and entry into a new solidarity with its privileges and obligations. As a ritual signifying personal renewal and new identity (cf.

Gal. 3.28), the liberating psychological impact of baptism is likely to have been profound.

Second, *commensality*. If baptism is generative of a transformative *habitus*, critical for sustaining that *habitus* is the bodily practice of eating together (cf. 1 Cor. 10.14–22; 11.17–34; also Gal. 2.11–21; Rom. 14.1–15.6). Just how critical is revealed at the point where the fellowship in food is put *at risk*, as at Corinth: 'When you come together, it is not really to eat the Lord's supper. For when the time comes to eat, each of you goes ahead with your own supper, and one goes hungry and another becomes drunk' (1 Cor. 11.20–22). Here, a ritual of solidarity around 'one bread' (cf. 1 Cor. 10.16–17), intended to bring the eschatological humanity into repeated connection with both the risen Lord (as host of the meal) and with fellow brothers and sisters, has been subverted into a ritual of competitive display. In sharp response, what Paul as psychagogue offers is a re-statement of honoured Jesus-tradition with a view to *re-situating* Corinthian commensality in the context of Jesus' past death and future coming (1 Cor. 11.23–32). What is at stake is 'the body and blood of the Lord' and its corollary, the proper recognition of 'the [ecclesial] body' (1 Cor. 11.27, 29).

Much more could be said of Paul's psychagogic efforts to build and sustain a *habitus* through the practices of the body, efforts (in the words of Bourdieu quoted earlier) 'capable of instilling a whole cosmology, an ethic, a metaphysic, a political philosophy'. My point is only to gesture towards dimensions – material as well as spiritual, social as well as individual – that may be reckoned as suggestive of what constitutes mental health in a Pauline perspective.

Conclusion

To go to Paul for insight and inspiration concerning mental health is a risky business! For Paul's primary concern is not mental health, but life 'in Christ': and that means a life of paradox and irony arising from a new way of seeing, knowing and feeling. What is central becomes peripheral; what is eccentric becomes the norming norm. Sensationally, Paul's *cursus honorum* of ascribed and acquired indicators of personal value and social capital is relegated to the dung-heap (cf. Phil. 3.4b–8a). It is displaced by a *cursus pudorum* of sufferings and hardships – matters of shame – now claimed as honourable on the basis of an apocalyptic hermeneutic according to which the whole of life, in all its joys and sorrows, is received as liberating gift through mimetic participation in the death and resurrection of Christ (cf. Phil. 1.21; 3.10–11).

In sum, given that mental health is a matter of *judgement* regarding the self and the self-in-relation in time and space, it is that *disruptive apocalyptic hermeneutic* which may constitute Paul's most enduring contribution. For in the light of the revelation of God's power to give life to the dead through the death and resurrection of God's Son, what it means to be truly human in every part of one's existence is neither determined by the past nor fixed in the present – nor, in the end, is it a matter of human estimation. Rather, in the light of faith, what it means to be truly human is a matter of dying and rising with Christ: the life begun in baptism (cf. Rom. 6.3–4). As such, it is a matter of ongoing discovery and creativity in openness to God's future and in relationship with others, inspired by the Spirit. It is no wonder that the ethos of Pauline spirituality is one primarily of joy, and that a mark of his prayers is thanksgiving and doxology (cf. Rom. 1.8; 7.25; 16.25–27).

Notes

1 For their advice in the shaping of this chapter, my thanks go especially to Robert Banks, James Harrison, Andrew Lincoln and Christopher Rowland.

2 K. Greene-McCreight, 2015, *Darkness Is My Only Companion. A Christian Response to Mental Illness*, Grand Rapids, MI: Brazos Press.

3 Cf. C. C. H. Cook, 2013, *Spirituality, Theology and Mental Health: Multidisciplinary Perspectives*, London: SCM Press.

4 Cf. J. Collicutt, 2012, 'Bringing the Academic Discipline of Psychology to Bear on the Study of the Bible', *The Journal of Theological Studies*, 63(1), pp. 1–48.

5 World Health Organization, 2004, *Promoting Mental Health*, Geneva: WHO.

6 F. Watts, 2018, 'Theology and Science of Mental Health and Well-Being', *Zygon*, 53(2), pp. 336–55, 341.

7 Cf. B. A. Strawn (ed.), 2012, *The Bible and the Pursuit of Happiness*, Oxford: Oxford University Press; M. C. Nussbaum, 1994, *The Therapy of Desire: Theory and Practice in Hellenistic Ethics*, Princeton, NJ: Princeton University Press; C. Gill, 2013, 'Philosophical Therapy as Preventative Psychological Medicine', in W. V. Harris (ed.), *Mental Disorders in the Classical World*, Leiden: Brill, pp. 339–60.

8 Cf. C. Shantz, 2012, '"I Have Learned to Be Content": Happiness According to St. Paul', in Strawn (ed.), *Pursuit of Happiness*, pp. 187–201.

9 Cf. C. Rowland, 1982, *The Open Heaven: A Study of Apocalyptic in Judaism and Early Christianity*, London: SPCK; B. E. Reynolds and L. T. Stuckenbruck, 2017 (eds), *Jewish Apocalyptic Tradition and the Shaping of New Testament Thought*, Minneapolis, MN: Fortress Press.

10 Cf. 1 Thess. 2.18; Gal. 4.8–9; 2 Cor. 4.4; 2 Cor. 11.14.

11 Cf. N. K. Gupta, 2017, 'Paul and the *Militia Spiritualis* Topos in 1 Thessalonians', in J. R. Dodson and A. W. Pitts (eds), *Paul and the Greco-Roman Philosophical Tradition*, London: Bloomsbury, pp. 13–32.

12 Cf. C. S. Keener, 2016, *The Mind of the Spirit: Paul's Approach to Transformed Thinking*, Grand Rapids, MI: Baker Academic, pp. 85–90.

13 Cf. J. Maston, 2018, 'Enlivened Slaves: Paul's Christological Anthropology', in J. Maston and B. E. Reynolds (eds), *Anthropology and New Testament Theology*, London: Bloomsbury T&T Clark, pp. 141–59.

14 Cf. on the latter, S. K. Stowers, 2016, 'Paul and Self-Mastery', in J. P. Sampley (ed.), *Paul in the Greco-Roman World*, vol. 2, 2nd edn, London: Bloomsbury T&T Clark, pp. 270–300.

15 Cf. J. Barclay, 2015, *Paul and the Gift*, Grand Rapids, MI: Eerdmans, where the *incongruity* of the divine gift and its unsettling implications for notions of value and worth are explored.

16 Cf. D. A. Black, 2012, *Paul Apostle of Weakness*, Eugene, OR: Pickwick Publications, pp. 84–111.

17 Cf. L. L. Welborn, 2011, 'Paul and Pain: Paul's Emotional Therapy in 2 Corinthians 1:1—2:13; 7:5–16 in the Context of Ancient Psychagogic Literature', *New Testament Studies*, 57(4), pp. 547–70.

18 Foundational is J. T. Fitzgerald, 1988, *Cracks in Earthen Vessels: An Examination of the Catalogues of Hardships in the Corinthian Correspondence*, Atlanta, GA: Scholars Press.

19 S. R. Garrett, 1990, 'The God of This World and the Affliction of Paul: 2 Cor 4:1–12', in D. L. Balch and colleagues (eds), *Greeks, Romans, and Christians*, Minneapolis, MN: Fortress Press, pp. 99–117, 103 (my emphasis).

20 Cf. J. P. Sampley, 1990, 'Faith and Its Moral Life: A Study of Individuation in the Thought World of the Apostle Paul', in J. T. Carroll and colleagues (eds), *Faith and History*, Atlanta, GA: Scholars Press, pp. 223–38.

21 Other pertinent texts include Rom. 1.16–17; 3.21–26; and 10.5–13, on which, see B. Dunson, 2012, *Individual and Community in Paul's Letter to the Romans*, Tübingen: Mohr Siebeck.

22 One could add here Paul's expressed concern for other individuals like Epaphroditus (Phil. 2.25–30), Euodia and Syntyche (Phil. 4.2–3), Timothy (1 Cor. 16.10–11), and Titus (2 Cor. 7.13b–15), to name but a few.

23 S. Grove Eastman, 2017, *Paul and the Person: Reframing Paul's Anthropology*, Grand Rapids, MI: Eerdmans, p. 9.

24 Cf. J. M. Scott, 1993, 'Adoption, Sonship', in G. F. Hawthorne and colleagues, *Dictionary of Paul and His Letters*, Downers Grove, IL: InterVarsity Press, pp. 15–18.

25 Cf. R. Aasgaard, 2004, *'My Beloved Brothers and Sisters!' Christian Siblingship in Paul*, London: T&T Clark.

26 Cf. M. M. Mitchell, 1992, *Paul and the Rhetoric of Reconciliation*, Louisville, KY: Westminster/John Knox, pp. 157–64.

27 For example, R. B. Hays, 1996, *The Moral Vision of the New Testament*, New York: HarperCollins, pp. 200–5.

28 Cf. Mitchell, *Paul and the Rhetoric of Reconciliation*, pp. 157–71, with examples of the variety of Greek and Latin words for 'love', at p. 167, n. 619.

29 Cf. M. Z. Rosaldo, 1984, 'Towards an Anthropology of Self and Feeling', in R. A. Shweder and R. A. Levine (eds), *Culture Theory: Essays on Mind, Self, and Emotion*, Cambridge: Cambridge University Press, pp. 137–57.

30 See further, S. C. Barton, 2011, 'Eschatology and the Emotions in Early Christianity', *Journal of Biblical Literature*, 130(3), pp. 571–91.

31 Cf. especially 2 Cor. 1.1–2.13, 7.5–16 and the discussion of *lupē* of a different kind (that is, 'godly grief' leading to repentance, in 2 Cor. 7.10), in Welborn, 'Paul and Pain'.

32 On the philosophers' ethic of 'self-mastery' as the basis for constraining – even extirpating – the passions in general, see Welborn, 'Paul and Pain', especially pp. 559–64.

33 M. Douglas, 1996, 'The Cosmic Joke', in *Thought Styles: Critical Essays on Good Taste*, London: Sage Publications, pp. 193–212.

34 P. Bourdieu, 1977, *Outline of a Theory of Practice*, Cambridge: Cambridge University Press, pp. 82–3, cited in Barclay, *Paul and the Gift*, p. 506.

35 Bourdieu, *Outline of a Theory of Practice*, p. 94.

36 On what follows, see W. A. Meeks, 1983, *The First Urban Christians*, New Haven, CT: Yale University Press, pp. 150–62.

5

Paul, the Mind and the Mind of Christ

PAULA GOODER

Introduction

We often talk about 'the mind' as though it were somehow tangible, a thing that we could indicate with an outstretched finger, pointing to its location within the body. Indeed, if invited to point to their mind most people would probably indicate their heads, implying an association with the brain. This would be one way of identifying the mind, but is not the only one. Roughly speaking, the mind is considered to be made up of a range of cognitive faculties, including memory, imagination, language, perception and consciousness, but also comprising thinking and the ability to make decisions. As a result, while we might imagine that much of what the mind does comes from the brain, it is not its only possible location within the body.

The mind is complex and giving anything more than a quite vague description of it can be hard to do. It is even quite challenging to identify who the study of the mind should belong to: it could be seen to fall within the remit of philosophers, psychologists or neurologists, though it would be very hard to get such specialists to agree on key questions such as whether our minds exist apart from our bodies (dualism) or as a fundamental part of the neurons in the brain (materialism).

These are only a few of the complexities that surround a modern understanding of the mind, and this is even before we have gone anywhere near asking how the mind relates to the soul. It is worth saying, however, that little of this modern discussion would have made much sense to the apostle Paul. Paul, like many people who were formed by a Hebrew worldview, thought of human beings as fundamentally embodied: to quote J. A. T. Robinson's famous phrase: in Hebrew thinking 'I am a body; I do not have a body'.[1] As a result, in a chapter exploring Paul and the mind, we need to begin with Paul's understanding of the body before we can ask the question of how Paul viewed the mind.

Embodiment and dualism

The reason why we need to begin with dualism is less to do with Paul than it is to do with modern thinking. Modern attitudes to the mind tend to split the human person into two: the material (that is, the body) and the non-material (that is, the mind, soul and spirit). Although we might point to where we imagine our mind to be in the body, many people would consider the mind to be separate and entirely different from their body. This kind of dualism has had many effects on how we view human beings. One, which is not the subject of this chapter, is that the human body – and embodiment – has not been regarded as important or, in fact, having much of a place in discussions about Christian spirituality; another effect has been to separate physical well-being from mental and spiritual well-being, assuming that the two have little to do with each other.

As indicated above, this attitude would have made little sense to some-one whose thinking was shaped more by a Hebrew worldview than a Platonic one. It is always dangerous to ask whether Paul's thinking is 'more Jewish' or 'more Greek', because even to ask the question is to misunderstand the complex culture of first-century Judaism, which drew profoundly on both Hebrew and Greek thinking and culture. It is possible, however, to ask whether there is evidence of the use of a particular philo-sophical tradition in the forming of certain attitudes. In the case of his attitudes to the body, the soul, the spirit and the mind, it is clear that Paul was closer to Hebrew thinking than to Greek.

His use of the word *psuchē* (often translated as 'soul') has much more in common with the Hebrew word (*nephesh*) than it has with Plato's use of *psuchē*, so that, for Paul, the soul is part of the body – its life force – not something separate from the body that leaves it at death.[2] What this means is that, in Paul's thinking, he does not separate the material from the immaterial, the body from the soul, spirit and mind in the way that we might. The material and immaterial are intimately interwoven in his thinking. This is important to remember as we explore the mind in the writings of Paul since it makes quite a difference to how we understand what he says.

The mind in Paul

We began this chapter by asking where in the body we might point to indicate the presence of the mind – the answer being that most people would point to their head. While asking this question at all might well have confused Paul, if he did respond it is unlikely that he would have pointed to his head; one place he might have pointed to was his heart. This indicates another layer of complexity in understanding the mind in Paul.

There is a main Greek word for mind (*nous*) but also a wide variety of others too (*sunesis, dianoia, noēma, ennoia, phronēma* and *phronēsis*). This is important. All these words have a vaguely similar resonance denoting some aspect of reason and thought process, but the sheer number of words that Paul used for similar ideas tells us that he was not using any particularly technical language to refer to the mind. Nor does he appear to have a high view of reason that would be comparable to certain strands of Greek philosophy, and which view the mind as that which relates to the divine.

Thinking and reason are, however, hugely important in Paul's theology. So much so that Albert Schweitzer dubbed him 'the patron saint of Christian thought'.[3] In Paul's writings you can see a perfect balance between experience and reason; the life of the Spirit and thought. Paul's experiences of the risen and ascended Christ had an overwhelming impact on Paul, his life and his mission (see, for example, 2 Cor. 12.1–10), but at the same time he dedicated his life to thinking through what this meant for him, for the Christian community, and for the world. As a result, one of Paul's great concerns was that Christians balanced their experience of the Spirit with rational thought. We can see this in places like 1 Corinthians 14.15 where he said: 'I will pray with the spirit, but I will pray with the mind also; I will sing praise with the spirit, but I will sing praise with the mind also.' This concern, responding to the Corinthians' over-emphasis on life in the Spirit, reveals the importance for Paul of balancing reason and experience in the life of faith.

Paul also seems to entwine his language about the mind with language about the body. Very strikingly, in Romans 12.1–2 he exhorted the Romans to do two things: present their bodies as a living sacrifice, holy and pleasing to God, AND not to be conformed to this world but transformed by the renewing of their minds. This twofold movement of the embodied dedication of the whole of life to God and the transformation that comes from the renewal of mind is important. The way in which this sentence is constructed makes it clear that these two are linked together closely: the one requires the other.

The problem, of course, is that rational thought processes do not encompass everything that *we* associate with the mind. Various other terms such as emotion, imagination, consciousness and perception all contribute to a modern understanding of the mind, but are not fully included in the Greek word *nous* or, indeed, the other words mentioned above. This reveals something important about Paul's attitude to the mind, which is that a simple word search on 'mind' will not provide all we need; we need other terms too. It is impossible in a chapter of this length to do justice to all the potential additional terms that would be needed to encompass fully our understanding of mind, but one particular word is worth a brief reflection – *kardia* (heart).

It is striking that whereas Paul only uses the word *nous* 21 times in his writing, he uses *kardia* 52 times. Even a brief exploration of these uses reveals that Paul's understanding of the heart and its place in human existence is very close to the Hebrew word *leb* (normally translated as 'heart'). One of the fascinating features to observe is that while *leb* is the seat of emotion as it is in modern thinking, it is also the place where understanding occurred (see, for example, Deut. 29.4: 'the Lord has not given you a mind [the actual word here is *leb* or heart] to understand'), but that is not all. Decisions were made in the heart ('The anger of the Lord will not turn back until he has executed and accomplished the intents of his mind [heart]', Jer. 23.20); God's laws were kept in the heart ('Give me understanding, that I may keep your law and observe it with my whole heart', Ps. 119.34); and meditation took place in the heart ('Let the words of my mouth and the meditation of my heart be acceptable to you', Ps. 19.14).

Paul's use of *kardia* (heart) was very similar to that of *leb*: he talked about decisions being made in the heart ('But if someone stands firm in his resolve [heart]', 1 Cor. 7.37); there being purposes of the heart ('the Lord ... who will bring to light ... and will disclose the purposes of the heart', 1 Cor. 4.5), and that the word is in the heart ('"The word is near you, on your lips and in your heart" (that is, the word of faith that we proclaim)', Rom. 10.8). This is why it is possible that, if asked to point to his mind, Paul might have pointed to his heart, as the place where thought and emotion intertwined. It is also possible, however, that he would have indicated the whole body as the place where reason, emotion, imagination, will and consciousness all reside and are expressed.

One thing that is clear is that our understanding of the 'mind' does not easily correlate to the Greek word *nous* or indeed to any other single word in Paul's writings. If we want to understand Paul's attitude to the mind we need to define what we understand mind to mean and then to explore the varying places where Paul refers to those different character-istics in his writings. A simple word search on the word 'mind' will not produce a full picture of Paul's attitude to what we would call 'the mind'.

The mind of Christ in Paul's writings

Another feature of Paul's references to 'mind' is that it is clear that his understanding is far less individual than ours. Two instances in his writing illustrate this well. In each of these, in different ways, Paul refers to having the mind of Christ.

1 Corinthians 2.15–16 states that we have the mind of Christ ('Those who are spiritual discern all things, and they are themselves subject to no one else's scrutiny. "For who has known the mind of the Lord so as to instruct him?" But we have the mind of Christ.') and Philippians 2.5 exhorts the Philippian Christians to 'Let the same mind be in you that was in Christ Jesus'. Each of these has a slightly different emphasis. In 1 Corinthians the emphasis is on seeing the world as God sees it. The logic is that until Christ no one was able to understand how God thought but now, through life in the Spirit, we have the mind of Christ and can comprehend what was before incomprehensible. In contrast, Philippians 2.5 places more emphasis on thinking as Christ did (the Greek here doesn't use the noun *nous* (mind) but the verb *phroneo* (to think)) with the consequent impact that this has on how we behave and what we do. As so often, Paul pulls us back to embodiment – having the mind of Christ is not just a concept, it affects what we do in the whole of life.

The importance of this is that it challenges our very individual notions of the mind. Descartes' famous adage 'I think, therefore I am' both consciously and unconsciously shapes much of our thinking about who we are as people and what this means for our minds. Most particularly it suggests that our own thought processes shape our identity in their entirety. Paul's theology – and in particular his references to having the mind of Christ – suggest that there is a corporate strand to the mind that our modern culture often overlooks. Thinking, feeling and imagining together as the body of Christ inspired by the Spirit can shape our minds so that we think and act like Christ, seeing the world as Christ did.

The corporate dimension to the mind, which we see in passages like these two, propose a significant shift in thinking away from our own minds as the entire focus and centre of identity to a shared identity as the body of Christ in the world.

Paul's mental health

Having explored Paul's attitude to the mind, and the complexities in definition that arise from this, we need to turn our attention to Paul's own mental well-being. As we have already observed, it is difficult to map modern categories of the mind on to the world and writings of Paul. For Paul, 'mind' probably would have, primarily, suggested reason and thought-processes not, as for us, a complex web of emotion, imagination and mental well-being.

Nevertheless, it is possible to observe in Paul's writings evidence of what might today be termed mental illness or depression. One of the most striking examples of this can be found woven through the epistle of 2 Corinthians, which refers on more than one occasion to Paul's despair and difficulty in ministry. In order to understand the references it is worth sketching out the background to 2 Corinthians and Paul's on-going relationship with the Corinthian Church.

Having founded the Church in Corinth Paul discovered, probably around 18 months later, that things had gone awry in a variety of ways. At this point he wrote them a letter (which is mentioned in 1 Cor. 5.9) in an attempt to correct them. The Corinthians responded to this initial letter with a letter of their own – and Paul responded to *this* letter with the letter that we now call 1 Corinthians, quoting parts of the letter that they had sent to him. At some point in this to-ing and fro-ing Paul managed to visit the Corinthians again, but the visit did not go well. It went so badly, in fact, that Paul referred to it in 2 Corinthians as a 'painful visit' (2.1). He followed this visit with a strongly worded letter (which he refers to as a severe and tearful letter, 2.4 and 2.9); 2 Corinthians, then, is written against the background of profound upset and a fragmented relationship between Paul and a church that he founded.

It is clear from the epistle as a whole that this breakdown of relationship, on top of numerous other calamities that marked Paul's ministry, has had a deleterious effect on Paul's physical and mental well-being. There are three key places in which this comes to the fore and we will explore them in turn.

The first passage occurs right at the start of the epistle in which Paul gives thanks after a time of great affliction. His accustomed opening benediction (1.3–11) weaves together the twin themes of suffering and consolation. It is clear from the language that he uses that Paul makes no particular distinction here between physical and mental suffering. This is also true in the other two passages we will explore as well (4.7–12 and 11.16—12.10). For Paul, the physical circumstances that brought about his 'affliction' also affected his mental well-being:

We do not want you to be unaware, brothers and sisters, of the affliction we experienced in Asia; for we were so utterly, unbearably crushed that we despaired of life itself. Indeed, we felt that we had received the sentence of death so that we would rely not on ourselves but on God who raises the dead. (2 Cor. 1.8–9)

Although Paul's language throughout is vague: he suffered affliction/pressure in Asia (probably the Roman province of Asia) to the extent that he 'despaired of life itself'. While some people interpret this as him fearing for his own survival, the phrasing suggests an emotional response, akin to the lowest moments of depression. Whatever it was that had happened affected his mental well-being so much that the sheer weight of the pressure cast him into despair.

One of the startling features of Paul's description of suffering in 2 Corinthians 1.3–11 is that he talks of it as Christ's suffering (in language reminiscent of Col. 1.24: 'in my flesh I am completing what is lacking in Christ's afflictions for the sake of his body, that is, the church'). In other words, his understanding of corporate identity that allows him to talk of being a part of the body of Christ and of having the mind of Christ also allows him to see his own sufferings as part of Christ's own suffering. Not only this, but it also allowed him to view consolation as shared too. This is important. One of the very difficult features of mental illness and depression is the sense of isolation that comes in its wake. Paul's profoundly corporate view of life and the mind led him to understand his own suffering and subsequent consolation as, ultimately, contributing to consoling the Corinthians. He wanted them to know that they were very much not alone in what they experienced.

This corporate view of suffering returns again in 2 Corinthians 4.7–12. Here, again, we see Paul interweaving physical and psychological suffering as though it were the same thing and, apparently, believing that his own suffering could bring greater life and hope to the Corinthians ('So death is at work in us, but life in you', 2 Cor. 4.12). One of the key features of Paul's language in 4.7–12 is his reference to having 'this treasure in clay jars, so that it may be made clear that this extraordinary power belongs to God and does not come from us'. Ben Witherington suggests in his commentary that, when hearing this reference to poor-quality jars made of clay (ostrakinos), the Corinthians might have thought of the oil lamps, famous in their city for being made of thin, delicate clay so that the light could shine more effectively through them.[4] If this is true then it implies that Paul did not view his frailties, both mental and physical, as a source of shame but as the means by which people could encounter, more fully, the glory of Christ. To misquote Leonard Cohen's line – there's a crack in everything, that's how the light of Christ shines out.

Probably the most iconic and most often quoted passage in Paul that has led people to wonder whether he did have some form of physical or mental illness is 2 Corinthians 12.7: 'a thorn was given me in the flesh, a messenger of Satan to torment me'. Speculation about the nature of this thorn in the flesh is almost endless but can be gathered into three main categories: spiritual or psychological anxiety; opposition to Paul and his ministry; and physical malady. Indeed, as in 2 Corinthians 1.8, Paul's reference to whatever it was is frustratingly so vague that it is almost impossible to come to a decision on what the nature of the 'thorn in the flesh' was.

As will be familiar by now, however, what is clear is that the physical ('in the flesh') is intertwined in Paul's mind with the psychological ('to torment me'). Whatever it was that was in the flesh caused him mental as well as physical torment. Also significant is the fact that the thorn in the flesh was not removed, no matter how often Paul begged. Again, as in 2 Corinthians 4.7, the torment revealed Christ's power – it 'was made perfect in weakness'. Paul's frailty was a part of him, something integral to the way in which he proclaimed the gospel.

Conclusion

This all too brief survey of the mind and Paul's own mental well-being has revealed a few strands that are worthy of further reflection. One of the foremost of these strands is the profound linkage in Paul's thinking between the body and the mind. So great is this connection that it is impossible to know whether, when Paul refers to crises in his life, they were physical ailments or the overwhelming despair of depression, or both. While we now know much more about mental well-being than used to be the case, it is worth reminding ourselves of the importance of this connection. Our minds, however we define them, exist within our bodies – whatever happens to our bodies will affect our minds too (and vice versa).

A second strand that emerges from Paul's thinking is the recognition that he saw minds as corporate as well as individual, so much so that he could say 'we have the mind of Christ'. This is very difficult for our individual culture to comprehend but is worth reflecting on further. Our culture places great emphasis on individual identity but sometimes that emphasis can feel too great a weight to bear, especially at a time when things that happen make us doubt who we really are. At times like this, resting in the knowledge of a corporate identity that finds its source in Christ could be both healing and reassuring.

A final strand that we can observe, particularly in 2 Corinthians, is the way in which Paul learns to live with his frailty. Whatever the cause of that frailty was – and it was probably a complex mix of physical, emotional and psychological issues – Paul learnt to live with it and even to recognize that it was because of the frailty that the light of Christ could shine through him and that Christ's power was made perfect in weakness.

Probably the most important issue that has emerged here is that Paul's categories and ours do not match. He would not ask the same questions about the mind as we do; he would not point to the same part of his body to identify it as we do. Nevertheless, there is much to learn from Paul's thinking about the mind and mental well-being, not least that if we frame our reflections in a different way we might have some very interesting new avenues to explore.

Notes

1 J. A. T. Robinson, 1952, *The Body: A Study in Pauline Theology*, London: SCM Press, p. 14.

2 For a fuller discussion, see P. Gooder, 2016, *Body: Biblical Spirituality for the Whole Person*, London: SPCK, pp. 15—42.

3 A. Schweitzer, 1931, *The Mysticism of Paul the Apostle*, London: A & C Black, p. 377.

4 B. Witherington, 1996, *Conflict and Community in Corinth: A Socio-Rhetorical Commentary on 1 and 2 Corinthians*, Grand Rapids, MI: Eerdmans, p. 387.

PART 2

Biblical Case Studies

6

Patient Job, Angry Job:
Speaking Faith in the Midst of Trauma

ISABELLE HAMLEY

There are few books in Scripture more puzzling than the book of Job. God misbehaves, Satan has free rein, the protagonist rants and raves for chapters on end, and the end seems to belong in fairy tales rather than Scripture. The Job of the beginning of the book has entered popular imagination as patient, long-suffering Job, who accepts his trials with grace and whose faith is unshaken. Sections of the poetry, such as chapter 38, have made it into songs and sermons for their sheer beauty, with stunning imagery of God's presence in nature, and power over it. Neither, however, really portrays the complexity, trauma and anguish of the book. The careful juxtaposition of prose and poetry suggests a man whose faith was anchored in his community's traditional expressions of spirituality. In the face of incomprehensible suffering, his certainties start to crumble, and his ability to articulate faith disintegrates. The book of Job therefore becomes a crisis of the language of faith, a crisis of theology, as well as a story of trauma and how the community of faith may facilitate or hinder constructive responses to psychological pain.

I do not intend to make a diagnosis of Job's distress, or identify modern-day mental health categories to map on to the text. Rather, I will seek to bring out the text's own language of mental distress in ways that suggest possible avenues of exploration for those seeking to understand how Scripture frames the experience of mental distress, and how Scripture itself provides resources to understand and respond to those who struggle. As such, I will follow a narrative approach to the text, as it enables a better exploration of interpersonal dynamics and of the inner life of the characters. Such an approach will naturally lead me to retrieve the beginning and end of the book, often dismissed by academic critics, as essential to the way in which the book can, and maybe should, function within a community of faith. Reading prose and poetry together, as literary critics have more recently started doing, reveals a complex picture, and one of relevance to those who seek to understand how the biblical text shapes our pastoral imagination in response to pain and suffering.

Job the patriarch: an anxious and driven man

The prose prologue of the book problematizes certain concepts of faith and the links between faith and blessing. We get a glimpse of Job's faith in 1.1–5. Verse 1 depicts Job as a patriarch of old, and over-emphasizes Job's righteousness. This is not innocent: the poetry sections will pick up on the notion of innocence, and the traditional tendency to think of suffering as punishment for wrongdoing. The prose narrative leaves us in no doubt that this link has no basis. Job is 'blameless and upright'. Then follows what any traditional reader would expect: for one as blameless as the patriarchs, Job was, naturally, blessed with all he could desire, from a perfect number of sons and daughters to great riches.

At this point, an unexpected little vignette occurs: Job's children feast together, they drink together, and Job offers sacrifices on their behalf. There are a number of features to note here. The presence of drink could be a sign of plenty and blessing, or it could be a warning sign. Job himself does not attend the party, and seems removed from his 'perfect' family. Instead, he offers sacrifices on their behalf, just in case: 'It may be that my children have sinned, and cursed God in their hearts' (v.5). Job neither socializes with his children, nor trusts them to follow in his pious foot-steps. We may wonder what kind of image of God underlies Job's piety at this point. A God who blesses him but would, with no doubt, strike his children for inebriated talk? A God who demands perfection? The sacrifices operate smoothly and mechanically, without the participation or consent of Job's children, and this mechanistic offering suffices to appease a potentially angry God. There is no dialogue between God and Job, and absolutely no suggestion that the sacrifices were necessary. Piety and faith function as a transaction through which the universe is made stable and predictable. It is a safe understanding of the world, but one that will not sustain Job through the events about to unfold. This 'is what Job always did' (v.5). His faith is based on routine practices which he performs almost obsessively.

It is interesting to note that the locus of Job's anxiety for his children is that they may '[curse] God in their hearts' (v.5). Here a central con-cept enters the narrative. First, Job's anxiety goes beyond what may be done or said, to the heart. Second, his anxiety is to do with words and language. The word for 'curse' in Hebrew is *barak*, a word better known for its meaning as 'bless'. Anxious scribes, whose anxiety about inadvertently committing blasphemy parallels Job's, often resisted using the normal word for curse (*qalal*) and replaced it with the euphemism *barak*. In many texts, it is reasonably straightforward to distinguish between the two usages. Here, the ambiguity becomes central to Job's struggles. Even here, the word itself echoes Job's uncertainty: did his children curse or not? And if they did not curse, did they bless? How do you know what is in the heart? Does it matter?

This introduction to Job has laid careful clues as to what is to come. The next scene will start problematizing the framework of traditional piety implicit in the patriarch-like beginning. A scene opens up in heaven, dramatizing an exchange between God (Yahweh) and the 'accuser' (*ha-satan*). There is ample critical work on parallels here with accounts and concepts from the Ancient Near East.[1] It is fascinating that an entirely separate universe is described, with no lines of communication between Job and Yahweh. Job is of course unaware of any heavenly happenings, a fact relevant to any pastoral reading of Job. Readers are invited into deeper complexity than the characters, so that when the poetic dialogues begin they cannot align their sympathies with the 'friends', however traditional and accepted their arguments may be. This insight into the fuller story prompts readers to empathize with Job, and cast Yahweh as a problematic character – the opposite of the friends' outlook. One of the pastoral functions and possibilities of the text therefore is to shape the ability to anticipate and perceive complexity, and discourage facile pastoral and theological answers. In addition, it sets up the question of how we understand the role of the divine within the context of suffering, rather than elide the question. God is not unambiguous – not simply portrayed as a God of love or justice. While the tale is not meant to be taken literally, it gives permission to readers to ask complex questions and, at times, potentially blasphemous ones. One of the key words in the heavenly dialogue comes with the accuser's question, 'Does Job fear God for nothing?' (1.9). *Hinnam*, translated here as 'for nothing', can have two meanings: either 'for no purpose', or 'without cause'. The question of the cause and purpose of suffering will be picked up again in the dialogues, with the friends arguing that Job's suffering either has a cause (his sin) or a purpose (God teaching him). Fundamentally, in relation to Job, who does not know the heavenly backstory, this is the question of meaning: does his suffering have meaning, or is it random? Can meaning be found, or is life random, unpredictable and meaningless? In relation to God and the accuser, something else is at stake. What is the nature of the human–divine relationship? Is it transactional and predictable? Is Job's piety merely mechanistic and self-interested? Or is there freedom on both sides of the Job–God relationship? Is there a spirituality that goes deeper than self-interest? Here we again come up against the blessing/ curse ambiguity of *barak*: does Job bless God because God blesses Job? And what is a blessing? Is a mechanistic exchange of blessings truly a blessing, or could it be its euphemistic opposite, a curse?

This introduction to Job therefore lines up a series of problematic concepts, not necessarily obvious on first reading. To start with, readers would expect a tale in line with those of the patriarchs, a story that reinforces traditional wisdom. This traditional wisdom will be echoed in the speeches of the friends.

The breakdown of God-talk in the face of trauma and grief

Tragedy now strikes – and Job loses everything, from his children, to his servants, to his entire fortune. Job's first response is the one that tradition has often remembered: 'the LORD gave, and the LORD has taken away; blessed be the name of the LORD' (1.21). It is interesting to wonder why this initial response has been recorded, sung, celebrated, yet his subsequent responses have not. Job's response is a ritual response; in the face of the unspeakable, he falls back on the language, rituals and categories of faith that have shaped him. Tearing his robe, shaving his head, falling to the ground, are all ways of processing grief that are culturally appropriate within an Ancient Near East setting,[2] and signify his deep grief in ways that keep him connected to the cultural and religious community around him. At the same time, his words strike a dissonant note for modern readers, as they seem to evidence denial and a lack of emotional engagement. We can read this at two different levels: on the one hand, Job is borrowing words much as we use liturgy or hymns in order to find words that connect him with God and the community of faith at a time when his own words fail. In this sense, noting this response is helpful in thinking how the words and habits of our own spiritual communities have the power to sustain those who face grief and trauma. On the other hand, the language that Job uses, the habits of faith and theology that have formed him, are actually preventing him from making a true connection with his own emotions, and therefore with others – human and divine – around him. The traditions of faith have become a substitute for truth-telling, and are unhelpfully reinforcing his distancing reaction. The text itself does not pass comment on whether this reaction is helpful, but the narrator merely states that Job 'did not sin or charge God with wrongdoing' (1.22). The comment is odd: is this a vindication of Yahweh's faith in Job? Is it approval for Job's reaction? Is it prompting the reader, who knows of the bargain between God and Satan, to question whether Job *should* have charged God with wrongdoing?

The story moves to a second heavenly scene which results in Job being physically afflicted. Job has sores 'from the sole of his foot to the crown of his head' (2.7). We are not certain about the nature of the disease, but skin diseases were often associated with social exclusion for fear of contamination. The story moves with an interesting slant on the way in which physical illness, as an internal trauma, affects Job differently from the loss of his children and fortune through a combination of natural disaster (whirlwind) and human action (robbers); both are traumatic, but they yield different (but cumulative) effects. Job now sits on 'a pile of ashes' – which may be an extension of the ashes of mourning rituals or may be the rubbish heap of the town, as an embodiment of the way in which trauma has isolated him from all he was previously connected to. Job now does not initiate worship, but simply sits in stunned silence, repeatedly scraping his sores. Language, even the language he has inherited, is starting to break down.

Job's wife now enters the stage. She has not been mentioned before, either in connection with her children, or with Job. She was not mentioned in times of plenty, and even though she shares in all of Job's misfortunes, her perspective was elided until now. The dialogue that ensues illustrates the alienation that trauma either has created, or strengthened. Translations have solidified her question to Job as 'Do you still persist in your integrity? Curse God, and die' (2.9). The translation, however, does not convey the ambiguity of the text. First, Hebrew does not have punctuation (hence no question mark), and there is no interrogative marker in the sentence. She may therefore not be accusing or mocking Job, but rather comforting him, or praising him, or simply reflecting back to him that he has kept integrity, despite everything. Her next comment, 'curse God and die', could equally be translated as 'bless God and die'. One may wonder whether Job's aggressive response is a function of his state of mind: he interprets her words and concerns negatively, and assumes she is advising him to curse. Job reinforces the alienation he feels in his response, and assumes she sees him as he sees himself – good enough for the rubbish heap. But her words alone do not warrant this interpretation. She could simply be stating her sadness before him, her fear that he is dying, her trust that he is facing death from a position of integrity. Or, she may be angry, feeling alienated and locked within her own grief, and seeing no future but death. The text as it is, with its ambiguity, enables readers to explore different responses, and the way in which relationships are affected by trauma.

Job's response also is more ambiguous than translations make it. Is he asking a question, or making a statement: 'we receive good at the hand of God, not receive the bad', or 'shall we receive the good, and not receive the bad?' (2.10 paraphrased). The theological meaning of the two alternatives is radically different; maintaining the ambiguity of the Hebrew again enables us to explore the potential gap between the statement of faith dictated by Job's theological outlook so far, and the questions prompted by his current predicament. The narrator is alert to this possibility: 'in all this, Job did not sin *with his lips*' (2.10). The addition is significant: at the end of the previous episode, there was no qualification. Job did not sin. Job had been worried about his children sinning *in their hearts*. Now Job does not sin *with his lips* – but is something else going on in his heart? And what would a potential 'sin' be at this point? Is this a judgement by the narrator or, more likely, a focalization of the narrative through Job's eyes? Job is obsessed with finding the right words, saying the right thing. This sentence may be a clue concerning his continuing anxiety, and this struggle to try and shore up his crumbling spirituality. In the face of trauma, faith is becoming a problem rather than a help or comfort.

Three more actors then enter: Job's three friends, ironically remembered as 'Job's comforters'. They are well-meaning, proactive, and know what is culturally expected of them (they weep, tear their robes, throw dust upon their heads). And yet … the reality of Job's condition takes them by surprise, and leads them into complete silence, even though their initial intent had been to speak words of comfort. The journey of the friends is significant. As we see most clearly in the poetry dialogues, they represent the community of faith – those who gather and are supposed to hold the member in distress. What the text portrays, however, is the ripple effects of trauma on others, and how observing trauma in Job threatens the friends' own settled spirituality. Hence Job and the friends, in the dialogue, will be wrestling with their existing spiritual categories. Yet instead of this wrestling bringing them together, it will be alienating, because they are coming from different angles, with different needs. The friends will consistently advocate for traditional philosophical/theological categories of thought; they explore the potential meaning of suffering within the framework of a cause and effect theology where good is rewarded and evil is punished, and God cannot be questioned. Job, in contrast, moves into the register of existential questioning, and argues from experience, using a different (but equally steeped in Israel's traditions) language, that of lament. The different modes of discourse yield an adversarial stance that at times becomes repetitive, and cannot draw conclusions or help move towards a different emotional space.

At the beginning of chapter 3, Job breaks the silence by cursing the day of his birth. The word for 'curse' here is unambiguous – *qalal*. Job has moved from blessing to curse, a move that church sermons on Job usually fail to make. Coming after the long period of silence, Job's curse on the day of his birth betrays a wish for nothingness and the depth of his despair. Language now moves into a different register. Job does not launch from silence, or from traditional categories, into new, spontaneous, or totally idiosyncratic speech. Instead, he draws on a different part of the social imaginary of Israel. While the friends, and early Job, drew on conventional wisdom, Job now draws on protest wisdom, the kind of wisdom found in psalms of lament. Hence Job is still drawing on his spiritual heritage, but a different part of it. Walter Brueggemann's categories of testimony and countertestimony in the life of Israel are illuminating here: the biblical witness is not contradictory, but it is multi-faceted.[3] Scripture, through the juxtaposition of texts in the canon, problematizes the simple use of different categories, and offers multiple ways of engaging with the reality of the human condition and, through this juxtaposition, invites us to reflect on how and why we may borrow certain categories at certain times.

The strand of conventional wisdom is important, and cannot simply be rejected. The depiction of a moral universe governed by laws of justice, where good leads to good outcomes and evil is not allowed to prevail, is essential to the formation of the moral imagination. The sense of an ordered world with a relationship between acts and consequences is foundational to a sense of security and the ability to form ethical norms. Conventional wisdom has the potential to cast a vision for what should be: norms that can be upheld, which can then enable human beings to identify when the 'right' order of things has been broken. The expectation of justice is what enables recognition of injustice, anger at oppression and unfairness, and a response aiming to achieve redress. If this vision of the world becomes mechanistic, however, it leaves no space for grace, and inadvertently enables those with power to justify their position, to theologize their privilege, and consign those without power to remain underprivileged. In isolation, the risk is significant. Within the canon as a whole, however, this type of text is set alongside other texts that modify, nuance and problematize them. Protest wisdom, which we find mostly in Psalms, Job and Ecclesiastes, clamours that this ideal picture simply is not the way of the world, and wrestles with how to speak of, and to, God from 'the abyss'. Protest wisdom takes issue directly with God for not delivering on promises, and not ensuring a world of justice. Here in Job, these two wisdoms are pitted against each other. The friends keep trying to explain away Job's suffering using the categories of traditional wisdom. Job dismisses their arguments and protests against God. Conventional wisdom on its own does not faithfully account for his experience. Protest on its own, however, leaves the world a random, disorienting and overwhelming place. What is at stake is both theology and spirituality. It is about how faith can speak authentically when in the midst of disorienting, disabling circumstances, when none of the traditional categories can help piece the world together. The question is acute – and remains, to a large degree, unresolved. The book of Job does not give an academic, intellectual answer to the problem of suffering. Instead, it journeys with one person through different stages of distress, and explores different ways of speaking within them, and their consequences not only for Job, but for the community of faith.

The problematic presence of Yahweh

The arrival of Yahweh as speaker interrupts the dialogues, and finally breaks the deadlock. The divine speeches have often been used negatively in traditional academic reflections to show Yahweh standing in judgement over a Job who had dared to question him. (This is a picture in keeping with the tendency to only quote Job's first response of 'perfect faith' – it would seem to say real faith does not question, real faith does not allow for distress, despair or trauma. Such a picture easily becomes damaging and destructive to anyone struggling with mental health challenges.) If we read Job within the context of the entire book, though, including the prologue and epilogue, this image does not withstand scrutiny – thankfully. First, we notice that God answers Job 'out of the whirlwind' (38.1). A 'great wind' (1.19), a natural disaster sent from God, had caused the death of Job's children. It is no coincidence that God speaks out of the wind now; not out of a utopian place of calm and detachment, but out of turmoil, pain and incomprehensible power. Symbolically, there is no need to look for places outside of trauma and pain for an encounter with God – the encounter can happen in the midst of confusion, wrestling, uncertainty, anger and rejection of faith as received.

The divine speeches do not answer Job's questions, nor do they address the friends' remonstrances. Instead, they are typical of an Old Testament theophany, a divine/human encounter that overwhelms and reveals the utter otherness and power of God. The book of Job is a text about how we speak to God, and about him. It is also a text that explores the nature of the relationship between the human and the divine, what is possible. Can humans and God be free within such a relationship, or are they tied by specific 'rules of engagement', by promises, by cause and effect? Can they love freely? Can God be God, and therefore free to act unexpectedly and outside of expectations (a precondition for the possibility of grace)? Here we come back to the accuser's wager in chapter 1, and the word *hinnam*. The God of chapters 38—41 is far bigger, far more powerful, and far more intimidating than the God Job worshipped in chapter 1. Hence Job's response – a response in line with the response of prophets meeting God (Moses, Isaiah, Ezekiel ...). Job acknowledges his own frailty, and the enormity of the God he simply did not know, a God who can do far more than what he had previously imagined. A theophany of this magnitude in the Old Testament is never an end, but a beginning. Job's response is in line with traditional prophetic responses in its awareness of the chasm of otherness, and the overwhelming holiness of Yahweh. And yet, the God that Job related to via sacrifices and rituals has now become a real-life interlocutor, both utterly other and yet utterly close, a change that becomes clear as we move into the epilogue.

The epilogue: a fairytale ending?

Prose resumes with the epilogue, and Yahweh speaking directly to the friends. While many critics have argued there is little relationship between the prose and poetry sections, the development of plot and character moves logically and coherently throughout the book. At the beginning, earth and heaven were completely separate; God was kept where God should be, and Job stayed where he belonged. As misfortune, pain and trauma took hold, the former categories of thought started breaking down, and so did the separation of earth and heaven. Here, in the final prose section, the world is being slowly put back together, but in different ways from the arrangement of the world of chapters 1 and 2. The clear boundaries of earth and heaven have collapsed, and Job and Yahweh relate directly rather than through sacrifices.

Yahweh takes the friends to task for '[not speaking] of me what is right' (42.7), but he commends Job for speaking rightly. What exactly is being referred to? Is Yahweh rebuking the friends for their incorrect theology? What 'speaking' is Yahweh commending Job for? His initial utterance? His long speeches of lament? His response to the theophany? Job does not speak consistently of God. Translation questions may help us here. While the conventional translation has been 'for you have not spoken *of* me what is right, as my servant Job has done', the Hebrew actually says 'you have not spoken *to* me what is right'. The difference is rather substantial; the question is not one of theology, but one of ontology. Job speaks to God, seeks to wrestle directly with God, by trying to match the reality of his experience with the reality of God as he has encountered him.

Furthermore, Yahweh's words go beyond a rebuke to the friends for their lack of pastoral understanding; it invites a social reintegration of Job to his community of faith, without leaving either untouched. They affirm that the trauma of one member has an impact on the entire community of faith, and that together they need to wrestle with how to speak to God within the whirlwind. The friends are not the only ones to be challenged, however. Job is invited to set aside the arguments with his friends and pray for them. He offers sacrifices for their misguided speech, just as he had for his (potentially innocent) children. Instead of a disconnected act on behalf of children he did not spend time with and whose guilt he had no proof of, he actually prays for the friends whom he knows have hurt him, and has to accept their donation towards the sacrifices. The picture of spirituality and the community of faith here is integrated, relational, and challenges all to let go of grudges and move towards reconciliation. For the community of faith to function properly, there needs to be an acknowledgement of failure, willingness for grace and openness to a new articulation of its journey with God. Job as a teaching book therefore takes seriously the fact that communities of faith will not respond well, and holds them responsible, but also prepares this same community to respond with grace to the failure of its members.

The portrait of Job in his old age is markedly different; there is little mention of piety, but much mention of community. Job now has friends and family gathered around him, and he interacts with them in a way he had not done before. The epilogue is not without shadows, however. Job's wife is not mentioned, a notable absence given the care taken by the narrator to have Job surrounded by all who loved him. A return to health and prosperity does not erase trauma and its long-term effects. Job has more children – but the ones he lost are not restored to life. He does, though, relate very differently to the children he has now. Not only does he spend time with them, but he values his daughters to the point that they are named and receive an inheritance – an unexpected and almost unthinkable detail in its cultural context. The detail is not theologically anodyne. A theology based on just deserts condemns those without power to stay without power – they are seen to deserve it. Elevating his daughters shows that Job has made a definite break with this theology, in a way that opens up possibilities for challenges to unhealthy uses and abuses of power in the wider community. The epilogue can appear fairytale-like, and indeed it is intended to make clear that this is not a true/real story, but a tale destined to shape the moral imagination. Despite the fairytale elements, though, we hear the note of warning held by the notion of Job being 'blessed' again; the word still holds the ambiguity of the prologue, and begs the attentive reader to ask, what really is a blessing? Are the wealth and riches the blessing, or does the blessing lie elsewhere?

Job, meanwhile, never blesses God in the epilogue.

Conclusion

This very cursory run through the book of Job reveals a complex, nuanced and sensitive book of great value for the Church, both theologically and pastorally. It is a book that legitimizes different discourses about God; at no point are we told that one of Job's pronouncements is right. The text does not condemn his initial reaction, or his reaction to the theophany, or his absence of blessing and prayer in the epilogue. Instead, the book takes us on a journey with Job and his friends as they grope towards a way of being, individually and collectively, in the face of deep grief and trauma. Job's experiences shake up the foundations not only of his own faith, but also that of the community. The portrayal of God, at times problematic and ambiguous, shows that faith itself, and one's understanding of God, are themselves part of the distress that Job is facing. And yet the book does not stop there, but it affirms the importance of exploring how to speak faith in the midst of disorientation and trauma, and affirms that this is the work of the community of faith. Despite its fairytale qualities, the book is deeply honest and realistic about human nature and the struggle of even the best-meaning friends to come alongside those whose world and faith are turned upside-down. As such, it is a hugely undervalued resource for engaging with trauma, but also for the pastoral and moral formation of communities of faith, so they can become communities of grace within which truth-telling can forge a way out of darkness and into new and unforeseen places of meeting with the overwhelming presence of a God who longs to bless.

Notes

1 N. Whybray, 2008, *Job*, Sheffield: Sheffield Phoenix, p. 105; D. J. A. Clines, 1989, *Job 1–20* (World Biblical Commentary 17), Grand Rapids, MI: Zondervan, p. 21.

2 J. G. Janzen, 2009, *At the Scent of Water: The Ground of Hope in the Book of Job*, Grand Rapids, MI: Eerdmans, p. 45.

3 W. Brueggemann, 1997, *Theology of the Old Testament: Testimony, Dispute, Advocacy*, Minneapolis, MN: Fortress Press, p. 391.

7

Anxiety: Some Perspectives
from the Old Testament

DAVID G. FIRTH

Anxiety is an issue of what we would call 'mental health' that is recognized in the Bible. Focusing on the Old Testament, we can see that anxiety can be expressed in a range of different contexts. In this chapter we will briefly note aspects of this range and then focus on the more particular ways in which it is expressed in the book of Psalms, particularly Psalms 38, 94 and 139. Anxiety is here understood as something that damages our relationship with God and others, but that can be put right in prayer.

Approaching the Old Testament

Consideration of biblical material on any mental health issue needs to begin by noting that the concept of mental health is a relatively modern construct. If we could go back to Israel in the time of the Old Testament and ask people about their mental health, we would probably receive some rather blank stares. Certainly, there is no Hebrew word that means 'mental health'. But the lack of an equivalent word or phrase to describe this is not the same as a lack of awareness of it. In part, this is because Hebrew frequently uses the word for 'heart' to refer to someone's intentions and, more specifically, to refer to their mind, even if it is not always evident in translation (e.g. Num. 16.28). So, when we are told that David's heart 'struck him' (1 Sam. 24.5) after he had cut off the corner of Saul's robe while in the cave, we need to understand that the reference is to a state of mental disturbance. It was not simply that he had an emotional response to this act, but that this also led to a condition of mental dis-ease. Without belabouring the point, this shows that within the Old Testament there is a fusion of emotional and mental distress. Lacking the need to divide these elements for analytical purposes, as is more common in the Western tradition, the Old Testament shows awareness that people can suffer from problems with mental and emotional well-being, even if it did not develop a technical terminology for this.

This general framework can be carried over to specific mental health problems that are identified today. That Israel did not develop a technical language for mental health issues means we need to be careful when we find broadly equivalent terms in the Old Testament for issues that might be diagnosed today. We can rightly recognize that the Old Testament accepts such matters in general, but comparatively few issues are addressed directly within it. Where we find terms that correlate to our modern language of mental health, we must understand that they do not offer a technical equivalence to our modern terms. We can, however, see a broad equivalence that exists between the language of the Old Testament and our modern suite of diagnostic terms.

One term that does occur in both modern discussion of mental health and the Old Testament is 'anxiety' (or sometimes its adjective, 'anxious'). Rather than attempting to correlate the Old Testament material with definitions from modern medicine, the aim here is to understand how the Old Testament understands this concept. This is not because Israel's concept is superior to ours, but rather because it is used in a non-technical sense. Hence, it correlates to more general use of the terms 'anxiety' and 'anxious' in English, without having to map precisely to a technical sense. That this is so can be seen from the fact that there are two main roots that are translated 'anxious' or 'anxiety' in the Old Testament, and although they have some overlap in meaning they are linguistically unrelated.[1] As Hebrew words can be traced back to a root, the meaning of which is broadly related across the verbs, nouns and adjectives that are derived from it, we will here focus on these two roots, while noting the distinction where relevant between the verb and other forms.

General observations on the language of anxiety

The first root to consider is *da'ag*. The verb of this root occurs seven times in the Old Testament,[2] while the related noun *de'agah* occurs a further six times.[3] Neither form is always translated as 'anxious' or 'anxiety' but this is routinely an element of the meaning, even if for various reasons it is translated otherwise. The root is sometimes used to indicate anxiety associated with a fear of some sort. That fear may or may not be appropriate. For instance, the noun occurs in Joshua 22.24 when the tribes living east of the Jordan express the fear that in subsequent generations those living to the west will forget their right to worship God. We may rightly regard this fear as an expression of anxiety, though since it refers to a possible future we have no way of knowing if their fear is appropriate. More immediately, in 1 Samuel 9.5 and 10.2, Saul is concerned that his father will become anxious because he and his servant have not returned from their search for some missing donkeys. In this case, the fear is real, though perhaps at a less substantial level than that expressed by the eastern tribes in Joshua 22.24. An equally immediate fear is expressed by Zedekiah in Jeremiah 38.19 when he refers to what he thinks the Judeans who have gone over to the Babylonians might do to him. By contrast, in Jeremiah 17.8, the prophet indicates that the person who trusts in God need not be anxious in difficult times. What unifies all these examples is that anxiety is associated with a fear about the future, a fear that may refer to something imminent and highly probable, or to something distant that cannot be proved.

The other root is not altogether clear – it is usually thought to be *sa'ap* – but the more important point is that the word *sar'apim* occurs twice, both times with the meaning of 'anxious thoughts'.[4] As we will look at both occurrences in our reflections on the book of Psalms and anxiety, we can leave discussion for now. However, it is worth noting that if the usual derivation of the root is correct, then it is related to the word *se'ipim* which occurs twice in Job.[5] Although the number of occurrences makes it difficult to be sure, it seems that in both texts it refers to thoughts that have been reached hastily and that might therefore need to be reconsidered. As we shall see, this is not inconsistent with the way the relevant word is used in Psalms.

As a final observation at this point, we should note that anxiety can be expressed without using the vocabulary that makes this explicit. This is particularly evident in the narrative texts of the Old Testament. For instance, Esther's deep distress over Mordecai's behaviour in the palace gate (Esther 4.4) could well include anxiety as an element of her distress because of the ramifications of such behaviour in the immediate presence of the king. So, there may be a much broader range of texts than we consider here that could be relevant, but the difficulty is to provide clear criteria. As such, we focus only on those texts that use explicit vocabulary associated with anxiety.

Psalms and anxiety

Rather than focusing only on more general observations, we turn now to consider three psalms that address the issue of anxiety in some way. Psalms is helpful because it includes all the relevant vocabulary, something true for no other book in the Old Testament. Although our comments are necessarily brief, it is hoped that providing this as a slightly more in-depth probe will show the important relationship the Old Testament demonstrates between anxiety and prayer. In particular, we note that genuine faith and anxiety are not set against one another; rather, faith names anxiety within prayer that begins to face up to the situations that generate anxiety.

Psalm 38

Psalm 38 has been interpreted in various ways. It has traditionally been read as part of the seven penitential psalms,[6] a group of psalms that receive a strong focus during Lent. That element is particularly important for our purposes since the element of anxiety receives particular expression in the confession of sin in verse 18. However, although this is an element within the psalm, in more recent years it has more commonly been read as a complaint psalm, perhaps associated with illness.[7] Certainly, the description of the psalmist's experience in verses 3–8 is consistent with this, though it is impossible to identify any one illness on the basis of the symptoms described here. But alongside this, the psalmist also discusses the problem of friends and companions standing aloof, a problem exacerbated by the fact that some were apparently keen to see the poet's downfall (vv.9–16). The situation that generated this prayer is thus complex, but it seems to represent a combination of factors, all of which contribute to the general lack of well-being experienced by the poet. The complexity means that there is no one element that defines the poet's suffering, but rather it is a combination of physical illness, social alienation and discipline from God. It is this combination that generates the psalmist's anxiety.

These elements come together in the appeal to God in verses 16–22. The psalmist here brings these complex matters before God, acknowledging the impact of sin, illness and social alienation. That alienation may have a legal background if the reference to the poet's foes lodging false accusations in verses 19–20 alludes to a court process, though this is not a necessary element of the language here. But even if there are no formal charges, the court of public opinion is certainly in view. Distress here comes from three sources – the psalmist's sin, the threat of others, and God's discipline (see v.2). The first and last are clearly linked, with the threats from others perhaps to be understood along similar lines to Job's experience of his so-called friends.

This provides the key background to the mention of anxiety in verse 18. Most translations offer something similar to the NRSV where, having acknowledged iniquity, the poet then expresses sorrow for sin. But this requires a meaning for *da'ag* that occurs nowhere else since sorrow is not expressed in any other occurrence. For this reason, the NASB's 'I am full of anxiety because of my sin' is to be preferred since it not only avoids the element of sorrow, but also brings the expression of anxiety into the open.[8] What might this anxiety mean? Since the psalmist has confessed, there remains the possibility of forgiveness, and the psalm as a whole hopes for this. But anxiety here represents the realization that sin damages the poet's relationship with God, just as the threats from others damage interhuman relations. Nevertheless, although anxiety is part of the distress experienced from which release is sought, there is no conflict between faith and anxiety. Rather, it is something that can legitimately be named in prayer.

Psalm 94

Psalm 94 is somewhat unusual in the part of the Psalter where it is found.[9] Psalm 92 emphasizes the importance of expressing thanksgiving, while Psalm 93 is the first of a collection of psalms reflecting God's kingship. The themes of Psalms 92—93 then dominate 95—100, as they move between summonses to sing God's praise and reflections on his reign. That this psalm is so distinctive, however, means that it is difficult not to notice it. Here, instead of celebrating the changes brought to the world by God's presence, we encounter a world where there is violence – and even the denial of any awareness on God's part (verse 7). Where Psalm 38 focused on an individual's distress, Psalm 94 is about a community that faces distress and violence, though from verse 16 the psalm does reflect the experience of an individual living in this world, and it is here that the language of anxiety is again expressed.

We can read this psalm in three main sections. In verses 1–7, while addressing God directly, the poet outlines the fundamental problem of the wicked and the need for God's vengeance to be expressed. Verses 8–15 draw on elements more typical of the Old Testament's wisdom traditions to provide an informed reflection on how God interacts with the world, and also on the certainty that ultimately God will act for his people. Here, those addressed are the psalm's human audience, indicating that those who hear this psalm are meant to learn from it. Finally, in verses 16–23 the poet draws on personal experience (expressed as testimony) to explain to the audience why God is the psalmist's refuge and why they too can trust God to act against the perpetrators of violence.

It is in the testimony that we find explicit reference to anxiety, though again there are numerous points where the distress described could cause this. Having posed the question in verse 16 of who would stand up for the psalmist against the wicked, each element of the testimony then demonstrates how God has helped resolve various expressions of distress. It is in verse 19 that the theme of anxiety (*sar'apim*) is raised.[10] Here, the psalmist looks back on times of significant anxiety, and testifies that God's comfort brought resolution. This is offered as a word of comfort to others who might currently feel anxiety, emphasizing that even in a world full of violence God is a refuge, and this provides hope that the violence described will not triumph. This does not mean the poet will not again feel anxiety in the face of such pressures, but it does model a way forward for all who do. Although the language here is different from Psalm 38, this psalm also shows that anxiety is not inconsistent with faith. But where it was enough for Psalm 38 to show this basic point, Psalm 94 encourages readers to see that God's comfort in the past continues to provide hope in each new experience of such distress.

Psalm 139

Where verses 1–18 of this psalm are much loved, the element of violence expressed in verses 19–22 means they are often omitted from public reading. Even when read, they are a source of much discomfort, though the final prayer to be searched by God in verses 23–24 is generally loved again. However, it is likely that verses 19–22 are vital for understanding this psalm and its presentation of anxiety. The psalm also plays an important part in this closing collection of Davidic psalms (138—145), which prepare for the burst of praise with which the book of Psalms closes (Psalms 146—150).

The psalm divides into two main sections, though unlike Psalms 38 and 94 where the main sections are of roughly equal length, Psalm 139's sections are unbalanced, with each subsection of the first part about the same length as the closing section. This is an important element in the psalm's form. Verses 1–18 focus on how God has known the psalmist. Here, the poet explores how God knows everything about the psalmist (vv.1–6), that there is nowhere that the psalmist could separate from God's presence (vv.7–12), and all that God has done has been for the poet's good (vv.13–18). The last two verses of the third subsection also sum up the whole of the first section as the psalmist expresses awe at the wonder of God's thoughts in such a context. All this changes radically in verses 19–24. In verses 19–22 the poet asks that God kill the wicked while also expressing absolute loyalty to God, before asking once again to be searched by God so that his own thoughts might be examined. Although God knows all about the poet, this new request to be searched occurs immediately after the request that God slay the wicked, making this a form of self-curse that might suggest the poet has been accused of a major crime, but for which a declaration of innocence is desired.

It is not necessary that the psalm reflect an actual court case (and in any case the Psalter does not provide details of this), but this sort of background provides a context for understanding the anxious thoughts mentioned in verse 23.[11] The anxious thoughts of which the poet speaks are those associated with elements that might trigger a 'guilty' verdict. But the freedom the psalmist seeks is not only related to a particular charge. Rather, in light of the fact that God is always searching the psalmist, the request must be that God bring to light those thoughts that are inconsistent with knowing God. Anxiety about thoughts that separate us from God are to be named in prayer so that God may resolve them. Just as Psalm 94 indicated that God provides comfort with other moments of anxiety, so this psalm expects that God will expose these anxious thoughts so they can be resolved. This is because anxious thoughts that take us away from God are inappropriate for faith, unlike all other expressions that can be named and from which we can learn. But we do not judge people for having such thoughts – rather, we ask that God bring these thoughts into the light so they can be addressed.

Conclusion

The number of texts in the Old Testament that speak directly about anxiety is relatively small, though there are numerous other places where we might detect it. Nevertheless, these texts provide an important pastoral resource for addressing anxiety. These texts understand that fear can trigger anxiety, and such fears may indeed be legitimate. In general, it is not inappropriate for believers to experience anxiety, and no one is criticized for experiencing anxiety. The only anxiety that is rejected is found in thoughts that lead us away from God, but even here the expectation is that in prayer it is God who can identify such thoughts and provide the comfort needed to go forward with confidence.

All of this does require considerable care from those providing pastoral support for those experiencing anxiety. Comparatively few are trained as counsellors, and those who are would need to reflect closely on this material in light of the more technical definitions of anxiety that are used there. Above all, we need to remember that none of these psalms was written specifically to address the issue of anxiety. However, there are some general signposts here that can help to shape pastoral practice and response to anxiety, and it may be helpful to outline these. Two such signposts can be noted here.

First, there is no necessary contradiction between anxiety and faith. Indeed, based on what we see in the book of Psalms, it is entirely possible for someone to be full of faith and yet at the same time to experience anxiety. Obviously, there is always a need for a case-by-case assessment, but faith in God does not mean that believers avoid various forms of threat, and threats can be a trigger for anxiety on particular issues. That is, these psalms recognize that particular threats can cause anxiety, but this does not mean that the person involved has a deficient faith. Rather, they may well be demonstrating a perfectly normal response to a threat. Faith may well suggest that certain forms of anxiety might be inappropriate, but because we are parts of imperfect communities it is likely that we will all face levels of threat that cause fear. For example, in the midst of economic upheaval, Christians are not intrinsically more likely to retain their jobs than are others (even if we might hope they will have better support systems through their church). In that things like the ability to maintain housing are often dependent upon keeping a job, a degree of anxiety where a business is failing is quite likely. Likewise, someone falsely accused of something may feel appropriate anxiety as this issue is worked through, and here Psalm 139 is an important resource. Faith in God does not make such fear inappropriate, and having anxiety under such circumstances should probably be expected. What matters, though, is that the anxiety be recognized for what it is – a natural expression of fear. Psalm 38 can then provide an appropriate resource that might shape the prayer of those experiencing this anxiety so that it is named in prayer. In this way, the anxiety is not belittled, and neither are those experiencing it asked to ignore it. But by seeing it as something to be prayed through (and not denied), anxiety can be seen as a means by which faith is in fact expressed.

Second, these psalms encourage those suffering from anxiety (and those who journey with them since the psalms were public prayers) to reflect on earlier points where God has helped. Psalm 94 is an important resource here since the anxious thoughts that trouble the psalmist are placed into a context of prior acts of God on behalf of both the psalmist and the community of which the poet is a part. This does not deny the reality of the anxiety, and neither does it regard it as inappropriate. But it places anxiety in a context where the fear that triggers anxiety might be managed. Again, prayer in the context of a believing community is an important mechanism for naming anxiety and for seeing it as normal. Anxiety is not removed through prayers such as this, but it is placed in a framework that does not allow it to be seen as ultimate. On the other hand, the placement of a psalm such as this in the midst of a group of poems that otherwise celebrate the reign of God means that triumphalism is also marginalized because although God's reign is rightly celebrated, it is acknowledged that this reign is experienced only imperfectly in our world.

Biblical reflection on the issue of anxiety needs to look more widely than the texts addressed here, and it is important to remember that each of the psalms considered is finally a prayer, not a case study in anxiety. But as long as this is properly noted, they provide an important pastoral resource for journeying with those experiencing anxiety.

Notes

1 There are a few other words translated in this way by some contemporary translations, but in each case alternatives exist that might be better because these are distinctive uses of terms that elsewhere are used in other senses. Because the exact sense in the instances is disputed, they are not considered here.

2 1 Sam. 9.5; 10.2; Isa. 57.11; Jer. 17.8; 38.19; 42.6; Ps. 38.18.

3 Josh. 22.24; Jer. 49.23; Ezek. 4.16; 12.18, 19; Prov. 12.25.

4 Pss. 94.19 and 139.23.

5 Job 4.13 and 20.2

6 The others are Pss. 6, 32, 51, 102, 130 and 133.

7 See Tremper Longman III, 2014, *Psalms: An Introduction and Commentary*, Nottingham: IVP, pp. 181–2.

8 The NIV's 'I am troubled by my sin' likewise moves in the right direction, though without naming the type of trouble expressed.

9 See G. W. Grogan, 2008, *Psalms*, Grand Rapids, MI: Eerdmans, p. 163.

10 The NRSV's 'cares of my heart' (so also ESV) is too general. The NIV's 'anxiety' is preferable, especially as the idiom here refers to the psalmist's inner being, and not just thoughts.

11 The NRSV only has thoughts, but again we follow the NIV as the element of anxiety is present. The psalmist does not ask for an assessment of all thoughts, only those causing anxiety.

8

Truth-Telling as Well-Making

WALTER BRUEGGEMANN

The lament psalms in the book of Psalms voice a clear, thick, deep, shrewd understanding of the processes that are indispensable for the transformation of the 'human condition' from death to life, from sorrow to joy, from anger to energy, from despair to hope. (A fresh understanding of these indispensable processes, so utterly Jewish, was reasserted in the modern world by Sigmund Freud.) These lament psalms offer rich variation in particulars. But the general flow of rhetoric that performs these indispensable processes is clear enough to trace, as scholarship has done, as a reliable, persistent pattern that amounts to a describable genre. This genre of speech features a human speaker who is filled with sufficient *chutzpah* to voice truth in honest ways before the Lord of the covenant. That recurring rhetoric is grounded in the conviction that God's covenant partners have entitlement in the covenant to address God. More than that, these entitled speakers seize the initiative in such speech, and dare to summon God into their vexation that is the subject of such lament, protest and complaint. They assume authority to state their case before God with expectation that God is willing, able and ready to engage with them in the vexation.

Drawing God into trouble

This recurring pattern of speech features the covenantal partner drawing God into trouble with an expectation that if God can be mobilized, the trouble can be assuaged! We may readily identify three features in this patterned speech. First, the psalmist regularly *addresses God by name*: 'LORD (YHWH)'. The utterance of the holy name affirms that the speaker is intimately and confidently connected to the God who is addressed – 'My God, my God' (Ps. 22.1), 'O LORD' (3.1), 'O God of my right!' (4.1), 'O LORD my God' (7.1). Second, the speaker voices a specific *complaint*, describing for God the particulars of trouble, often an attack by enemies, being shamed and slandered, being abandoned, being sick, being vulnerable, or being weak:

> O Lord, how many are my foes!
> Many are rising against me. (3.1)

> I am distraught by the noise of the enemy,
> because of the clamour of the wicked.
> For they bring trouble upon me,
> and in anger they cherish enmity against me. (55.2–3)

> People trample on me;
> all day long foes oppress me;
> my enemies trample on me all day long,
> for many fight against me. (56.1–2)

> I lie down among lions that greedily devour human prey;
> their teeth are spears and arrows,
> their tongues sharp swords. (57.4)

The descriptions are vivid and specific; they are, at the same time, open and imaginative enough that in our use of these psalms we may fill them with imagery from our own experience.

Third, when the complaint has been sufficiently detailed to move God, it is accompanied by vigorous *imperatives* that ask God to act to rectify circumstances that are unmerited and unbearable before which the speaker is helpless:

> Rise up, O Lord!
> Deliver me, O my God! (3.7)

> Answer me when I call, O God of my right!...
> Be gracious to me, and hear my prayer. (4.1)

> Be gracious to me O Lord, for I am languishing;
> O Lord, heal me, for my bones are shaking with terror. (6.2)

> Rise up, O Lord, in your anger;
> lift yourself up against the fury of my enemies;
> awake, O my God. (7.6)

> O God, break the teeth in their mouths;
> tear out the fangs of the young lions, O Lord! (58.6)

It is to be noted that these imperatives are unrestrained in their vigour, in their emotional force, and even in their violence. These are acts of urgency that, in so far as they are imperatives, issue commands to God expecting that this covenant partner addressed will be attentive and responsive.

These three elements together amount to framing the God-relationship around the needs of the speaker, thus in contrast to doxologies in which all the attention is given over to God. Thus provisionally, in the lament psalms, the speaker assumes the dominant and primary role in the relationship, able to take a daring and necessary initiative.

Honest speech

There are two recurring elements in this patterned speech to be noticed because they constitute difficulty for those who want pastoral care (and Christian piety in general) to be 'nice'. First, the lament psalms are permeated with *motivations* that give God reason to be attentive and to act. It is as though when God heard the unrestrained imperatives, God responds, 'Now why should I bother to answer your demand?' Such motivations may seem ignoble to us, because they sound like bargaining that ought not to happen with God. They are, however, efforts to make clear to God that God has something at stake in the vexation of the speaker and should act for God's self-interest. Or, as we say, 'For your name's sake' – that is, for the sake of your reputation. God should act on behalf of the speaker and so be on exhibit as a trustworthy God. This act will maintain and enhance God's reputation (about which God is thought to care!) as a faithful covenant partner. Thus, for example, the speaker may remind God of God's previous fidelity that ought now to be continued in present circumstances:

> In you our ancestors trusted;
> they trusted, and you delivered them.
> To you they cried, and were saved;
> in you they trusted, and were not put to shame. (22.4–5)

Most daringly, the psalmist warns God that if the speaker dies, there will be one less voice to praise God. This is on the assumption that God relishes praise and enjoys it:

> What profit is there in my death,
> if I go down to the Pit?
> Will the dust praise you?
> Will it tell of your faithfulness? (30.9)

Do the shades rise up to praise you?
Is your steadfast love declared in the grave,
or your faithfulness in Abaddon?
Are your wonders known in the darkness,
or your saving help in the land of forgetfulness? (88.10–12)

The hope is that God will act for the speaker in God's own self-interest.
In dire straits it is not a surprise that the petitioner will engage in regres-
sive speech!

The other 'objectionable' element in the lament psalms are what scholars
term *imprecation* – that is, a wish for vengeance on one's enemies. Most
notoriously, in Psalm 109 the speaker inveighs against the enemy at
length:

May his days be few;
may another seize his position.
May his children be orphans, and his wife a widow.
May his children wander about and beg;
may they be driven out of the ruins they inhabit.
May the creditor seize all that he has;
may strangers plunder the fruits of his toil.
May there be no one to do him a kindness,
nor anyone to pity his orphaned children.
May his posterity be cut off;
may his name be blotted out in the second generation. (109.8–13)

Or, quite viciously:

Break the arm of the wicked and evildoers;
seek out their wickedness until you find none. (10.15)

Let them vanish like water that runs away;
like grass let them be trodden down and wither.
Let them be like the snail that dissolves into slime;
like the untimely birth that never sees the sun. (58.7–8)

Some strands of piety will think that the faithful should not talk in this
way, and certainly not in the presence of the Holy One. Behind that is the
notion that the faithful should also not *think* that way or *feel* that way.
But we do! Israel knew, from the outset, that what is felt and thought
must be said; it must be said out loud, and it must be said out loud
in the presence of God. This is the God from whom no secret 'can be

hid'.[1] Truth-telling through such laments is completely without restraint or reservation because it is truth-telling that goes to the very heart of the speaker. It will be noted, of course, that the speaker does not act out these violent wishes for vengeance but only voices them to God, in whom the speaker has complete confidence.

When we consider these five elements together –

address to God
complaint
petition
motivation, and
imprecation –

we are able to see that this is honest speech in the process of truth-telling. It is an act whereby the self, diminished by many 'toils and snares', is now reclaimed and restored in the presence of God. The utterance amounts to a moment of 'omnipotence' for the speaker in which the speaker dares presume that the speaker's cause deserves – and will receive – the full attention of the holy God.[2]

This moment of utterance is an instance of *being heard* – that is, being heard back to full personhood. Thus the opening imperative of such speech is often: 'Listen to me!'

Answer me. (4.1)

Give ear ... give heed. (5.1)

Hear O LORD. (30.10)

Hear my prayer. (54.2)

Give ear to my prayer ...
attend to me and answer me. (55.1–2)

Self-announcement is the first step in the recovery of a self that has been depleted. But self-announcement counts only if it is addressed to someone in whom there is confidence of being taken with utmost seriousness. Utmost seriousness on the part of God grounds this daring, unrestrained speech of the self who is ready to risk full exposure.

Risky speech

At this point in the patterned speech there is often a turn in rhetoric or at least a pause. One can see this in the abrupt newness of 13.5–6 and 22.21a, in which there is inexplicable resolution for the speaker. It is as though the speaker has spent his energy and has no more to say. Or perhaps the speaker pauses in the hope of receiving a response from the one addressed. The outcome of such speech is not automatic or guaranteed. It is a leap to the faithfulness of God that God enacts in freedom. It is risky speech, given fidelity-in-freedom on God's side, but these prayers characteristically end in a good resolve of being heard by God:

[T]he LORD has heard the sound of my weeping.
The LORD has heard my supplication;
the LORD accepts my prayer. (6.8–9)

In my distress I called upon the LORD;
to my God I cried for help.
From his temple he heard my voice,
and my cry to him reached his ears. (18.6)

But you heard my supplications
when I cried out to you for help. (31.22)

This poor soul cried, and was heard by the LORD,
and was saved from every trouble. (34.6)

I waited patiently for the LORD;
he inclined to me and heard my cry. (40.1)

I love the LORD, because he has heard my voice and my supplications.
Because he inclined his ear to me,
therefore I will call on him as long as I live. (116.1–2)

Being heard when engaged in truth-telling is a moment of verification, recognition, valorization – being taken seriously! It is an act of emancipation. This is indeed truth-telling that makes free and that makes well. Such a prayer characteristically ends in joyous thanksgiving, perhaps expressed in a thank-offering:

What shall I return to the LORD for all his bounty to me?
I will lift up the cup of salvation

and call on the name of the LORD.
I will pay my vows to the LORD
in the presence of all his people. (116.12–14)

Or it may issue in glad testimony to the community:

I have told the glad news of deliverance
in the great congregation;
see, I have not restrained my lips, as you know, O LORD (40.9)

Or endless doxology into future generations:

From you comes my praise in the great congregation;
my vows I will pay before those who fear him ...
Posterity will serve him;
future generations will be told about the Lord. (22.25, 30)

In a variety of forms these laments culminate in gladness, well-being, and readiness for a new life fully in sync with the faithful God who has restored. The truth that makes someone free and makes them well is a part of the process of *the reconstitution of the self* that has been depleted by a variety of assaults.

Of course we must reckon with the occurrences of this patterned speech when it does not eventuate in such good resolve. This is evident in the individual laments of Psalms 39 and 88, and in the communal lament of Psalm 44. These psalms serve as reminders that in the free interaction of covenant partners there are no guarantees. The entire interaction is risky. That same risk, of course, is present in every serious relationship of honest truth-telling.

Liturgical practice

How odd it is that these rich resources of the community of faith that occupy so much of the book of Psalms have been almost completely lost in the life of the Church, being absent (except for Psalm 22) in the liturgical sequence of the Church.[3] Such an absence from the liturgy is in the interests of a polite spirituality that thinks that such abrasive truth-telling has no proper place in the life of the congregation. Such an absence in the practice of the Church is an invitation to denial, the bet that such truth-telling is inappropriate before the God of all truth.

The Church has devised two strategies for embarrassed silencing of these best texts and their best practice. The positive strategy is the development of pastoral care and particularly (at least in the USA) the 'Pastoral Care Movement', with its protocols and accrediting apparatus. In a segue from the lament psalms to pastoral care, the Church has made two bargains. First, it has moved the indispensable truth-telling processes from the congregation into 'private practice' so that the normative form has become one-on-one counselling. There are, to be sure, some remaining practices of group interaction as in recovery groups, but those tend to be at the margins of congregational life. The *privatism* of such pastoral care is most often done in a vacuum, as though the resources of the community do not matter to well-being. Second, we have agreed to a *secular* form of truth-telling with a *human listener*, because the notion of *God as listener* is too embarrassing for us because we imagine that God is too timid or too fragile for such abrasive interaction. (I do not denigrate such a privatized secularized practice, because I have benefited greatly from such interaction.) But we may be aware that entrusted to us (and only to us) is a reliable script for a more public practice of voiced 'I's who receive fresh valorization from this Holy Thou who is made available through the practice of the congregation. Recovery of such public practice is, in my judgement, a powerful desideratum.

The other less noble strategy for scuttling the lament psalms is that the Church, in its practice, has taken the full range of emotional needs and extremities and reduced them all to only one note – namely, guilt. Thus liturgically the only aspect of the complexity of the human self about which we regularly tell the truth concerning our guilt is in the regularity of confession; we tend, moreover, to do even that in rote innocuous articulation. Such a singular accent reduces to silence all the other undeniable dimensions of the self that concern our life with one another and with God.

The contemporary Swedish interpreter Fredrick Lindstrom has carefully and compellingly shown that in the 50 or so lament psalms there is not one admission of guilt.

> It is highly doubtful if we can speak of a motif of sin in the individual Psalms ... The confession of sin is not an element in the classical individual complaint Psalms, and the motif of sin, in the few cases in which it occurs, hardly functions as indication of the reason for the affliction.[4]

In its lament-protest-complaint, Israel is not willing to accept responsibility for what has gone awry in its life. Often the fault is assigned to unnamed adversaries. Sometimes the fault is said to belong to God as the trouble-maker through acts of infidelity towards Israel. It would be good, in my judgement, if the Church moved in intentional ways beyond such reductionism and created room in the liturgy for the full truth-telling of the diminished self without such reductionism. Among other liabilities in an excessive focus on guilt is that it amounts to collusion with the political-economic oligarchy. That oligarchy of money and power is wont to 'blame the victim' for his/her sorry state of disadvantage and vulnerability, when in fact the oligarchy itself is most often the perpetrator of such vexation for the vulnerable. Israel in its prayer will have none of that!

Conclusion

For this reason I suggest that the Church could well recover the truth-telling processes of the lament psalms because a greedy culture of despair will never make free and will never make well. The oligarchy, with its passion for control, predictably ends in despair, whereas the laments are acts of hope that God will make all things new.

In the 'post-history' of the laments, we may refer to Jesus' parable in Luke 18.1–8 in which Jesus instructs his disciples to pray like a nagging widow who insists on justice before a cynical indifferent judge. Her insistence on justice sounds very much like a lament psalm! When Jesus taught his disciples in this way, he might have said to his early Jewish followers, 'Pray like you know to do in the lament Psalms.' Jesus does not assure us that such prayer will be answered. Rather, he assures us that with such prayer we will never 'lose heart'. Tepid practices of prayer, like so much prayer in the life of the Church, end in denial about what dare not be uttered, and become a sure way to 'lose heart'. What is required in order not to lose heart is engagement in self-announcement before one who reliably listens in a way that valorizes. The widow insists on being heard, and finally *is* heard by the judge: 'I will grant her justice, so that she may not wear me out by continually coming' (Luke 18.5).[5]

When the Church loses heart, its witness is tepid, its mission is weak, its courage is limited, and its imagination is domesticated. At the end of the text Jesus wonders if the coming Son of Man will find faith to pray as truth-tellers. That same question is put to us. How we answer that question indicates a great deal about our practice of pastoral care. There is no other resource that is so rich and inexorable in its prospect for truth-telling that makes for well-being.

Notes

1 See W. Brueggemann, 2014 (ed. B. A. Strawn), *From Whom No Secrets are Hid: Introducing the Psalms*, Louisville, KY: Westminster John Knox Press.

2 On the cruciality of an experience of omnipotence for personal health, see D. W. Winnicott, 1965, *The Maturational Processes and the Facilitating Environment: Studies in the Theory of Emotional Development*, Madison, CT: International Universities Press, p. 180 and throughout.

3 See W. Brueggemann, 1995, 'The Costly Loss of Lament', *The Psalms and the Life of Faith*, Minneapolis, MN: Fortress Press, pp. 98–111.

4 F. Lindstrom, 1994, *Suffering and Sin: Interpretations of Illness in the Individual Complaint Psalms*, Stockholm: Almqvist and Wiksell International, p. 350.

5 J. R. Donahue, 1988, *The Gospel in Parables*, Philadelphia, PA: Fortress Press, p. 183, translates the response of the judge: 'Because this widow is "working me over" I will recognize her rights, so she doesn't give me a black eye by her unwillingness to give up.'

9

Spirituality from the Depths: Responding to Crushing Circumstances and Psychological and Spiritual Distress in Jeremiah

JILL FIRTH

'My anguish, my anguish! I writhe in pain!' (Jer. 4.19). Jeremiah suffers along with his people, shares God's tears, enters into complaint, dialogue and debate with God, and offers insight into future hope. The book of Jeremiah offers many resources for suffering people today. Writings in spirituality, discipleship and theology by John of the Cross, Dietrich Bonhoeffer and Kazoh Kitamori have embraced suffering in Jeremiah. In recent years, Kathleen O'Connor, Emmanuel Katongole and others have examined Jeremiah through lenses such as resilience, trauma and lament, and the book could be useful in the newer field of moral injury. I will first highlight Jeremiah's difficult circumstances and mental and spiritual pain in the biblical text, then I will consider these pastoral applications of the book.

Jeremiah's crushing circumstances and psychological and spiritual pain

As a result of his calling as God's prophet, Jeremiah was rejected by his family, hometown, close friends (11.21; 12.6; 20.10), other prophets (26.11; 28.10–11), priests (20.20–21), and national leaders (36.19). He experienced death threats (11.19; 20.20; 26.8; 38.25), plots (18.18), public mocking (20.2, 7, 10), assault, unjust arrest and imprisonment (20.2; 37.15, 21), danger of starvation (37.20–21; 38.9), kidnap, and forced migration to Egypt (43.4–7). Jeremiah's call was in tension with his loyalty to his people (15.16–18; 17.17–18; 20.7–10), and his summons to the nation to submit to Nebuchadnezzar was at odds with government policy and public sentiment (21.9; 25.9; 27.5; 38.2, 17; 42.11; 43.10). He was called a 'madman' (אִישׁ מְשֻׁגָּע, 29.26).[1] Jeremiah experienced a whole lifetime of personal suffering, including social exclusion, because God prohibited him from joining communal events such as feasts, weddings and funerals (16.5–9). His celibacy and lack of descendants added to his loneliness and to his loss of status in a society that esteemed marriage and children (16.2). Jeremiah survived, though everything had been stripped from him except his life and his trust in God.[2]

Jeremiah also shared the sufferings of his people, including the violence, exploitation and oppression of Judah's leaders (22.13–17), drought (14.1–6), warfare, exile and the direct rule of foreign powers (52.28–30). Using imagery of the reversal of creation and the pain of childbirth from Genesis 1—3, Jeremiah grieved over the total destruction of his people's way of life: 'I looked on the earth, and lo, it was waste and void ... I heard a cry as of a woman in labour, anguish as of one bringing forth her first child' (4.23, 31). The fall of Jerusalem was not a mere battle or invasion, but 'the collapse of Judah's once stable world', including loss of temple, land, and dynasty.[3]

Jeremiah's suffering mirrors the suffering of God.[4] The tears of God and Jeremiah mingle over the people's sufferings and their refusal to accept God's help. 'My joy is gone, grief is upon me, my heart is sick' (8.18). 'O that my head were a spring of water, and my eyes a fountain of tears' (9.1; see also 13.17; 14.17). 'My heart is crushed within me, all my bones shake' (23.9; see also 4.19). There is anguish about the war (4.19), the devastation of the land (4.23–26; 12.4), the hurt of people (8.21), the slain (9.1; 14.17–18), the captivity of the people (13.17), and starvation (14.18). God calls for the mourning women to bring a dirge for the devastation of the earth and for the many deaths (9.10, 17–22).

Jeremiah wrestles with God in his 'confessions' (11—20) which include laments and complaints in dialogue with God.[5] He pours out his fears for his life (11.19; 20.10), and of being publicly cursed (קלל, 15.10), and even sees God as a potential terror (מְחִתָּה, 17.17). Jeremiah interrogates God's justice (12.1–2), and complains of 'unceasing pain' (15.18). In reply to Jeremiah's fears for his life, God assures him of his protection and judgement on the wicked (11.21–23; 14.10). In reply to Jeremiah's distress at injustice, God shares his own pain in seeing his people turn to evil (12.5–12; 14.17–18). When Jeremiah complains of 'unceasing pain' and accuses God of being an unreliable and untrustworthy 'deceitful brook' (15.18), God reminds Jeremiah of his earlier promise to strengthen him and to be with him (1.18–19; 15.20).

In his final confession (20.7–18), Jeremiah's emotions swing from lament to praise and then back to a deep distress about his life. He questions his call, fearing public humiliation (20.7, 10), then after expressing confidence and praise (20.13) he curses the day he was born (20.14–18), because his life seems so full of toil (עמל), sorrow (יגון) and shame (בשת). Federico Villanueva observes that a shift back to complaint, after an initial movement from lament to praise, is also found in some psalms, such as Psalms 12 and 28.[6] Maureen Conroy describes a similar process in spiritual direction, where deeper issues can be uncovered after painful feelings are explored and resolved.[7]

Hope

Alongside the descriptions of suffering in the book of Jeremiah are many promises of hope. The early chapters of the book contain hope for a return to the land after exile (3.15–19; 12.14–17; 16.14–15; 27.22; 29.10–14; 30.1—33.26), and offers of forgiveness are connected to prophecies of judgement (17.24–26; 18.8; 24.4–7; 22.4–5; 25.4–6; 26.12–13; 38.2–3, 20–23). Later in the book, the exile is unexpectedly portrayed as a place of thriving (29.4–7), and those who surrender to Nebuchadnezzar are promised their lives as a 'prize of war' (21.9; 38.2). The promise of return to the land specifically includes vulnerable people, including the blind and lame, and women who are pregnant and giving birth (31.8).[8] The new covenant of Jeremiah 31 promises future blessing, and Jeremiah buys a field as an earnest that 'houses and fields and vineyards shall again be bought in this land' (32.15). Under Governor Gedaliah, those who remain in the land after the fall of Jerusalem find themselves in an Edenic plenty of wine and summer fruits (40.9–12).[9] Several of the oracles about the nations even include promises of restoration for Israel's enemies (46.26; 48.47; 49.6, 39).

People today may relate to Jeremiah's rejection by family, struggles with authorities, assault, persecution, imprisonment, hunger, war, loss of country or forced migration, or to his loneliness, grief or spiritual distress. The book of Jeremiah is soaked in the tears of Jeremiah, God and the nation. We now turn to some uses of the book of Jeremiah in spirituality, discipleship and theology.

Jeremiah and spirituality, discipleship and theology

From New Testament times, the Christian tradition has embraced suffering (Mark 8.34; 1 Pet. 2.21). Early Christian martyrs were willing to suffer with Christ, like the slave Felicitas: 'Now it is I that suffer what I suffer, but there will be another in me, who will suffer for me, because I also am about to suffer for him'.[10] John of the Cross, Dietrich Bonhoeffer, Kazoh Kitamori and Jürgen Moltmann drew from the book of Jeremiah in their reflections on spirituality, discipleship and theology.

Spirituality

Like Jeremiah, John of the Cross was imprisoned and placed in solitary confinement.[11] He welcomed discomfort and hardship, as he wrote to Madre Leonor Bautista, because 'an apostolic life ... is a life of contempt'.[12] He approved the perseverance of Madre María de Jesús in visiting the poor, as they would 'know what you profess, which is the naked Christ'.[13] In *The Living Flame of Love* (2.27), John cited Jeremiah's life as an exemplar of suffering, quoting Jeremiah 12.5 to invite aspirants to be willing to accept 'common trials' in order to be able to endure 'spiritual tribulations and trials that are deeper'.[14] In *The Ascent of Mount Carmel* (2.20.6), John refers to Jeremiah's 'severe trial' in Jeremiah 20.7–9, when people mocked him when the fulfilment of his prophecies was delayed.[15]

John of the Cross also saw suffering as a way into spiritual growth, through the darkening of the senses. To Doña Juana he writes, 'thus God does one a great favor when he darkens the faculties and impoverishes the soul'.[16] To Doña Juana de Padraza, he says, 'I have felt your griefs, afflictions and loneliness,' and compares these to 'knocks and rappings at the door of your soul'.[17] In *The Dark Night* (1.8.1), John uses Jeremiah as an example in explaining 'two kinds of darkness'.[18] First, John describes the dark night of the senses which 'is common and happens to many'.[19] He cites Jeremiah 31.18 in describing this first night, where a person is 'chastened and buffeted'.[20] In explaining the second night, the dark night of the spirit, which 'is the lot of very few',[21] John celebrates God's love, and quotes Jeremiah 2.2: 'For this immense love that Christ, the Word, has cannot long endure the sufferings of his beloved without responding. God affirms this through Jeremiah: *I have remembered you, pitying your youth and tenderness when you followed me through the desert.*'[22]

Discipleship

Dietrich Bonhoeffer's discipleship was influenced by Jeremiah's life and words. Both Jeremiah and Bonhoeffer experienced conflict between loyalty to God and their political leaders.[23] Each had to pray for the military defeat of his nation, was imprisoned, and was under sentence of death.[24] Each chose to share the difficulties of his people, rather than live safely on foreign soil: Jeremiah chose to stay behind with the people in the land after the fall of Jerusalem (40.2–6), and Bonhoeffer elected to return to pre-war Germany from the USA.[25]

Bonhoeffer's 1942 hope for renewal in his nation was inspired by Jeremiah 32.15, 'living every day as if it were our last, and yet living in faith and responsibility as though there were to be a great future: "Houses and fields and vineyards will again be bought in this land" proclaims Jeremiah (32.15)'.[26] Jeremiah 32.15 also underlies Bonhoeffer's 1943 affirmation to his fiancée, Maria von Wedemeyer, 'our marriage will be a yes to God's earth'.[27]

In Jeremiah 45, Bonhoeffer found inspiration for renunciation of worldly advancement and wealth.[28] Writing from Tegel prison on 5 September 1943, he quotes Jeremiah 45.4–5, 'Behold, what I have built I am breaking down ... And do you seek great things for yourself? Seek them not ... but I will give your life as a prize of war.'[29] On 30 April 1944, he wrote, 'We shall have to repeat Jer. 45.5 to ourselves every day.'[30] In May, citing Jeremiah 45: 'If we can save our souls unscathed out of the wreckage of our material possession, let us be satisfied with that.'[31] On 16 July, reflecting on Luther's *theologia crucis*, Bonhoeffer reminded himself that 'the Bible directs man to God's powerlessness and suffering: only the suffering God can help'.[32] On 21 July, the day after the failed attempt to assassinate Hitler, he linked sharing God's sufferings to Jeremiah 45, sharing the 'sufferings ... of God in the world – watching with Christ in Gethsemane ... that is how one becomes a man and a Christian (cf. Jer. 45)!'[33]

Theology

Theologians responding to the trauma of World War Two integrated the book of Jeremiah with Luther's theology of the cross. Kazoh Kitamori argues that 'Jeremiah may be called the Paul of the Old Testament ... "God on the cross" for Paul is "God in pain" for Jeremiah'.[34] 'The "pain" of God reflects his will to love the object of his wrath.'[35] Kitamori's 'theology of the pain of God' developed from his understanding of God's mercy for Ephraim in Jeremiah 31.20, 'I am deeply moved [המה] for him', as the Hebrew verb המה is used elsewhere in the psalms and prophets for heartfelt pain.[36] Building on Kitamori, Luther and Bonhoeffer, Jürgen Moltmann's understanding of 'the crucified God' was shaped 'in the shadow' of Auschwitz.[37] Moltmann comments: 'A theology which did not speak of God in the sight of the one who was abandoned and cruci-fied would have had nothing to say to us then.'[38]

Jeremiah has been linked with the suffering servant in Isaiah as there are many parallels in thought and wording with the servant songs.[39] Katharine Dell defines the suffering servant in Isaiah as 'a male individual who suffered uncomplainingly even when faced with death'.[40] Jeremiah 'may have been the historical figure most likely to have been in mind', but there are also differences, as Jeremiah complains about his fate, and his suffering is not redemptive.[41] No individual human figure adequately fulfils the role of the suffering servant except Jesus, who took all our sins and suffering (Isa. 53.4, 12; Acts 8.35). All Christians are called to share in Christ's sufferings, and Jeremiah's life of suffering and exile shows that God goes with us.[42]

The book of Jeremiah has been significant in Christian spirituality, dis-cipleship and theology in learning to accept and find meaning in pain and suffering. We now turn to applications of the book of Jeremiah in healing and survival, in the fields of resilience, trauma, lament and moral injury.

Jeremiah and resilience, trauma, lament and moral injury

In recent decades, the book of Jeremiah has been used in strategies for survival and healing, though previously Isaiah and Ezekiel were more commonly used for reflection on hope.[43] The book of Jeremiah contains a rich presentation of personal struggle, but we must observe due caution in developing pastoral applications from its pages.

First, a biographical approach to Jeremiah is not straightforward, as evidenced by the many different interpretations of his personality.[44] Carl Friedrich Keil (1807–88) imagined Jeremiah as 'naturally of a yielding disposition, sensitive and timid',[45] and Abraham Heschel (1907–72) thought Jeremiah's 'own heart was rich in tenderness and sensitivity to other people's suffering'.[46] On the other hand, Robert Carroll sum-marized mid-twentieth-century views of Jeremiah as 'a classic figure of promethean strivings with the deity ... in keeping with a gloomy existentialism'.[47] Gerhard von Rad pictured Jeremiah moving 'step by step into even greater despair',[48] because of 'scepticism about his office'.[49] Mary Callaway helpfully warns against making Jeremiah in our own image.[50]

Second, we should be careful of imposing an overly definite chronology on Jeremiah's experiences. The text of Jeremiah is unclear whether the emotional turmoil of the confessions (11—20) is confined to Jeremiah's early years, or if it also forms a backdrop to the later narratives (37—44), which lack such accounts of emotional distress.[51] Corrine Carvalho considered that 'the basic elements of his personality remain consistent',[52] but Mary Mills proposed that under the 'traumatic stress' of social fragmentation, Jeremiah became 'a bleak, disordered and paranoid persona ... an emotionally unstable character who can be described as "disabled"'.[53] Jeremiah may have been incurably wounded, like Frodo: '"Alas! there are some wounds that cannot be wholly cured," said Gandalf. "I fear it may be so with mine," said Frodo',[54] or he may have been 'used up to the last drop', like Merlin in *That Hideous Strength*.[55] The later narratives may reflect a more settled attitude to suffering, or Jeremiah may be 'ebbing away in God's service'.[56]

Resilience

Michael Moore regards the book of Jeremiah as a 'premier text' in considering ministry burnout, because of the rare 'inscaping' of Jeremiah's personal emotions, especially in Jeremiah's confessions.[57] Trust in God is essential to surviving the conflict Jeremiah experiences when Judah fails to respond to the political crisis of Babylonian threat.[58] Russell Davis brings the perspective of depth psychology, observing that as Jeremiah pushes back against God in the confessions, he develops the ego strength that will be necessary for his mission, and this struggle is also the place where his true self emerges.[59] Ronald Cook observes the value of a call from God, and the comfort of the presence of God, for resilience. Jeremiah's confidence in God and perseverance under trial enable him to go the distance.[60]

Studies in resilience have used Jeremiah's story to invite individuals to persevere and trust in God, though the cost may be great. Trauma studies direct our attention to suffering and healing within a whole community.

Trauma

Kathleen O'Connor describes Jeremiah as the 'ideal survivor' of trauma, because he survives, though he has lost everything, and is 'a flesh and blood figure with whom readers can identify'.[61] Jeremiah 'embodies their fate and the ethical behaviour they need for their survival'.[62] He models how to respond, showing engagement, trust, resistance, cooperation, and his life embodies God's word for people.[63]

O'Connor also identifies a trauma response in the book's structure.[64] The 'dystopian' vision of the early chapters moves from family poems featuring Israel as a failed wife and son (2.1—4.2), through war poems (4.3—6.30), to weeping poems (8.18—9.2). This grounds the 'utopian' vision of Jeremiah 30—31, where the exiles return in safety.[65] The seemingly chaotic arrangement of the book may be 'replicating the interpretive turmoil' of the exiles, but also offers the reader an opportunity to 'make sense of the confusion'.[66] O'Connor argues that the lack of chronological ordering fits with the disordered chronology that is experienced in trauma.[67]

Lament

Emmanuel Katongole emphasizes the value of lament in dealing with trauma, and its links to hope. *Born from Lament* opens with the abduction of schoolgirls by the Lord's Resistance Army,[68] and incorporates laments that express unimaginable horrors of violence and cruelty in Northern Uganda and the Congo.[69] Laments '(1) give voice to the grief of the community; (2) name what is going on; and (3) express the longing for restoration and social healing'.[70] Katongole contests the claim that an 'inner quality' of resilience is 'the key to social healing', noting the value of turning to God, as evidenced in the 'sense of utter helplessness' and 'anguished turning to God' of these popular laments.[71]

Tears in Jeremiah are linked to the tears of Jesus as he wept at the tomb of Lazarus and over Jerusalem (John 11.35; Luke 19.41–42).[72] Jeremiah is 'the wailing prophet par excellence', whose laments function '(1) as a social critique; (2) to mourn the covenant; (3) as a reflection of Yahweh's tears; and (4) to announce the newness of restoration'.[73] 'There are things that can be seen only with eyes that have cried,' according to Archbishop Christopher Munzihirwa, who was martyred in 1996.[74] These include a new vision for society, the way of non-violence, the suffering of God, and the invitation to share his suffering.[75] Katongole highlights the memory of Rachel's tears in Jeremiah (31.15) in the story of the slaughter of the innocents in Matthew 2.17–18, invoking 'God's own anguish' and connecting these tears to the new hope that comes through Jesus.[76]

Moral injury

Recent research in PTSD (Post Traumatic Stress Disorder) has observed that some emotions such as guilt and shame are not successfully addressed by therapies focusing on physical and emotional reactions to prolonged danger.[77] 'Moral injury' results in shame and guilt from 'perpetrating, failing to prevent, bearing witness to, or learning about acts that trans-gress deeply held moral beliefs and expectations'.[78] Moral injury is seen as the 'signature wound' of recent morally ambiguous wars such as Iraq and Afghanistan,[79] but is relevant to other settings. People may also carry shame and guilt for failing to prevent atrocities to the self or others, such as rape and incest,[80] sex trafficking,[81] or indigenous dispossession and social disruption.[82]

The book of Jeremiah may become a useful resource in conversations about moral injury because of its setting in social disruption, violence and war, its rich vocabulary of shame, and its portrayal of people confront-ing morally complex circumstances.[83] In his confessions, Jeremiah fears shame and dismay (בוש, חתת, 17.18), and suffers insult (חרפה, 15.15; 20.8), derision (קלס, 20.8), shame (בשׁת, 20.18), being a laughing stock (שׂחוק, 20.7), and being mocked (לעג, 20.7). Though Jeremiah's own actions may not have transgressed his sense of 'what's right',[84] he feels caught in a power struggle between God and the people, who are both using per-suasion (פתה, 20.7, 10) and seeking to prevail over him (יכל, 20.7, 10). His best efforts fail to prevent the abuse of the poor and needy (22.3; 23.13–14), the destruction of the land, and violence (4.23–31; 15.8–9), and he is an observer of distressing events such as the desecration of dead bodies (8.1–3), and the destruction of the temple (52.13). Other case studies of moral decision making include the contrasting stories of Ebed-Melech the Ethiopian, who risks his own safety to rescue Jeremiah (38.7–13), and King Zedekiah who sacrifices his own wives and children along with the security of the nation, because he is afraid of his political opponents (38.19–23).

The pastoral use of the book of Jeremiah today is complicated by the differences between Jeremiah's historical setting and our own. God's judgement was coming on Judah in the sixth century BC after decades of specific warnings (25.1–7), but today's refugees and displaced indigen-ous people are not under God's judgement. The Jews of Jeremiah's time were promised safety and security in their temporary accommodation in Babylon, and a return from exile after 70 years (29.5–11), but today's refugees and displaced indigenous peoples may face daily abuse, dis-respect, multigenerational trauma, and permanent exile or loss of homelands.[85] Persecuted people today may not gain their lives as a prize of war, but lose their lives for Christ's sake.[86] In addition, the book's depictions of violence and use of feminine imagery may require careful treatment.[87]

Conclusion

The book of Jeremiah displays Jeremiah's psychological and spiritual pain as he wrestles with God and with his family, community and nation under extreme circumstances of war, displacement and drought. Through the tears of God and Jeremiah, the book offers hope for restoration of the nation, and mercy for enemies after judgement. Jeremiah has been an exemplar of suffering in spirituality, discipleship and theology, as well as resilience, lament and trauma. Recent studies in moral injury may open up further relevance for this text. The book of Jeremiah deepens our understanding of sustained suffering, and invites us to put our trust in the God who shares our pain:

There are things that can be seen only with eyes that have cried.
(Oscar A. Romero)

Notes

1 See H. W. Wolff, 1986, 'Prophets and Institutions in the Old Testament', *Currents in Theology and Mission*, 13, p. 5.

2 K. M. O'Connor, 2005, 'Jeremiah as Ideal Survivor', *Journal for Preachers*, 28, pp. 21–2.

3 L. Stulman, 2005, 'Conflicting Paths to Hope in Jeremiah', in C. R. Yoder and colleagues (eds), *Shaking Heaven and Earth: Essays in Honor of Walter Brueggemann and Charles B. Cousar*, Louisville, KY: Westminster John Knox, p. 47.

4 H. Rowold, 2004, 'Theology of the Pain of God: Reflections from Scripture', *Missio Apostolica*, 12, p. 19.

5 P. J. Scalise, 2001, 'The Logic of Covenant and the Logic of Lament in the Book of Jeremiah', *Perspectives in Religious Studies*, 28, p. 400.

6 F. G. Villanueva, 2008, *The Uncertainty of a Hearing: A Study of the Sudden Change of Mood in the Psalms of Lament*, Leiden: Brill, p. 250. Villaneuva analyses Jeremiah 20.7–18 in detail.

7 M. Conroy, 1995, *Looking into the Well: Supervision of Spiritual Directors*, Chicago, IL: Loyola Press, pp. 40–8.

8 K. M. O'Connor, 2005, 'Jeremiah's "Prophetic Imagination": Pastoral Intervention for a Shattered World', in Yoder and colleagues (eds), *Shaking Heaven and Earth*, p. 68; S. M. Olyan, 2008, *Disability in the Hebrew Bible: Interpreting Mental and Physical Differences*, Cambridge, MA: Cambridge University Press, p. 82.

9 See L. Stulman, 2004, 'Jeremiah as a Polyphonic Response to Suffering', in J. Kaltner and L. Stulman (eds), *Inspired Speech: Prophecy in the Ancient Near East: Essays in Honor of Herbert B. Huffmon*, London: T&T Clark, pp. 302–18.

10 Tertullian, *c.*160–*c.*230, 'The Passion of the Holy Martyrs Perpetua and Felicitas'. For an English translation see *Latin Christianity: Its Founder, Tertullian*, Vol. III in A. Roberts, J. Donaldson and A. Coxe (eds), *The Ante-Nicene Fathers*,

Grand Rapids, MI: Eerdmans, 1885, pp. 609–706. This quote may be found on p. 704.

11 K. Kavanagh and O. Rodriguez (eds), 1991, *The Collected Works of St John of the Cross*, rev. edn, Washington, WA: ICS, p. 18.

12 Kavanagh and Rodriguez (eds), *Collected Works*, p. 742.

13 Kavanagh and Rodriguez (eds), *Collected Works*, p. 751.

14 Kavanagh and Rodriguez (eds), *Collected Works*, p. 668.

15 Kavanagh and Rodriguez (eds), *Collected Works*, p. 222.

16 The majority of the extant letters of Saint John of the Cross are addressed to women. He also drew the sketch of Mount Carmel for Magdalena del Espíritu Santo (Kavanagh and Rodriguez (eds), *Collected Works*, p. 752, n. 36), and wrote *The Living Flame of Love* for Ana de Jesús (p. 742, n. 14).

17 Kavanagh and Rodriguez (eds), *Collected Works*, p. 744.

18 Kavanagh and Rodriguez (eds), *Collected Works*, p. 375.

19 Kavanagh and Rodriguez (eds), *Collected Works*, p. 375.

20 *The Dark Night* 1.14.4, in Kavanagh and Rodriguez (eds), *Collected Works*, p. 393

21 *The Dark Night* 1.8.1 in Kavanagh and Rodriguez (eds), *Collected Works*, p. 375.

22 *The Dark Night* 2.19.4 in Kavanagh and Rodriguez (eds), *Collected Works*, p. 443.

23 I. Stockton, 1999, 'Bonhoeffer's Wrestling with Jeremiah', *Modern Believing*, 40, p. 50.

24 Stockton, 'Bonhoeffer's Wrestling', pp. 52–4.

25 D. W. Shriver Jr, 1981, 'Jeremiah, Prophet of the Eighties', *Review & Expositor*, 78, p. 400.

26 D. Bonhoeffer, 1971, *Letters and Papers from Prison: The Enlarged Edition*, ed. Eberhard Bethge, London: SCM Press, p. 15.

27 Bonhoeffer, *Letters and Papers*, p. 415.

28 Bonhoeffer, *Letters and Papers*, p. 219.

29 Bonhoeffer, *Letters and Papers*, p. 105.

30 Bonhoeffer, *Letters and Papers*, p. 279.

31 Bonhoeffer, *Letters and Papers*, p. 297.

32 Bonhoeffer, *Letters and Papers*, p. 369. See also R. Bauckham, 1984, '"Only the Suffering God Can Help": Divine Passibility in Modern Theology', *Themelios*, 9, pp. 6–12.

33 Bonhoeffer, 1971, *Letters and Papers*, p. 370.

34 K. Kitamori, 1965, *Theology of the Pain of God*, Richmond: John Knox Press, p. 20.

35 Kitamori, *Theology of the Pain of God*, p. 21.

36 Kitamori, *Theology of the Pain of God*, p. 152.

37 J. Moltmann, 1993 (trans. R. A. Wilson and J. Bowden), *The Crucified God: The Cross of Christ as the Foundation and Criticism of Christian Theology*, Minneapolis, MN: Fortress Press, pp. x–xi.

38 Moltmann, *The Crucified God*, p. 1. The term 'the crucified God' occurs in Luther's discussion of Psalm 118.28 in *Luther's Works* 14.105 (Martin Luther, 1958, Psalm 118, in J. Pelikan and D. E. Poellet (eds), *Luther's Works*, vol. 14, St Louis, MO: Concordia Publishing House, p.105).

39 W. L. Holladay, 1986, *Jeremiah 1: A Commentary on the Book of the Prophet Jeremiah Chapters 1—25*, Philadelphia, PA: Fortress Press, p. 359, and M.

Schreiber, 2009, 'The Real "Suffering Servant": Decoding a Controversial Passage in the Bible', *Jewish Bible Quarterly*, 37, p. 36.

40 K. J. Dell, 2010, 'The Suffering Servant of Deutero-Isaiah: Jeremiah Revisited', in K. J. Dell, G. Davies and Y. Von Koh (eds), *Genesis, Isaiah, and Psalms: A Festschrift to Honour Professor John Emerton for his Eightieth Birthday*, Leiden: Brill, p. 122.

41 Dell, 'The Suffering Servant', pp. 120, 132–3.

42 Shriver, 'Jeremiah, Prophet of the Eighties', p. 403.

43 Stulman, 'Conflicting Paths', p. 45, n. 6.

44 The book of Jeremiah does not set out to give a full biography, but a 'selective account' of the prophet which gives 'an interpretation of his role and significance' (T. E. Fretheim, 2002, *Jeremiah*, SHBC, Macon, GA: Smyth and Helwys, p. 11). Scholars also debate whether the presentation of Jeremiah is historical, or a constructed persona (see A. R. Diamond, 1987, 'The Confessions of Jeremiah in Context: Scenes of Prophetic Drama', *JSOT Supplement*, 45, Sheffield: Sheffield Academic Press, pp. 11–16).

45 C. F. Keil, 1988, *Jeremiah, Lamentations*, Grand Rapids, MI: Eerdmans (reprinted), p. 18.

46 A. J. Heschel, 1962, *The Prophets*, New York: Harper and Row, p. 120.

47 R. P. Carroll, 1986, *Jeremiah*, OTL, London: SCM Press, pp. 55–6.

48 G. von Rad, 1965, *Old Testament Theology: The Theology of Israel's Prophetic Traditions*, vol. 2, London: SCM Press, p. 204.

49 Von Rad, *Old Testament Theology*, p. 206.

50 M. C. Callaway, 2004, 'The Lamenting Prophet and the Modern Self: On the Origins of Contemporary Readings of Jeremiah', in Kaltner and Stulman (eds), *Inspired Speech*, p. 50.

51 Holladay argues for a basically chronological account (Holladay, *Jeremiah 1*, pp. 1–6). Diamond suggests that there are 'two progressive cycles' in the confessions, from 11.18 to 15.21, and from 18.18 to 20.18 (Diamond, 'The Confessions', p. 177).

52 C. Carvalho, 2016, *Reading Jeremiah: A Literary and Theological Commentary*, Macon, GA: Smyth & Helwys, p. 11.

53 M. E. Mills, 2007, *Alterity, Pain, and Suffering in Isaiah, Jeremiah, and Ezekiel*, New York: T&T Clark, p. 123.

54 J. R. R. Tolkien, 1974, *The Return of the King*, London: Unwin, p. 236.

55 C. S. Lewis, 1955, *That Hideous Strength*, London: Pan, p. 234.

56 G. von Rad, 1984, 'The Confessions of Jeremiah', in L. G. Perdue and B. W. Kovacs (eds), *A Prophet to the Nations: Essays in Jeremiah Studies*, Winona Lake, PA: Eisenbrauns, p. 346.

57 M. S. Moore, 1992, 'Jeremiah's Identity Crisis', *Restoration Quarterly*, 34, pp. 135–49; C. Norma, and M. Tankard Reist (eds), 2016, *Prostitution Narratives: Stories of Survival in the Sex Trade*, North Melbourne: Spinifex, p. 138.

58 Moore, 'Jeremiah's Identity Crisis', pp. 135–49.

59 R. H. Davis, 1997, 'Calling a Divine Summons: Biblical and Depth Psychological Perspectives', *Union Seminary Quarterly Review*, 51, pp. 136–7.

60 R. L. Cook, 2016, 'Running the Distance: A Call to Perseverance', *Review & Expositor*, 113, pp. 397–400.

61 O'Connor, 'Jeremiah as Ideal Survivor', p. 19.

62 O'Connor, 'Jeremiah as Ideal Survivor', p. 20.

63 O'Connor, 'Jeremiah as Ideal Survivor', p. 24.

64 O'Connor, 2005, 'Jeremiah's "Prophetic Imagination"', pp. 60–4.

65 O'Connor, 'Jeremiah's "Prophetic Imagination"', p. 66.

66 K. M. O'Connor, 2012, *Jeremiah: Pain and Promise*, Minneapolis, MN: Fortress Press, p. 128.

67 O'Connor, *Jeremiah*, p. 132.

68 E. Katongole, 2017, *Born from Lament: The Theology and Politics of Hope in Africa*, Grand Rapids, MI: Eerdmans, p. xi.

69 Katongole, *Born from Lament*, pp. 62–100.

70 Katongole, *Born from Lament*, p. 63.

71 Katongole, *Born from Lament*, pp. 98–9.

72 Katongole, *Born from Lament*, pp. 145–7.

73 Katongole, *Born from Lament*, pp. 151–2.

74 Katongole, *Born from Lament*, p. 164.

75 Katongole, *Born from Lament*, pp. 155–7.

76 Katongole, *Born from Lament*, p. 195.

77 R. Nakashima Brock and L. Gabriella, 2012, *Soul Repair: Recovering from Moral Injury after War*, Boston, MA: Beacon Press, p. xiii.

78 B. Litz and colleagues, 2009, 'Moral Injury and Moral Repair in War Veterans: A Preliminary Model and Intervention Strategy', *Clinical Psychology Review*, 29, p. 695.

79 R. Emmet Meagher and D. A. Pryer, 2018, 'Introduction', in R. Emmet Meagher and D. A. Pryer (eds), *War and Moral Injury: A Reader*, Eugene, OR: Cascade, p. 1.

80 Norma and Tankard Reist (eds), *Prostitution Narratives*, pp. 146, 164.

81 M. Theocharous, 2016, 'Becoming a Refuge: Sex Trafficking and the People of God', *JETS*, 59, pp. 314–15.

82 J. Atkinson, 2002, *Trauma Trails, Recreating Song Lines: The Transgenerational Effects of Trauma in Indigenous Australia*, North Melbourne: Spinifex, pp. 98–145.

83 Discussions of shame can be framed differently within a majority world or a Western cultural setting (J. Georges and M. D. Baker, 2016, *Ministering in Honor-Shame Cultures: Biblical Foundations and Practical Essentials*, Downers Grove, IL: IVP Academic, p. 19). Brené Brown distinguishes humiliation from shame in a Western context (B. Brown, 2018, *Dare to Lead: Brave Work: Tough Conversations. Whole Hearts*, London: Vermilion, pp. 128–30).

84 J. Shay, 1994, *Achilles in Vietnam: Combat Trauma and the Undoing of Character*, New York: Scribner, p. xiii.

85 Atkinson, *Trauma Trails*, pp. 5–11; B. Boochani, 2018 (trans. Omid Tofighian), *No Friend but the Mountains: The True Story of an Illegally Imprisoned Refugee*, Sydney: Picador, p. 357.

86 Kim-Kwong Chan and A. Hunter (eds), 1991, *Prayers and Thoughts of Chinese Christians*, London: Mowbray, p. 19; G. Francis-Dehqani, 2018, 'Firewords: Voicing the Pain: Response 1,' in M. Dale, C. Hine and C. Walker (eds), *When Women Speak …*, Oxford: Regnum, pp. 156–62.

87 L. J. M. Claassens, 2014, 'The Rhetorical Function of the Woman in Labor: Metaphor in Jeremiah 30—31: Trauma, Gender and Postcolonial Perspectives', *Journal of Theology for Southern Africa*, 150, pp. 67–84, and T. E. Fretheim, 2013, 'Violence and the God of the Old Testament', in M. Zehnder and H. Hagelia (eds), *Encountering Violence in the Bible*, Sheffield: Sheffield Phoenix, pp. 108–27.

What Did Jesus Have to Say About Mental Health? The Sermon on the Mount

CHRISTOPHER C. H. COOK

What did Jesus have to say about mental health? This may seem like an odd question to ask, and in some ways it is. The concept of 'mental health', as we understand it, is a modern one and we cannot expect to find Jesus talking about it in the Gospels in these terms. If Jesus did talk about mental health, he would be using a different vocabulary than we do. However, I think that the question also sounds odd to us for other and more important reasons. In the Western world, we have separated out mental and spiritual well-being as separate domains of concern, addressed by different professionals. Mental health belongs to the world of science and medicine. Spirituality belongs to an unscientific and transcendent world of faith and prayer. Such a separation would be completely alien to first-century Palestine (and to many today in other cultural traditions), whether in the mind formed by reading the Hebrew Scriptures or the classical thinking of the invading Roman civilization.

This chapter takes just one passage of Jesus' teaching, from Matthew's Gospel, in order to reconsider the question of what Jesus had to say about mental health. If we stop thinking of spirituality and mental health as different things, and if we look behind the vocabulary that Jesus (or Matthew) uses, might we find that Jesus actually had quite a lot to say on this topic? I write as a Christian priest and theologian, but also as a psychiatrist and a scientist reading Matthew's Gospel. I do not pretend to be a biblical scholar, in the narrow specialist sense, but I do find that Jesus addresses many matters that are familiar to me in my dual roles and in the different perspectives that they bring to my reflections on the nature of mental health and the cure of souls.

The Sermon on the Mount

The passage that we know as the Sermon on the Mount is the first of five discourses by Jesus in Matthew's Gospel. It is understood by many as a summary of Jesus' moral teaching. It has been the subject of a vast literature, offering widely differing interpretations, and is seen by some as providing an ideal that sets the standard so high as to be virtually impossible in practice. It has been described as the 'epicentre of Christianity's self-understanding throughout the Church's history'.[1] While its approach to ethical teaching includes commandments, it has also been read from the perspectives of virtue ethics and the ethics of intention.[2] Notably for our present purpose, Jonathan Pennington has argued that it provides a vision of human flourishing which sees inner qualities as the basis for ethical behaviour. It thus provides resources for a Christian positive psychology that prioritizes love of God and neighbour within the context of eschatological concerns.[3]

The Sermon clearly has a sophisticated structure, but there is much debate about how best to organize discussion of the material within it. For the present purpose, I will follow the structure proposed by Luz.[4] Although, to some extent, this is arbitrary, it has the advantage of organizing the material relationally, with the Lord's Prayer (6.7–15) – representing, as Luz puts it, the 'interior of faith',[5] or nearness to God – at the centre. Either side of this are various concerns regarding relationships with other people and things (5.21–48; 6.19—7.11) that challenge and clarify fundamental human priorities and concerns. These are respectively introduced (5.17–20) and concluded (7.12) with reference to the law and the prophets of the Hebrew religion. The Sermon as a whole is introduced (5.3–16) and concluded (7.13–27) with a description of the paradoxical nature of life in the kingdom of heaven.

Life in the kingdom

After the opening frame provided by 5.1–2 (which corresponds to the closing provided by 7.28—8.1), the Sermon begins with a series of eight beatitudes. Each of these highly paradoxical sayings refers to particular groups of people as 'blessed'. While the English word 'blessed' has been the most popular translation of the Greek *makarios*, and is the word that I will use here, it is not entirely satisfactory and various translators have rendered the sense as happy, fortunate or flourishing.[6] The present psychological implications of the term cannot be completely avoided. However, this term is also theologically loaded, and has – at least to some degree – a forward-looking dimension in relation to the eschato-logical fulfilment of God's kingdom. Commentators vary in the extent to which they associate it with a realized or unrealized eschatology. Jesus proclaims as blessed the very people whom we would not normally con-sider to be blessed in any sense. Those who are poor in spirit, those who mourn, and those who are meek head the list.

At least three of the beatitudes contain ethical imperatives, but they are not primarily concerned with injunctions to moral behaviour; instead, they are more concerned with a reversal of our perceptions concerning the identity of those judged by God to be blessed. They have a strongly relational theme, reflecting our estimation of ourselves and of our rela-tionships with God and others. They reverse our evaluations of present disharmony, low self-esteem, grief and misfortune, setting these in a theo-logical and eschatological context that subverts our prejudices. According to certain readings,[7] they might be interpreted as narrowly applicable to Christian disciples in particular contexts, but I suggest that this should not permit us to reject out of hand the relevance to those who, as a result of traumatic events, genetic inheritance, socio-economic deprivation, or other factors, suffer from the poverty of spirit that is associated with much mental disorder. The beatitudes concern themselves with the kind of things that people struggle with in the course of mental illness and it would seem to represent a certain kind of special pleading to deny this by asserting that they apply only to Christians or only to particular spiritual concerns. Indeed, it is hard to see that it would be conducive to the general message of the Sermon to argue that those who suffer from depression are not poor in spirit. In what way would this show mercy (5.7) or love (5.43)? While the use of the Greek word *pneuma* (spirit) might have other senses, it seems here most obviously to refer to an inner attitude, or state of mind.

The blessings of 5.3–12 are balanced by the warnings of 7.13–27. Con-trasts are presented between a narrow road that leads to life and a broad one that leads to destruction, between a good tree that bears good fruit and a bad one that bears bad fruit, and between a wise man who builds his house on a rock and a foolish one who builds his house on founda-tions of sand. What we do in this life has eternal consequences, and Matthew does not pull any punches about eternal judgement. It matters what you believe, and what you do, in this life.

The law and the prophets

The affirmation and particularity of the Hebrew law and prophets in
5.17–20 is balanced in 7.21 by the so-called 'golden rule' – to 'do to
others as you would have them do to you'. This rule, found in a variety
of other faith traditions, is here said to be 'the law and the prophets'. In
terms of our interest in mental health, 5.17–20 – with its strict ethical
imperatives – presents a problem for those with obsessive-compulsive
traits or disorders, or those whose mental state makes them prone to
guilt. Religious rules and commandments can easily become the focus of
anxiety, guilt and dysphoria. In contrast, the latter passage – 7.21 – provides a compassionate reminder that we should care for others who suffer
(for example, from mental disorders) as we would wish others to care for
us. In both passages, the Sermon makes clear that what we do with our
lives, the way that we live, is important. Life in the kingdom is concerned
with actions, not merely words or good intentions.

Psychiatry has only relatively recently recognized that mental health
is adversely affected by inability to be compassionate towards oneself
and that compassion may provide an important element of psychological
therapies.[8] Some might argue that its professional, scientific and technical
perspectives have historically militated against any emphasis on love. The
recognition by psychiatrists and psychologists that compassion is, in fact,
crucial in healthcare provides opportunity for an important rapproche-
ment. Within the Sermon, there is a recognition that an emphasis on rules
alone is not helpful. Mental, as well as moral, well-being requires that we
understand commandments within the context of compassion towards
ourselves and others.

Desires of the heart

The teachings of 5.21–48 are concerned primarily, in various ways, with
anger, lust and love. Those of 6.19—7.11 are concerned with anxiety and
worry about fundamental human needs, and with the human tendency to
judge others more harshly than ourselves. Together, these comprise the
bulk of what Luz refers to as the 'main section' of the Sermon, and they
provide metaphorical 'bookends' on either side of the central teaching on
prayer. These teachings focus – in broad terms – on aspects of the inner
life that might interfere with prayer.[9] They are, however, not only concerned with impediments to prayer. They address fundamental human
thoughts and desires that have the power either to help us to flourish or
else to preoccupy us and dominate us, poisoning our relationships with

one another, denying us peace, and alienating us from ourselves and from God.

The antitheses of 5.21–48 track murder back to anger, and adultery to lust. They challenge the human tendency to feel unfairly treated by others with an injunction to prefer such injustices rather than feed the vicious cycle that results from responding angrily. Going further than this, Jesus instructs his disciples even to love their enemies. Seeming in places to contradict the preceding affirmation of the Hebrew law (5.17–20), and going much further than that law, these verses set a very high moral standard indeed and this standard is psychologically problematic. Sexual desire, labelled as lust, easily becomes the focus of obsessional ruminations or a cause for guilt. The injunction to accept injustice is easily misused to justify submission to violence in cases of abuse, or else feeds the guilt experienced by victims of such abuse.

Issues of sexual desire, anger, injustice and marital disharmony are among those matters commonly addressed within counselling and psychotherapy, whether or not these psychological interventions are provided within the context of a faith community. Jesus' teaching in the Sermon presents them as key issues for Christian discipleship. Contemporary psychological therapies address them as matters that may be understood within the scientific paradigm and, perhaps in reaction to this, some Christian approaches to counselling have emerged that reject the insights of psychology. On the other hand, secular psychological interventions are frequently offered without addressing the spiritual/religious challenges that arise for Christians (or others), and this is also unhelpful. Happily there is increasing recognition of the need for spiritually/religiously integrated therapies.[10]

Verses 29 and 30 of Matthew 5, taken invariably as metaphorical by almost all readers, are usually understood as encouraging men to take responsibility for their own desires and actions, rather than blaming women. In caring for victims, and in working with offenders (for example, in domestic violence), this has important implications for counselling and therapy. However, it has also provided the basis for acts of self-harm by some people suffering from psychotic delusions and hallucinations.[11] Major mental illness seriously distorts the human ability to contextualize, critically interpret, and prioritize religious teachings in relation to the things that we desire most, and yet it is – at least sometimes – also deeply concerned with religious themes. Religious content is commonly a feature of psychotic delusions and hallucinations especially, but not only, for those who were 'religious' prior to the onset of their illness.[12]

In 6.19—7.11 the Sermon gets to the heart of what it is that we are most concerned about – our deepest desires. The trouble is that we worry about the people and things that we care about, and so Jesus' teaching here addresses the vexed issue of anxiety. It is paradoxically easy to get into a condemnatory cycle of anxiety and guilt generated by the injunctions in 6.25–34 not to be anxious.

The passage starts (6.19–21) with the observation that we invest our wealth in those things that we value most, and that we easily become enslaved by wealth (v. 24). It quickly moves on to the fundamental needs of life – food and drink, clothing (vv. 25 and 31), and length of life (v. 27). All of these are set in the context of the need to strive first for God's kingdom, and (echoing the fourth beatitude in 5.6) his righteousness (v. 33). In the central section of the Sermon, on prayer, Jesus' disciples are encouraged to ask for their 'daily bread', but not before they have asked that God's kingdom will come. The reader of the Sermon is thus challenged about her/his order of priorities. It is not that the basic needs of life are not important. God knows that we need these things (6.32) and wants to give them to his children (7.11). While a certain kind of reading of this passage can make it seem unrealistic (we can't simply 'turn off' our worries), it proves on deeper reflection to be challenging, psychologically wise, and practical. It invites us to question what we care most about, and to turn these concerns into prayer.[13] Prayer, we might say, is the psycho-spiritual therapy for worried Christians.

In this section of the Sermon we also find an interesting passage about judging, or criticizing, others (7.1–5). In some ways, this passage seems out of place here, and it appears to represent a move of topic from what went before. Almost all commentaries[14] remark on the humour of the parable (the idea of getting a large building plank into your eye!), the need to distinguish between fair and unfair ways of judging others, and the danger of hypocrisy. Interestingly, none that I have found observe the obvious (to a psychiatrist or psychotherapist[15]) similarity to the psychodynamic defence mechanism of projection. In projection, unacceptable aspects of the self – thoughts, desires or feelings – are disowned and attributed to others.[16] Thus one becomes blind to one's own failings but sees them clearly in others. This psychological process, first described in detail in psychoanalytic literature by Sigmund Freud, and further developed by his daughter Anna, provides a defence against the anxiety that conscious recognition of one's own faults might cause. It is therefore psychologically highly appropriate that this passage is to be found in the Sermon immediately after a passage dealing with anxiety. It is ironic that this relevance seems to be universally unnoticed by biblical scholars and positively appreciated only by secular therapists.

Intrinsic and extrinsic religiosity

In Matthew 6.1–18, Jesus deals with three important religious practices: almsgiving (vv. 1–4), prayer (vv. 5–15) and fasting (vv. 16–18). In each case, Jesus' teaching concerns the motivation for religious piety. The section as a whole is summarized in verse 1: 'Beware of practising your piety before others in order to be seen by them; for then you have no reward from your Father in heaven.'

In general, research suggests that religious practices are good for health and well-being, including mental health. Of course, this does not mean that one should pursue Christian life so as to be healthy, or to live longer. The teaching of the Sermon is that one should strive above all for God's kingdom, and seek to be righteous for his sake; but perhaps health and well-being are among 'all these things' (6.33) that Jesus promises to those who first seek the kingdom? Within the Sermon, 6.1–18 functions to question our motivation for religiosity.[17] Are we doing it because we value God's reward, or are we doing it for the sake of appearances before other people?

In a seminal and widely cited paper, Allport and Ross distinguished between intrinsic and extrinsic religious orientation. Extrinsic orientation serves a purpose. Among the purposes that it may serve, Allport and Ross included 'security and solace, sociability and distraction, status and self-justification'. 'In theological terms', they suggested, 'the extrinsic type turns to God, but without turning away from the self.'[18] This is not exactly the same as 'practising your piety before others in order to be seen by them', but such piety certainly would offer one example of extrinsic religiosity. Intrinsic orientation, in contrast, finds its motivation in religion itself. In the terminology of Matthew's Gospel, we might say, it seeks first the kingdom of heaven. Subsequent research has confirmed that intrinsic, and not extrinsic, religiosity is associated with better mental health.

Prayer

A discourse on prayer lies at the very heart of the Sermon (6.5–15). Following on from the verses (5–6) that I have characterized as a warning against extrinsic religiosity, there is a warning against using too many words in prayer (v. 7), and then a reminder (v. 8) that God already knows what our needs are before we pray. Apart from the injunction to pray for those who persecute you (5.44), this is the first point in the Gospel where Jesus' teaching on prayer is addressed. It is immediately followed by a model prayer, which we know as the Lord's Prayer (vv. 9–13). In this prayer, there are three petitions on behalf of God, and three on behalf of those who pray.[19] Interestingly, petitions are not included on behalf of others, albeit the prayer is framed in the first person plural (thus implying that we ask these things for others who pray with us, and not for ourselves alone). The initial requests – that God's name should be hallowed (or held in reverence), that his kingdom should come, and that his will should be done – clearly set the theological priorities for Christian prayer. They are an implementation in prayer of the teaching of the preceding parts of the Sermon.

The Lord's Prayer, at the very centre of the Sermon, reflects many of the themes that precede and follow it, both in the Sermon itself and in the Gospel more widely. This has made it theologically significant through the history of the Christian Church, both in instruction in the faith and in the formation of doctrine. Ulrich Luz has suggested, however, that its primary function is 'to make possible prayer, not theology'.[20] Further, it does this in such a way as to integrate the more outward/practical and inward/mental aspects of the teaching of the Sermon:

> For Matthew, prayer is not a flight from, but the inner side of, practice. Prayer makes it possible for Jesus' disciples to understand his demands as the Father's will and to draw strength from that understanding. Prayer is not made superfluous by action; instead, action is constantly dependent on prayer.[21]

The theological significance of such an understanding of prayer seems to have been missed entirely by much of the scientific research that has taken place in relation to prayer and mental health. The focus of such research has generally been very instrumental. For example, prayer has been found to be an effective coping strategy in the face of illness, and is associated (in retrospective and cross-sectional studies) with lower rates of depression.[22] When offered as an intervention, prayer has been found to produce significantly greater improvements in depression and anxiety in comparison with control interventions.[23] Among members of Alcoholics Anonymous, prayer has been found to effect a reduction in craving.[24] Among undergraduate students it has been shown to facilitate empathy and forgiveness.[25] In one longitudinal study of older people, trust-based prayer was associated with greater life satisfaction across time.[26]

In some ways, all of this research is encouraging. It seems to suggest that prayer is good for mental health. However, if the objective in praying is simply the same as the objective in prescribing an antidepressant, this clearly misses the point entirely so far as the Sermon is concerned.

Prayer is not about trying to manipulate God to a particular medical end. Nor is it legitimate to abstract prayer from its proper context as a way of life in the kingdom that Jesus announced. The parallels between the Lord's Prayer and Jesus' prayer in Gethsemane demonstrate that the outcomes may not always be those that we would choose.[27]

Forgiveness

The Lord's Prayer provides the first point of reference in Matthew's Gospel to the importance of forgiveness, and this is immediately reinforced by the teaching in verses 14–15. The need for God's forgiveness, which we are directed to seek in prayer, is linked with the injunction to forgive others, an injunction that is further reinforced, later in the Gospel, by the parable of the two debtors (18.23–35). This link between prayer and action in relation to forgiveness is challenging. Forgiveness is made conditional upon being forgiving, and yet forgiveness is humanly difficult, and sometimes seemingly impossible. What should be said to the woman, repeatedly and brutally sexually abused as a child, who finds it impossible even to *want* to forgive the perpetrator? This question is especially acute given research that now shows that childhood trauma (especially, but not only, sexual abuse) is a significant and common risk factor for adult mental illness.[28]

An enormous amount of scientific and clinical research has now been undertaken in relation to forgiveness and there is an extensive evidence base to suggest that forgiveness, as an intervention, has therapeutic efficacy in a wide range of mental disorders, including anxiety disorders, depression, bipolar affective disorder and addiction.[29] Forgiveness therapy especially addresses unhealthy anger, a kind of abiding, misdirected, and extreme anger which is encountered in a range of common mental disorders. Within therapy it is recognized that forgiveness is not easy, and that it represents a process that takes place over time. It has cognitive, emotional, behavioural and spiritual dimensions.

Forgiveness therapy focuses on the action of forgiveness within human relationships, rather than on the need to be forgiven by God. The Sermon, however, suggests that these are interrelated, and in mental disorders both can be important. Sometimes we find it humanly impossible to forgive, just as we may find it humanly impossible to receive forgiveness. The Lord's Prayer reminds us that we need to seek divine help with both, and that we can take neither for granted.

Mental health and the Sermon on the Mount

As a psychiatrist reading the Sermon on the Mount, I am struck by the great extent of its attention to the same things that I have been concerned with in my clinical practice in the past, and in my ongoing academic work in the field of mental health. Of course, my interests have been particularly at the interface between spirituality and psychiatry, and so I may well not be completely representative of mental health professionals in this regard. There is significant ongoing professional debate about the nature of the boundaries between spirituality and psychiatry.[30] However, the very fact that there is such a debate is to some extent evidence of the overlap of concerns between spirituality and psychiatry and the difficulty of disentangling them.

As a priest and theologian seeking to find wisdom in Jesus' teaching about the human condition, I am struck by the extent to which he was (at least according to Matthew's account of his teaching in the Sermon) psychologically perceptive. It is easy to reduce the concept of poverty of spirit to the virtue of humility, but is that ethical reading of the text simply the reading in of a Christian concern with virtue, rather than to take seriously Jesus' compassion towards those whose inner experience was of depression, or other forms of emotional emptiness? Jesus shows awareness in the Sermon of the problems with laws and commandments that enslave people. He does not deny the importance of obedience to them, but he reinterprets them both more generously and more rigorously in such a way as to move us beyond the service of rules for their own sake.

Jesus probes us with questions about why such things are important, about what we really desire, and about why we worry about the things that we do, all of which are central to what we would call mental well-being. He asks difficult questions about how we relate to one another, and to God, when we face conflict, failure and human selfishness (our own, or that of others). When Jesus talks about forgiveness, he does not centre this on theories of the atonement, but on the reality of our need for divine help to give and receive forgiveness. Forgiveness has the power to heal us, but it is also sometimes simply beyond human grasp.

Prayer is at the heart of the Sermon on the Mount. I would go so far as to suggest that it is at the heart of the therapy that Jesus offers for the human condition.

Conclusion

The Sermon on the Mount has a lot to teach us about mental health. It is not really possible to separate out mental health and spiritual well-being as though they were separate concerns; they are far too inextricably intertwined. In a secular culture that has none the less designated the one a professional and scientific domain, and the other a largely private and religious matter, this presents us with a challenge. Obedience to Jesus' teaching has never been easy, but we have opportunities to engage with the relevance of this teaching for mental health in a way that previous generations did not. We need to have a vision of the relevance of the Sermon that will enable us to grasp these opportunities creatively in the face of the needs presented to us by the burden of mental ill health in our society.

Notes

1 J. T. Pennington and C. H. Hackney, 2016, 'Resourcing a Christian Positive Psychology from the Sermon on the Mount', *The Journal of Positive Psychology*, 12(5), pp. 427–35, 429.

2 For a recent account from the perspective of virtue ethics, see W. C. Mattison, 2017, *The Sermon on the Mount and Moral Theology: A Virtue Perspective*, Cambridge: Cambridge University Press.

3 Pennington and Hackney, 'Resourcing a Christian Positive Psychology'.

4 U. Luz, 2007, *Matthew 1–7*, in H. Koester (ed.), *Hermeneia – A Critical and Historical Commentary on the Bible*, Minneapolis, MN: Fortress Press, pp. 172–4. See also the account of this structure, as modified slightly, by D. C. Allison, 2016, *The Sermon on the Mount*, in *Companions to the New Testament*, New York: Herder & Herder, pp. 27–40.

5 Luz, *Matthew 1–7*, p. 172.

6 See helpful discussions by R. T. France, 2007, *The Gospel of Matthew*, in G. D. Fee (ed.), *New International Commentary on the New Testament*, Grand Rapids, MI: Eerdmans, pp. 160–1; S. McKnight, 2013, *Sermon on the Mount*, in T. Longman and S. McKnight (eds), *The Story of God Bible Commentary*, Grand Rapids, MI: Zondervan, pp. 32–6; J. T. Pennington, 2017, *The Sermon on the Mount and Human Flourishing*, Grand Rapids, MI: Baker, pp. 41–67.

7 The first beatitude is particularly interesting in this respect. Almost all commentators seem to understand poverty of spirit in relation to a humble desire for God on the part of those who are aware of their own need for God. Luz, however, drawing on Meister Eckhart, suggests that the one who is poor in spirit wants nothing, knows nothing, and has nothing – not even in relation to God (Luz, *Matthew 1–7*, p. 192).

8 P. Gilbert, 2009, 'Introducing Compassion-focussed Therapy', *Advances in Psychiatric Treatment*, 15, pp. 199–208.

9 In the fourth century, Evagrius of Pontus identified eight kinds of thoughts that he considered to be impediments to prayer, which share significant common ground. These were: gluttony, fornication, avarice, anger, sadness, acedia, vainglory, and pride. See: C. C. H. Cook, 2011, *The Philokalia and the Inner Life: On Passions and Prayer*, Cambridge: James Clarke, pp. 23–30.

10 For examples of spiritual/religious contextualization and engagement, see K. Pargament, 2011, *Spiritually Integrated Psychotherapy*, New York: Guilford; H. G. Koenig, 2005, *Faith and Mental Health*, Philadelphia, PA: Templeton Foundation Press; R. F. Hurding, 1985, *Roots and Shoots: A Guide to Counselling and Psychotherapy*, London: Hodder & Stoughton.

11 J. P. Schwerkoske, P. Caplan, and D. M. Benford, 2012, 'Self-mutilation and Biblical Delusions: A Review', *Psychosomatics*, 53, pp. 327–33; H. L. Field and S. Waldfogel, 1995, 'Severe Ocular Self-injury', *General Hospital Psychiatry*, 17, pp. 224–7.

12 C. C. H. Cook, 2015, 'Religious Psychopathology: The Prevalence of Religious Content of Delusions and Hallucinations in Mental Disorder', *International Journal of Social Psychiatry*, 61(4), pp. 404–25.

13 I have explored these issues in greater depth elsewhere: C. C. H. Cook, 2021, 'Worry and Prayer: Some Reflections on the Psychology and Spirituality of Jesus's Teaching on Worry', in R. Re Manning (ed.), *Mutual Enrichment between Psychology and Theology*, London: Routledge.

14 See, for example, D. A. Hagner, 1993, *Matthew 1–13*, in B. M. Metzger and colleagues (eds), *Word Biblical Commentary*, Volume 33A, Dallas, TX: Word, pp. 167–70; H. D. Betz, 1995, *The Sermon on the Mount*, in A. Y. Collins (ed.), *Hermeneia – A Critical and Historical Commentary on the Bible*, Minneapolis, MN: Fortress Press, pp. 486–93; J. Nolland, 2005, *The Gospel of Matthew*, in I. H. Marshall and D. A. Hagner (eds), *The New International Greek Testament Commentary*, Bletchley: Paternoster; France, *The Gospel of Matthew*, pp. 273–6, Luz, *Matthew 1–7*, pp. 349–53.

15 Psychotherapists, in contrast, not uncommonly comment on this. See, for example, D. Brown and J. Pedder, 1980, *Introduction to Psychotherapy*, London: Tavistock, or the Wikipedia article on psychological projection: https://en.wikipedia.org/wiki/Psychological_projection (accessed 16.4.20).

16 See the helpful discussion by J. Sandler and M. Perlow, 1988, 'Internalization and Externalization', in J. Sandler (ed.), *Projection, Identification, Projective Identification*, London: Karnac, pp.1–11.

17 'Religiosity' is used here in a technical sense of meaning measurable levels of engagement in religious activities. For example, frequency of church attendance, bible reading, or prayer, might all constitute measures of religiosity in research.

18 G. W. Allport and J. M. Ross, 1967, 'Personal Religious Orientation and Prejudice', *Journal of Personality and Social Psychology*, 5(4), p. 434.

19 A shorter version is to be found in Luke's Gospel (11.2–4), in which there are only five petitions.

20 Luz, *Matthew 1–7*, p. 325.

21 Luz, *Matthew 1–7*, p. 326.

22 A. L. Ai and colleagues, 2010. 'Long-term Adjustment after Surviving Open Heart Surgery: The Effect of Using Prayer for Coping Replicated in a Prospective Design', *The Gerontologist*, 50(6), pp. 798–809; M. E. Johnson and colleagues, 2009, 'Centering Prayer for Women Receiving Chemotherapy for Recurrent Ovarian

Cancer: A Pilot Study', *Oncology Nursing Forum*, 36(4), pp. 421–8; P. S. Possel and colleagues, 2014, 'Do Trust-based Beliefs Mediate the Associations of Frequency of Private Prayer with Mental Health? A Cross-sectional Study', *Journal of Religion and Health*, 53(3), pp. 904–16.

23 P. A. Boelens and colleagues, 2009, 'A Randomized Trial of the Effect of Prayer on Depression and Anxiety', *International Journal of Psychiatry in Medicine*, 39(4), pp. 377–92; P. A. Boelens and colleagues, 2012, 'The Effect of Prayer on Depression and Anxiety: Maintenance of Positive Influence One Year after Prayer Intervention', *International Journal of Psychiatry in Medicine*, 43(1), pp. 85–98.

24 M. Galanter, and colleagues, 2017, 'An Initial fMRI Study on Neural Correlates of Prayer in Members of Alcoholics Anonymous', *The American Journal of Drug and Alcohol Abuse*, 43(1), pp. 44–54.

25 S. L. Vasiliauskas and M. R. McMinn, 2013, 'The Effects of a Prayer Intervention on the Process of Forgiveness', *Psychology of Religion and Spirituality*, 5(1), pp. 23–32.

26 N. Krause and R. D. Hayward, 2013, 'Prayer Beliefs and Change in Life Satisfaction over Time', *Journal of Religion and Health*, 52(2), pp. 674–94.

27 Allison, 2016, p. 119.

28 A. Rossiter and colleagues, 2015, 'Childhood Trauma Levels in Individuals Attending Adult Mental Health Services: An Evaluation of Clinical Records and Structured Measurement of Childhood Trauma', *Child Abuse and Neglect*, 44, pp. 36–45.

29 R. D. Enright and R. P. Fitzgibbons, 2015, *Forgiveness Therapy: An Empirical Guide for Resolving Anger and Restoring Hope*, Washington DC: American Psychological Association.

30 See, for example, C. C. H. Cook, and colleagues, 2011, 'Spirituality and Secularity: Professional Boundaries in Psychiatry', *Mental Health, Religion and Culture*, 14(1), pp. 35–42; R. Poole, C. C. H. Cook and R. Higgo, 2019, 'Psychiatrists, Spirituality and Religion', *British Journal of Psychiatry*, 214, pp. 181–2.

11

The Gerasene Demoniac

CHRISTOPHER C. H. COOK

The story of the Gerasene demoniac stands out as being the only detailed account in the canonical Gospels of Jesus' encounter with a person who may have been suffering from a major mental disorder. Despite this, commentators typically say little or nothing about the mental health issues that the story addresses.[1] The present chapter will seek to remedy this neglect by viewing the narrative specifically from a mental health perspective. In doing so I do not presume that mental health concerns are the only, or even the main, purpose of the story. The story demonstrates, first and foremost, Jesus' power over the forces of evil. Ironically, it is the demons within the narrative who recognize Jesus' true identity. The story shows Jesus engaged in mission among Gentiles and it ends with the man – a Gentile – telling others the good news of what Jesus has done for him. Anything that we may learn from the story about Jesus' healing someone with a mental illness must therefore be set firmly within this context. The healing of the Gerasene demoniac is a visible and tangible demonstration of the coming of the kingdom of God.

The story in outline

The story opens with Jesus crossing the Sea of Galilee together with his disciples.[2] As soon as he steps out of the boat he encounters a man from the country of the Gerasenes (or – in Matthew – two men, from the country of the Gadarenes). In Mark and in Luke we are given a relatively detailed description of this man's disturbed behaviour (albeit much less information than we might like from our mental health perspective). In all three Gospels, we are told from the outset that the man is in some way afflicted by a demon (or demons), or unclean spirit. Jesus' initial command to the demon to leave the man (omitted in Matthew) evokes a request by the demons that Jesus should not torment them. In this, the demons acknowledge Jesus' authority and name him as Son of God. Jesus asks the man his name (also omitted in Matthew), but we never really learn the man's name as it is the demons who respond. They are called 'Legion', for there are many of them. They ask to be sent into a nearby herd of pigs (numbered by Mark as being about 2,000). Jesus gives permission for this, and the pigs promptly run down a steep bank into the sea and are drowned. The swineherds run off to tell people what has happened and a large crowd gathers. When they see the demoniac 'clothed and in his right mind', they are afraid (although this detail is also omitted by Matthew) and they ask Jesus to leave. In Mark and in Luke the man begs to go with Jesus but is told to go and tell others what God has done for him, which he does. In Matthew, the story concludes with Jesus getting back into the boat. In Mark and Luke, the story concludes with the man's obedience to Jesus' command to proclaim what God has done for him. In all three Gospels we are left with a narrative within which Jesus has crossed the Sea of Galilee for the sole purpose of healing this man.

The critical context

The Markan version of the story is generally assumed to be the earliest of the three synoptic Gospel accounts, and almost certainly draws on an unknown pre-Markan source or sources. Luke and Matthew each make significant changes to the text that they received from Mark.[3] There is no evidence of additional sources that Luke or Matthew may have drawn upon other than that provided to them by Mark. The story of the Gerasene demoniac is not told by the fourth evangelist. We therefore really have only one account of the story – albeit retold in interesting ways by Matthew and Luke.

In all three synoptic Gospels Jesus crosses the Sea of Galilee by boat and immediately steps out into the country in which the story is set. Further affirmation of the proximity of the location to the sea is provided at the end of the story, when the demon-infested pigs rush down a steep bank into the sea. In Mark and Luke the country in question is said to be that of the Gerasenes, and in Matthew it is the country of the Gadarenes. However, Gerasa is 30 miles from the sea and Gadara is 5 miles away. Added to this, literary analysis suggests that there has been considerable pre-Markan elaboration of an original text, or texts.[4]

Biblical scholarship does not provide any conclusive reason why we may not understand the story as being based upon an historical incident in which Jesus encountered, and healed, a man with a major mental disorder. However, scholars dispute this. Stevan Davies, for example, asserts that 'It is an imaginative allegory, not a historical reminiscence.'[5]

Michael Willett Newheart (2004) suggests that the event, as narrated by Mark, 'probably did not happen'. None the less, he also concedes that Jesus clearly did encounter 'deeply disturbed people', some of whom were thought to have demons or unclean spirits, and that 'perhaps' some historical incident of this kind may have lain behind the story of the Gerasene man. The assumption here will be that there was such a historical event, and there is reasonable evidence to support this view.[6] Even if the historicity of the event were to be denied, the story still tells us some important things about the evangelists' understanding of Jesus' mission in relation to (what we would call) mental illness.

Mark's account of the story (5.1–20) immediately follows his account of the stilling of the storm on Galilee (4.35–41), and then is immediately followed by the raising of Jairus' daughter from the dead and the healing of a woman with a gynaecological condition (5.21–43). It is thus one of a series of examples of Jesus' command over the forces of death and disorder, be they natural or spiritual. Similarly, in Luke and in Matthew, the story is one event in a series of events that provide evidence of the power of Jesus' ministry.[7] Jesus heals those whom society holds in low esteem, an 'unclean' woman, and a man with an unclean demon, thereby showing his concern for those who are subject to stigma and social exclusion.

The demonology of the story is said by some to reflect popular superstitions of the time, and this raises interesting questions concerning the extent to which Jesus adopts or accepts culturally prevailing views on such things. It is therefore particularly important to consider the wider context of Jesus' ministry of healing and exorcism.

Healing and exorcism in the synoptic Gospels

None of the specific accounts of healing miracles in the synoptic Gospels clearly involve a mental disorder. Jesus heals two people with a fever (on separate occasions), eleven people with leprosy (one on one occasion and ten on another occasion), a paralysed man, four or five blind men (on three separate occasions), two men with different kinds of paralysis (on different occasions), a deaf mute man, a woman with a gynaecological problem, a man with oedema (probably due to heart disease), and a traumatic injury to the ear of the high priest's slave in Gethsemane. The widow of Nain's son and Jairus' daughter are raised from the dead. The woman with the 'spirit of weakness', whose story is found in Luke 13.10–16, clearly experienced psychological as well as physical distress, but the general consensus seems to be that she suffered from a primarily musculo-skeletal disorder, probably ankylosing spondylitis. Usually,

Jesus heals someone in response to a request to do so, or else asks their permission to heal them. The wide range of conditions and people that Jesus is said to have healed suggest he was open to healing any type of sickness, and any person wishing to be healed. We may, therefore, assume that this included people with mental illnesses, but we are given no detailed account of any healings of this kind.

The synoptic exorcism narratives include the exorcism of 'an unclean demon',[8] a boy with convulsions,[9] various cases of mutism and/or blindness,[10] and the daughter of the Syrophoenician woman (whose symptoms are unspecified).[11] Again, there are also various references to Jesus casting demons out of other people, about which we have no specific information. The only individual narrative that might reasonably be understood as involving someone whom a psychiatrist today might consider to have a mental disorder is that of the Gerasene demoniac. Despite this, there have long been controversies as to whether or not the Gospel accounts of demonic affliction might be considered to be analogous, or perhaps equivalent, to mental illness. These debates go back to at least the sixteenth century,[12] with a widespread assumption that in the Middle Ages psychiatric disorders were uncritically understood to be due to demon possession.[13]

Exorcism was a common, although probably not everyday, practice in Judaism at the time of Jesus.[14] Demons were understood as causing physical affliction, as well as behavioural disturbance, and were sometimes associated with particular sins. Demons were understood variously as destructive spirits, or else as disembodied souls and thus sometimes associated with burial places (as in the story of the Gerasene demoniac). Jesus' practice of exorcism is distinctive by virtue of the lack of reference to magical techniques, incantations, and other practices that characterized Jewish exorcisms of the time. The practice of exorcism overlaps with that of healing in the New Testament accounts so that, for example, Luke can refer to those who are afflicted by unclean spirits as being 'cured' by Jesus.[15]

In Mark's Gospel (chapter 3), Jesus is accused of being out of his mind or demon possessed and, like the Gerasene demoniac, is also thought to be in need of restraint. This suggests on the one hand that mental illness and demon possession were distinguished in New Testament times but also, on the other hand, that there might sometimes be scope for doubt about whether someone was suffering from one rather than the other. We should therefore be wary of accepting any simplistic assumptions that the Gospel writers did not critically distinguish between these conditions, but equally, when reading the text, we should be willing to suspend our modern assumptions as to the relationship between them.

Stuckenbruck has argued that three features of the Gospel exorcism narratives stand out.[16] First, they are understood as acts of divine power; they are demonstrations of God's dispossession of evil forces in the world. Second, there is a vocabulary of terms that is used more or less interchangeably by the evangelists, including that of demons and unclean or evil spirits. Third, demons were understood to have the capacity to enter – and leave – human bodies. While Stuckenbruck does not specifically explore this, we might say that the story of the Gerasene demoniac demonstrates that this entering of bodies may be understood (by us, as modern readers) to have an impact on both mind and brain. It might be easy to dismiss the language of demonology as premodern, metaphorical or mythical (and Stuckenbruck identifies a variety of ways in which such views are argued), but in fact there are important points of common ground. Stuckenbruck argues that Jesus' approach was realistic within his Jewish context. Evil cannot be removed, and should not be ignored; it can only be relocated, not destroyed, within our present world. The perspective of faith looks beyond this to God's ultimate victory over evil, but does not deny present realities within which recovery may be partial or faltering.

Taking a less nuanced approach than Stuckenbruck advocates, there have been attempts to argue that much of Jesus' ministry – both in healing and exorcism – was addressed to mental disorder, and that the cases of healing/exorcism of seemingly physical conditions actually addressed psychosomatic complaints, in response to which Jesus acted as an effective psychotherapist.[17] This seems an unlikely explanation on purely scientific grounds, and goes counter to what the Gospel texts clearly imply regarding the nature of the underlying conditions. However, it is true to say that Jesus is portrayed by the evangelists as addressing all aspects of the human condition, including physical illness, social exclusion and prejudice, and psychological distress, as well as spiritual need. The paralytic man in Capernaum,[18] for example, is forgiven as well as enabled to walk. The Gerasene demoniac was living among the tombs, excluded from human society. Similarly, those who suffered from leprosy lived on the margins of society (see Lev. 13.46; Num. 5.2–3). In the case of the Syrophoenician woman,[19] Jesus at first seems to collude with social prejudice, but the eventual outcome is that the woman is commended for her faith and her daughter is healed.

The plight of the Gerasene demoniac

We clearly need to be cautious in relying too much upon the text as providing anything that we might regard as a 'scientific' or medical account of the man's behaviour or mental state. On the other hand, it is reasonable to assume that the text does provide some information relevant to our understanding of his mental health.

Mark tells us that the man who, we may reasonably assume, was a Gentile has 'an unclean spirit' (v. 7, πνεύματι ἀκαθάρτῳ), later identified as many unclean spirits (plural). This accords both with his dwelling among the tombs at the outset of the story, and the eventual transfer of the spirits to the pigs, all of which would have been associated with uncleanness in Jewish thought. From a contemporary mental health perspective, the significant feature here is the stigma, marginalization and isolation of the man due to his condition. He was excluded from society, just as many people with mental health conditions today experience stigma and exclusion as a result of their illness.

Mark provides more detail about the man's condition than in some other comparable narratives (e.g. 1.21–28; 7.24–30), but frustratingly little information from the modern clinical perspective. We learn that there had been attempts to restrain the man, but that even shackles and chains had proved ineffective. The man was evidently strong, as 'no one had the strength to subdue him' and he had broken his physical restraints. We are told that he was howling loudly, and harming himself with stones. He was evidently sleeping little, or at least poorly, given that this behaviour continued through the night. When he greets Jesus, he is shouting loudly (v. 7). By implication, he was naked or scantily dressed.[20]

Usually, psychiatrists are very interested in what people say. Amongst other things, this provides information about self-perception, the content and form of thought, and the nature of beliefs. According to what the Gerasene man says in Mark's Gospel, his perception of his own identity is somewhat confounded with that of the spirits by whom he was said to be afflicted. Jesus commands the spirit to come out of him (v. 8) and the man responds in the first person singular (v. 7).[21] Jesus asks the man his name, and he replies (in the first person, plural) that his name is Legion 'for we are many' (v. 9). The voices of the spirit and of the man are not distinguished in the narrative. Jesus' command to the spirit is perceived by the man as tormenting. To the extent that Jesus' dialogue is with the spirit(s) rather than with the man, this passage (and its synoptic parallels) is unique. Nowhere else does Jesus engage in an extended dialogue with a spirit/demon in this way. However, there are similarities with the story of the exorcism of the man with an unclean spirit in Capernaum (Mark

1.21–28) who – also giving voice to the spirits within – similarly responds in the first person plural. The man in Capernaum and the Gerasene man both respond to Jesus with formulaic utterances which acknowledge Jesus' superiority and reveal knowledge of his identity.[22] Despite these similarities, there is no reason to identify the man in Capernaum as suffering from a mental illness. We should therefore be cautious about inferring too much about the Gerasene man's mental state on the basis of what he says to Jesus.

The information provided by Mark – particularly the disruption of sleep pattern, and disruptive behaviour – seems to indicate that the man was suffering from a mental disorder acccording to the understanding of his time.[23] This view is further reinforced once the man is delivered by Jesus, as he is then referred to as being 'in his right mind' (v. 15). Nowhere else in the Gospels do we have such a statement following a healing or exorcism. However, the man is also explicitly understood to be demon possessed, and so the two states were clearly not understood by Mark to be incompatible.

Luke's account (8.26–39) rearranges the material somewhat, employs slightly different vocabulary, and offers a shorter version of the man's condition, but comprises an essentially similar picture. From the outset, Luke refers to demons (δαιμόνια) in the plural (v. 27). Luke makes it explicit that the man had not worn clothes (v. 27) and that he did not live in a house, both of which are left implicit in Mark's account. Luke adds a reference to the long duration of the condition of the man (v. 27). In Luke's account it is possible to see evidence of an episodic course to the condition, although this is debatable.[24] Luke does not provide the 'night and day' reference that Mark provides, and so the disruption of sleep pattern is not evident. In Luke's account it is the demon who is said to drive the man into the wilderness (v. 29) and when the demons have been expelled he is eventually said to be healed, or saved (ἐσώθη). Healing, salvation and deliverance are all closely interrelated in Luke's thinking (both here and elsewhere).

Matthew's account (8.28–34) is considerably shorter than either Mark's or Luke's. Most notably, the single man referred to in Mark and Luke now appears as two demoniacs, who are said to come from the country of the Gadarenes rather than the Gerasenes.[25] Matthew omits almost all of the details of the men's condition, both before and after their deliverance, but does refer to them as 'fierce', or 'extremely violent',[26] so that 'no one could pass that way'. If we only had Matthew's account, it would not be at all obvious that these men might be suffering from a mental health problem. Matthew also omits most of the dialogue between the man/demons and Jesus.

There is much that we are not told about the Gerasene man, including most of the things that would be central to any assessment of mental state or differential diagnosis within modern clinical practice. There is no clear evidence from the Gospel narratives of thought disorder or hallucinations, very little information about mood or affect, and there are only minimal hints concerning the course and duration of the condition. However, we are left in no doubt as to the severity of his mental distress, and we are given a vivid picture of the impact of this upon the man and his community.

Diagnoses

It is hard to find any critical or detailed account of what the diagnosis of the Gerasene demoniac might have been, if indeed he had any psychiatric condition that might – at least in theory – have been diagnosable. Many commentators refer to the matter uncritically, or merely in passing. For example, Weatherhead, in a long but rather speculative account, suggests that the Gerasene demoniac was suffering from a psychosis induced by childhood trauma.[27] Pesch suggests that some will see here a case of 'manic-depressive insanity',[28] but gives no account of why this might be a plausible diagnosis. Mackrell refers to the 'Gadarene Maniac' without explanation or justification.[29] Guelich finds within the Lukan text four characteristics of insanity as understood in Judaism of the time, but does not offer any comment on what these might mean for diagnosis within modern taxonomies.[30] Edwards suggests that, 'The demoniac is not a split-personality but a multiple- or shattered personality'.[31] Commenting further in a footnote on the 'plethora of psychological interpretations', Edwards almost completely ignores any consideration of mental illness, but expresses concern that many such interpretations do not 'do justice to the text'. Does it do 'justice to the text', we might ask, to devote two long paragraphs to geographical questions concerning the location of Gerasa/Gadara, and only a short footnote to the human condition that Jesus addresses as a central concern of the narrative?

One of very few articles that gives anything like detailed attention to the question of diagnosis is that provided by the Reverend T. Hawthorn. Drawing only on quotations from Henderson and Gillespie's then influential *Textbook of Psychiatry*, he suggests that it is 'easy enough to find evidence for a diagnosis of mania'.[32] He goes on to suggest that in some features of the biblical account 'we may more easily recognize a schizophrenic'. While he notes that Henderson and Gillespie observe that the clinical presentations of these two conditions can be difficult to differentiate, Hawthorn seems to prefer the diagnosis of schizophrenia. Interesting though Hawthorn's analysis is, it now appears very dated and it shows a lack of medical understanding of diagnostic criteria even according to prevailing medical knowledge at the time.

Medical commentators typically, but not always, have more to say about the matter than biblical scholars. An early detailed account is provided by the medical missionary, later Professor of Divinity, William Menzies Alexander in his book *Demonic Possession in the New Testament*. Alexander was confident that the Gerasene demoniac suffered from acute mania, citing in support of this evidence from the Gospel accounts of his irritability, loss of self-control, 'ungovernable fury', and rapid changes of thought, affect and behaviour during the course of the encounter with Jesus. For Alexander, 'the conclusion is eminently beyond dispute. The whole of the symptoms point to acute mania of a formidable, but not of an exceptional, type'.[33]

S. Vernon McCasland, a professor of religion, included consideration of the diagnosis of the Gerasene demoniac within his monograph *By the Finger of God*. McCasland discussed his draft manuscript with two eminent psychiatrists of the time, one of whom, Professor Cole Wilson, wrote an introduction to McCasland's book. McCasland seems to have been in no doubt that the Gerasene demoniac was suffering from a manic episode in the context of a diagnosis of manic-depressive psychosis. Wilson, in the introduction, equivocates rather more, initially saying that 'one would hesitate to make a final diagnosis', but then goes on to agree with McCasland and to state that, 'It is quite safe to conclude that Christ cured a case of acute mania in this instance.'[34]

More recent medical writers have generally been more cautious. Sims, a professor of psychiatry, drawing on the story of the Gerasene demoniac only as a passing example in a longer article about demon possession, makes clear that we do not have enough information either to make or exclude particular diagnoses. He suggests that the biblical description is 'quite compatible with schizophrenia, but far from pathognomonic'.[35] Wilkinson, a physician who gives detailed accounts of possible differential diagnoses for most other Gospel narratives in his 'medical and theological commentary', alludes only briefly to the possibility that this man might have been suffering from mania in the context of a bipolar affective disorder.[36]

Overall, mania seems to have been the more popular diagnosis among medical and non-medical commentators. However, the evidence for this is tenuous. What we do have is evidence that the condition was severe and prolonged, and that it was associated with self-harm and social exclusion. The lack of evidence to support a particular diagnosis should not be allowed to obscure the evidence that suggests that this man was indeed suffering from a major mental disorder. The differential diagnosis includes principally bipolar disorder and schizophrenia. However, it might also be possible to see here evidence for dissociative identity disorder, and perhaps (more speculatively) the military connotations of 'legion' hint towards a history of post-traumatic stress disorder. More obviously, the man's condition might be understood as a culturally determined possession state, with or without any underlying psychiatric diagnosis.[37]

In fact, it is not necessary to 'diagnose' the Gerasene demoniac at all. Diagnostic criteria are contested, taxonomies are subject to constant revision and change, and the conferral of a diagnosis may be associated with stigma, prejudice and harm of various kinds. While the negative is not always stated or affirmed, it may well be that many commentators do not consider the Gerasene demoniac to be 'ill' in any medical sense, or else consider that a diagnosis is inappropriate. Girard provides a sophisticated (if speculative) analysis of the scapegoating of the Gerasene man, based on his theory of mimetic rivalry, within which the psychological dynamics may be accounted for without any psychiatric diagnosis.[38] Horsfield finds within the narrative both 'mythological and dynamic' parallels with contemporary experiences of women and children subject to sexual abuse.[39] Hughes discovers insights into the inner chaos of desires that are the human condition, assuming that we have the courage to engage in the necessary introspection to identify them.[40] Any, or all, of these might be valid accounts of the plight of the Gerasene demoniac.

In an interesting psychoanalytic interpretation of the narrative, Uleyn argues that the story touches upon our sense of the 'uncanny', as understood within the Freudian technical sense of that term.[41] Jesus' power over evil echoes with a repressed infantile sense of omnipotence; he does what we, as adults, cannot do. When the people of Gerasa send Jesus away, they give voice to their disenchantment, they reject Jesus, foreshadowing the climax of the Gospel when the vulnerability of Jesus is revealed in his passion. For Uleyn, the story is uncanny; it disturbs our sense of ourselves and reawakens our fears of our powerlessness over evil. In a similar way, but taking up a Jungian perspective, McGann argues that the demons of Gerasa represent the unacceptable 'shadow' of our unconscious self, which we disown and project on to others (represented in the narrative by the pigs).[42] Both Uleyn and McGann turn the focus away from diagnosis in the traditional medical sense; the Gerasene demoniac is no more or less mentally ill than any of us. Using the theoretical frameworks of the depth psychotherapies, they turn the spotlight upon the human condition. The Gerasene demoniac is every man, and every woman.[43]

Diagnoses are useful in medical practice because they provide guidance to correct treatment and likely prognosis. However, people are not defined by diagnoses; nor are they defined by their demons. In an age when treatments for major mental disorders were completely lacking, Jesus shows compassion to a tormented man excluded from his community. Whatever the diagnosis may have been, Jesus redefines the prognosis.

Healing and salvation

The Gerasene man is 'restored to his right mind', clothed, and able to return to his home. He is healed. As we might say, he is in recovery, although the Gospel texts imply a more permanent and complete restoration to well-being than may be experienced by many people with a major mental disorder today. When he is said to be 'sitting at the feet of Jesus', we see a man who has at last found mental peace, but we also might read here an inference of discipleship, of wanting to learn from the one who brought him healing. The man begs to go with Jesus but, instead, is sent to tell the good news to others. The transformation that he undergoes is not only one of mental healing; it is spiritual salvation and the finding of a new vocation in sharing the good news with others. The mental and the spiritual dimensions of well-being are interwoven here, both in sickness and in health, and the evangelists do not give us any cause to separate them out.

The move from the biblical text to the pastoral practice of churches today is not an easy one. Our society understands mental health differently from first-century Palestine and, notwithstanding the widespread belief in demon possession worldwide, the prevailing Western view is of a disenchanted world, within which demons are not usually evoked as causal agents. It is unhelpful (and potentially dangerous) to dismiss the insights of medicine and the social sciences, but it does not do justice to the spirituality of the human condition to reduce everything to a medical or psychological account. If contemporary pastoral or clinical practice is to have integrity, it needs to address the spiritual, psychological and physical unity of the human condition.

Demon possession, exorcism and mental health

The 'case study' in this chapter started with Scripture, and has sought to read the text (and commentaries on the text) from a mental health perspective. In doing so, it draws attention to some of the ways in which contemporary medical and social scientific understandings might throw light upon the human condition as it is portrayed within the text. It is recognized that this kind of reading of the text may run the risk of anachronism, and that the evangelists were not writing from this perspective. However, it may also be argued that the human condition has not changed greatly over the last two millennia, and that we have every reason to expect that Jesus would have encountered people who suffer from conditions that we would recognize today as mental disorders. The Gerasene demoniac may well have been one of them.

We might have started a similar case study from the perspective of contemporary experience. Exorcism and deliverance ministry have been practised widely within Western Christian churches in the twentieth century and remain popular in many churches.[44] Christian opinions on how demon possession should be understood in relation to mental health today range from the extreme of completely rejecting any demonic reality on the one hand, to complete rejection of the insights of the medical and social sciences on the other. Some would argue that mental health problems need to be distinguished from demon possession, whilst others argue that they can co-exist. Across this spectrum of opinion, opposing interpretations of the New Testament exorcism narratives are cited as authority for opposing views. This hermeneutical evidence is often prioritized over empirical scientific research.[45] The story of the Gerasene demoniac is not merely of academic interest, it also impacts upon contemporary clinical and pastoral practice.

Among the implications of this story for clinical practice must be the importance of affirming the spiritual worldview of patients and recognizing the need to work with this. This has received increasing attention in recent years from mental health professionals, many of whom are only too willing to discuss the ways in which spiritual and religious concerns arise for their patients during treatment.[46] Conversely, the need for priests, chaplains and pastors to work with mental health professionals should be reaffirmed. Neglect of, or antagonism towards, medical and psychological care does not do justice to the way in which spiritual needs are entangled with the well-being of both mind and brain. The story of the Gerasene demoniac is set within a context of religious pluralism (Jewish, Gentile and Roman) not unlike ours, and Jesus shows willingness to accept and adapt to this in his response to the human need with which he is confronted. Jesus does not impose a theological understanding of demon possession; he responds effectively, and with compassion, to the request of a man who believes himself to be possessed.

This story, as a part of a recurring theme within the Gospels, understands the Gerasene man within the context of his community. The healing and salvation that he finds brings reintegration into that community, just as it brings reintegration of mind and spirit. He is not healed only to go back to life as usual. He finds a new vocation and purpose which transforms his life within the community to which he now more fully belongs than ever before. Even though Jesus does not allow the man to go with him, the man becomes a follower of Jesus – a disciple – in the truest sense. Both clinical and pastoral care need to give much more attention to the reintegrative and vocational aspects of recovery from major mental disorder than they currently do. Christian churches are in a unique position to facilitate this.

Conclusion

The story of the Gerasene demoniac provides tangible evidence within the Gospel texts of the power of Jesus to restore the human mind and soul. Within our culture, this story of healing and new life most directly speaks to the conditions that we know as bipolar affective disorder and schizophrenia, but its relevance is wider than that. We should not imagine that it is only a story of restoration of mind. Nor is it only a story about 'deliverance ministry'. It is a story about finding new life through the power of Jesus to set people free from spiritual, mental and social forces that enslave, exclude and condemn.

Notes

1 See, for example, R. Pesch, 1971, 'The Markan Version of the Healing of the Gerasene Demoniac', *The Ecumenical Review*, 23, pp. 349–76; W. L. Lane, 1974, *The Gospel of Mark*, Grand Rapids, MI: Eerdmans; J. Nolland, 1989, *Luke 1–9:20*, Nashville, TN: Thomas Nelson; C. F. Evans, 1990, *Saint Luke*, London, SCM Press; J. B. Green, 1997, *The Gospel of Luke*, Grand Rapids, MI: Eerdmans; I. H. Marshall, 1998, *The Gospel of Luke*, Grand Rapids, MI: Eerdmans; R. T. France, 2002, *The Gospel of Mark*, Grand Rapids, MI: Eerdmans.

2 Mark 5.1–20; Luke 8.26–39; Matt. 8.28–34.

3 See, for example, summaries of the debate by R. T. France, 1989, *Matthew – Evangelist and Teacher*, Exeter: Paternoster Press; J. D. G. Dunn, 2003, *Christianity in the Making*, Grand Rapids, MI: Eerdmans.

4 For helpful analyses of these issues, see Pesch, 'The Markan Version of the Healing of the Gerasene Demoniac'; R. A. Guelich, 1989, *Mark 1–8:26*, Dallas, TX: Word; Nolland, *Luke 1–9:20*; Marshall, *The Gospel of Luke*.

5 S. L. Davies, 1995, *Jesus the Healer: Possession, Trance, and the Origins of Christianity*, New York: Continuum, p. 79.

6 For further discussion, see Pesch, 'The Markan Version of the Healing of the Gerasene Demoniac'; Nolland, *Luke 1–9:20*.

7 Thus Marshall, in *The Gospel of Luke*, suggests that this is the second of a consecutive series of three 'mighty works' in Luke's Gospel. For Nolland, in *Luke 1–9:20*, it is the second in a series of four mighty works in Luke's Gospel, culminating in Peter's confession of Jesus as Messiah. For France (R. T. France, 2007, *The Gospel of Matthew*, Grand Rapids, MI: Eerdmans), commentating on Matthew's Gospel, it is the second of a series of three 'demonstrations of authority'. And for Hagner (D. A. Hagner, 1993, *Matthew 1–13*, Dallas, TX: Word), also commentating on Matthew, it is the second of a group of three miracle narratives.

8 Mark 1.21–28; Luke 4.33–36.

9 Matt. 17.14–21; Mark 9.14–29; Luke 9.37–43.

10 Matt. 9.32–34; 12.22–24; Luke 11.14–26.

11 Mark 7.24–30.

12 H. C. E. Midelfort, 2012, 'The Gadarene Demoniac in the English Enlightenment', in *A Linking of Heaven and Earth: Studies in Religious and Cultural History in Honor of Carlos M. N. Eire*, E. Michelson, S. K. Taylor and M. K. Venables (eds), Farnham: Ashgate, pp. 49–66; A. Ossa-Richardson, 2013, 'Possession or Insanity? Two Views from the Victorian Lunatic Asylum', *Journal of the History of Ideas*, 74, pp. 553–75. See also W. M. Alexander, 1902, *Demonic Possession in the New Testament: Its Relations Historical, Medical, and Theological*, Edinburgh: T&T Clark; S. V. McCasland, 1951, *By the Finger of God; Demon Possession and Exorcism in Early Christianity in the Light of Modern Views of Mental Illness*, New York: Macmillan, for examples of such arguments from the twentieth century.

13 C. E. Forcén and F. E. Forcén, 2014, 'Demonic Possessions and Mental Illness: Discussion of Selected Cases in Late Medieval Hagiographical Literature', *Early Science and Medicine* 19(3), pp. 258–79.

14 See M. J. Borg, 1987, *Jesus: A New Vision. Spirit, Culture, and the Life of Discipleship*, San Francisco, CA: Harper & Row; Davies, *Jesus the Healer*; C. S. Keener, 1999, *A Commentary on the Gospel of Matthew*, Grand Rapids, MI: Eerdmans; E. Sorensen, 2002, *Possession and Exorcism in the New Testament and Early Christianity*, Heidelberg: Mohr Siebeck.

15 Luke 6.18. See discussion by Sorensen, *Possession and Exorcism*.

16 L. T. Stuckenbruck, 2013, 'The Human Being and Demonic Invasion: Therapeutic Models in Ancient Jewish and Christian Texts', in C. C. H. Cook (ed.), *Spirituality, Theology & Mental Health*, London: SCM Press, pp. 94–123.

17 D. Capps, 2008, *Jesus the Village Psychiatrist*, Louisville, KY: Westminster John Knox; cf. Davies, *Jesus the Healer*.

18 Matt. 9.1–8; Mark 2.1–12; Luke 5.17–26.

19 Matt. 15.21–28; Mark 7.24–30.

20 In verse 15, one of the signs of his recovery is that he is clothed.

21 There is a kind of 'flashback' within the narrative, so that Jesus' command is reported only after the account of the man's response.

22 Guelich, *Mark 1–8:26*.

23 See, for example, Guelich, *Mark 1–8:26*.

24 Verse 29 – see Nolland, *Luke 1–9:20*, and Marshall, *The Gospel of Luke*.

25 Matthew seems to 'double up' in a number of his accounts, and there are various theories as to why this may be. For a helpful discussion of this in relation to the present narrative, see Hagner, *Matthew 1–13*; France, *The Gospel of Matthew*.

26 Hagner, *Matthew 1–13*.

27 L. D. Weatherhead, 1955, *Psychology, Religion and Healing*, 2nd edn, London: Hodder & Stoughton.

28 Pesch, 'The Markan Version of the Healing of the Gerasene Demoniac'.

29 G. F. Mackrell, 1975, 'The Gadarene Maniac', *New Blackfriars*, 56(656), pp. 32–5.

30 Guelich, *Mark 1–8:26*; cf. Lane, *The Gospel of Mark*.

31 J. R. Edwards, 2002. *The Gospel according to Mark*, Leicester: Apollos.

32 T. Hawthorn, 1954, 'The Gerasene Demoniac: A Diagnosis', *Expository Times*, 66, pp. 79–80.

33 W. M. Alexander, 1902, *Demonic Possession in the New Testament*, p. 80.

34 McCasland, *By the Finger of God*, p. x.

35 A. Sims, 1986, 'Demon Possession: Medical Perspective in a Western Culture', in B. Palmer (ed.), *Medicine and the Bible*, Carlisle: Paternoster, pp. 165–89.

36 J. Wilkinson, 1988, *The Bible and Healing: A Medical and Theological Commentary*, Grand Rapids, MI: Eerdmans. Bipolar affective disorder is the current preferred terminology for the condition previously known as manic-depressive psychosis.

37 For a helpful psychiatric account of possession states as culture-bound psychiatric syndromes, see R. Littlewood, 2004, 'Possession States', *Psychiatry*, 3(8), pp. 8–10. Davies, in *Jesus the Healer*, argues that demon possession in the New Testament context was of two sorts. More commonly, it might occur as a culturally affirmed coping mechanism for dealing with family conflict. In other cases, it might have been a dissociative state – which we would diagnose as dissociative identity disorder – arising as a result of childhood abuse.

38 R. Girard, 1986, *The Scapegoat*, Baltimore: Johns Hopkins University Press; R. Girard, 1990, 'The Demons of Gerasa', in R. Detweiler and W. G. Doty (eds), *The Daemonic Imagination: Biblical Text and Secular Story*, Atlanta: Scholars Press, pp. 77–98.

39 P. Horsfield, 1993, 'The Gerasene Demoniac and the Sexually Violated', *St Mark's Review*, 152, pp. 2–7.

40 G. W. Hughes, 1996, *God of Surprises*, 2nd edn, London: Darton, Longman and Todd.

41 A. J. R. Uleyn, 1986, 'The Possessed Man of Gerasa (Marc 5, 1–20)', in A. van Belzen and J. M. van der Lans (eds), *Current Issues in the Psychology of Religion: Proceedings of the Third Symposium on the Psychology of Religion in Europe*, Amsterdam: Rodopi, pp. 90–6.

42 D. McGann, 1985, *The Journeying Self: The Gospel of Mark through a Jungian Perspective*, New York: Paulist Press.

43 For further narrative and psychological analysis of the story, see also M. W. Newheart, 2004, *'My Name is Legion': The Story and Soul of the Gerasene Demoniac*, Collegeville, MN: Liturgical Press.

44 M. W. Cuneo, 2001, *American Exorcism: Expelling Demons in the Land of Plenty*, New York: Broadway; J. M. Collins, 2009, *Exorcism and Deliverance Ministry in the Twentieth Century: An Analysis of the Practice and Theology of Exorcism in Modern Western Christianity*, Eugene, OR: Wipf & Stock. There is also an extensive anthropological literature on possession as a global phenomenon. See, for example, E. Bourguignon, 1968, 'World Distribution and Patterns of Possession States', in R. Prince, *Trance and Possession States*, Montreal: R. M. Bucke Memorial Society, pp. 3–34; F. D. Goodman, 1988, *How about Demons? Pos-*

session and Exorcism in the Modern World, Bloomington, IN: Indiana University Press.

45 There has, in fact, been a surprising paucity of such research. See C. C. H. Cook, 2020, *Christians Hearing Voices*, London: Jessica Kingsley, for a review in relation to the specific issue of research on people who hear demonic voices. Anecdotal evidence would suggest that the harms to mental health caused by ill-judged exorcism and deliverance ministry heavily outweigh any benefits. Within the Church of England deliverance ministry is only permitted when undertaken by a person authorized by their bishop, and then only in collaboration with medical professionals.

46 See, for example, C. C. H. Cook, 2013, *Recommendations for Psychiatrists on Spirituality and Religion*, London: Royal College of Psychiatrists, p. 12; C. C. H. Cook, 2016, 'Narrative in Psychiatry, Theology and Spirituality', in *Spirituality and Narrative in Psychiatric Practice: Stories of Mind and Soul*, C. C. H. Cook, A. Powell and A. Sims (eds), London: Royal College of Psychiatrists, pp. 1–13; A. A. Moreira-Almeida and colleagues, 2016, 'WPA Position Statement on Spirituality and Religion in Psychiatry', *World Psychiatry*, 15(1), pp. 87–8.

PART 3

Practical Focus

12

The Bible in Pastoral Care of Christians Living with Mental Health Challenges

JOHN SWINTON

In his essay 'The Strange New World within the Bible', Karl Barth provides us with a fascinating perspective on the imaginative function of Scripture.[1] He argues that the Bible is not simply a place that we go in order to find moral frameworks, rules and ways of conforming to God's will. It may be that, but it is much more. The Bible is the point of revelation that introduces us to a strange new world. When we enter into this strange new world, we begin to see the world that we used to know quite differently. As we read the stories of Abraham, Moses, Paul and Jesus, we come to realize that their stories are our stories; they are a part of our Christian inheritance. As we use the strangeness of the Bible to illuminate the experience of living within God's creation, so we are enabled to see and imagine things in ways that were simply unavailable to our previous modes of seeing and imagining. Scripture profoundly changes the way in which we encounter the world.

The context of reading Scripture

There is a great beauty and liberation in looking at Scripture in this way. To have our minds transformed and our imagination renewed in ways that shift us away from the pattern of this world, and allow us to test and approve God's pleasing and perfect will (Rom. 12.2), is potentially a wonderful thing. However, while it is true that Scripture may open a new world, coming to understand, interpret and live faithfully within that new world remains a complex hermeneutical enterprise. Scripture does not reveal its pearls of wisdom in a straightforward manner. Barth, like many modern theologians, had a limited audience in mind when he was reflecting on the hermeneutical wonder of the Bible. The constitution of the 'we' whom Barth assumes will interpret Scripture and help to reconstruct our understanding and imagination of that strange new world is inevitably limited. The breadth of our understanding of Scripture is to a greater or lesser extent determined by who is doing the interpreting. One of the lessons we have learned from those who work with a dynamic influenced by some mode of liberation theology is that all knowledge, including theological and biblical knowledge, is value laden and con-textual. The context from which we read Scripture is highly influential in relation to the ways in which we interpret texts and the interpretative conclusions – theological and practical – that we come to.

A *disability hermeneutic*

Within the field of disability theology writers focusing on disability have argued that in order for the text to be authentically interpreted, the experi-ences of people living with disabilities need to be taken into consideration as a hermeneutical key.[2] For example, the practical theologian John Hull, who went blind in his early fifties, argues that we need to be more critical of the use of visual metaphors in the Bible. When blindness is repeatedly associated with darkness and a lack of knowing, it doesn't take much for that understanding to be extended to interpret the lives of those who are blind.[3] Similarly, assuming that the healing ministry of Jesus provides a template for the Church's response to people living with disabilities often serves to exclude those who don't receive healing. Insisting on healing as spiritual normalization and proof of faithfulness is deeply oppressive for those who desire to live well *with* their disabilities.[4] There are other ways in which we can think about healing that remain true to the text, but do not exclude the human experience of disability.[5]

In response to potentially destructive interpretative practices, some dis-ability theologians have developed a *disability hermeneutic*.[6] A disability hermeneutic insists that it is the responsibility of the exegete to take into consideration the human experience of disability as a significant dynamic for interpreting Scripture. These scholars argue that assumptions about the primacy of ablebodiedness have historically provided the often hidden hermeneutic that lies behind, and within, many interpretations of Scripture in relation to issues of disability. Shifting the focus towards the interpretive significance of disability helps to reveal and transform this bias in order that the full range of human experience is represented in the process of biblical interpretation. By addressing this implicit bias, we should end up with a more accurate, inclusive and arguably more faithful interpretation.

A mental health hermeneutic

What is true for people with disabilities is also true for people living with mental health challenges. Certain interpretations of Scripture can be deeply damaging for people with mental health challenges.[7] There is a need for a mental health hermeneutic that takes into consideration the life experiences of those living with mental health challenges. Such a hermeneutic strives to bring the experience of people living with mental health challenges into critical conversation with the interpretation and usage of Scripture, with a view to more accurately understanding the meaning and the scope of the text and enabling the recipients of our interpretations to live well even in the midst of difficult experiences. Such a hermeneutic strives to take seriously Barth's suggestion that the Bible opens up a strange new world, but allows the experience of people with mental health challenges to participate in its construction. Such a hermeneutic is *contextual, critical, prophetic* and *faithful*. It is *contextual* in that it takes the experience of mental health challenges seriously as a location for understanding the function of the Bible and the nature and practical power of the revelation that it offers. It is *critical* in so far as it seeks to challenge modes of interpretation that implicitly or explicitly misrepresent mental health issues. A mental health hermeneutic is *prophetic* in the sense that it disturbs the complacency of generalized assumptions about mental health and seeks to overcome cultural distortions by measuring interpretations against the vision of the gospel. Prophets remain close to people, particularly those who are oppressed and downtrodden – the victims of systems and ways of seeing that are damaging. Such a hermeneutic is *faithful* in that it strives to bring clarity to the revelation that comes through Scripture and to provide fresh understanding and new ways of being in the world that reflect this emerging reality.

In what follows I will sketch out some aspects of what I will describe as a *pastoral mental health hermeneutic*. The focus here will be on the ways in which understandings of Scripture impact upon people with mental health challenges both positively and negatively. It is pastoral in the sense that it focuses both on what Scripture *does*, what it *means*, and what it *can come to mean* within a pastoral context. The key question will be: how does Scripture inform the ways that we listen, hear and respond to the experiences of mental health challenges within a pastoral context? As will become clear, the 'we' here is inclusive of all people and not confined to those who do not live with mental health challenges. What follows emerges from a wider project on theology and mental health challenges that has been carried out by the author over the past three years; it has focused on trying to understand the spiritual experiences of Christians living with depression, bipolar disorder and schizophrenia. The quotations from research interviews are presented with permission from the participants.[8]

Mental health as shalom

A useful place to begin developing our pastoral hermeneutic is with the question of precisely what mental health is. It is interesting to note that the Bible has no word for 'health' in the sense that some of us have come to use the term within biomedicine – that is, as the absence of disease, suffering or distress. The closest term is the Hebrew word *shalom* which occurs 250 times in the Hebrew Bible. The basic meaning of the word *shalom* is peace. This peace involves physical and psychological well-being. It is not, however, defined by such goals. The root meaning of the word *shalom* is wholeness, completeness and well-being. *Shalom* is primarily a relational term that has to do with a restoration of relationships. More specifically, it relates to the restoration of human relationships with God. To be at peace – to be healthy – is to be in right relationship with God. Such relationship is not determined by particular states of physical or psychological well-being, desirable as such experiences may be. *Shalom* is determined by our relationships with God.[9] *Shalom* has several subsidiary meanings that emerge from this primary relational intention:

• Security
• Friendship
• Prosperity
• Justice
• Righteousness
• Salvation

These secondary meanings should be understood theologically as flowing from the primary relationship that God has with human beings.

Shalom *is a person*

Theologically, then, health in general and mental health in particular is not best conceived as a biomedical category. It is rather a theological statement. Mental health in particular is not something that a person develops in their own strength or according to personal desires. Health (*shalom*) is a gift of God's self to human beings. *Shalom is thus seen to be a person.* Health is not a state of mental, emotional or physical well-being (although it may include these things). Rather, health understood as *shalom* is a gift that God gives to his creation: a gift of God's self. Within this frame, mental health is a *theological* concept. Mental health is not an ideal, a concept or a goal, it is a *relationship*; it is not the *absence* of anything – it is the *presence* of Jesus.

The dangers of shalom?

It could of course be argued that such a reinterpretation of mental health could have potentially dangerous pastoral connotations in so far as it might be used to reinforce spiritually prescriptive antidotes to people's mental health struggles. For example, if we define mental health as 'right relationship with God', people who are struggling with mental health might be viewed by some as 'not being in right relationship with God'. The solution to their problems then becomes a spiritual one. 'If you are experiencing depression or anxiety, you are doing something wrong in your relationship with God.'

Such a concern is valid. However, it is important to note that *shalom-as-mental-health* is not intended to be an *explanatory* framework for the causes of mental health challenges. Such challenges have multiple causes and require a broad range of understanding and forms of intervention. This way of thinking does not insinuate that a person's mental health experiences are caused by a flaw in their relationship with God. The idea of mental health as *shalom* points us towards the *goal* of mental health care for Christians (and it should be noted that this chapter is specifically focused on Christians). Shalomic mental health care[10] has to do with helping people to hold on to God's presence at all times, even in the midst of symptoms and difficult experiences that may be interminable. The ultimate goal of mental health care is not simply the eradication of symptoms, but the facilitation of God's presence.

I remember talking at a mental health conference in Edinburgh a few years ago on the topic of *shalom* as mental health. After the talk a man came up to me and said, 'I have lived with schizophrenia all of my life. I always thought it was because I was a bad Christian, but now I see things differently.' When one allows one's mind to be transformed by the strange new world within the Bible, some apparently 'obvious' things begin to look different.

With this basic understanding of mental health in mind we will now turn to the ways in which the Bible works itself out within the lives of people living with mental health challenges. Rather than focusing on these challenges in general terms, it will be helpful to focus on the experience of depression as a particularly fruitful context for the development of a pastoral mental health hermeneutic.

When reading the Bible can be helpful: a positive mental health hermeneutic

Jane is 32 years old, and a mother of two young children. She is a social worker, but has taken a career break in order to be with her children. She is a devout Christian and has been since she was a child. Jane has lived with major depression for over ten years, and her journey into depression has profoundly impacted the way she understands her faith and how she approaches the Bible. As a charismatic evangelical Christian, she was always encouraged to pray and read the Bible in order that God would heal her of her depression. This was painful advice, as God never did. She had to think again:

> I think sometimes I've wanted God to intervene in a big, loud, miraculous way, and in healing: I just wanted to wake up one morning and not feel depressed any more. But I now know that isn't going to happen any time soon. Does that mean God has abandoned me? No. I think God has very much been there in my friends who have been really supportive, and in the psychotherapist I see who's a Christian, and who has just been so helpful, especially over the last three years which have been particularly difficult ... I also have a really good psychiatrist and I eventually got on to a drug that really worked for me. I think God has been there in the everyday – sort of not big, supernatural things but just in the everyday-ness, he's been there.

It was within this complex combination of Christian friends, therapists and psychiatrists that Jane found healing, not in the sense that she was cured of her depression. Rather, hers was an interdisciplinary mode of healing that meant that, at the very least, she had learned what it might mean to live well with her depression. The idea of living well and living faithfully with mental health challenges is important.

In John 10.10 Jesus says: 'I have come that they may have life, and have it to the full.' But what does that mean when you are depressed? Jane continued:

> I guess in some ways it [depression] has made me wonder how to understand this whole abundant life thing. I just struggle with, 'You're a

Christian, you're meant to delight in the Lord, rejoice in the Lord, just have this vibrancy in life that attracts other people to actually want to come and experience this abundant life and everything is fine.' I guess I've struggled a lot with thinking how actually do you experience that, how do you embody that while being depressed? My experiences kind of struggle against each other; they are kind of the opposite of each other. But I guess I've sort of learnt to maybe be a little bit more compassionate with myself, even when I'm not out telling everyone about how amazing Jesus is and how wonderful it is to be his child, but sometimes actually just the simple act of getting up in the morning or keep doing life that day is abundant enough.

Jane's perspective on abundant life is, or rather has become, not that she has to be freed from depression in order to be with God. Instead, she recognizes that she has to learn to see God differently in order to understand what it might mean to live faithfully with depression. She finds abundance not in ridding herself of her depression, but in her friends, her relationships, the small things in life. Such everyday abundance is inspired by a particular way of reading the Bible:

I've kind of discovered God in the small things in life. I think also I've really started to resonate much more with parts of the Bible that I probably would have avoided beforehand. Like Lamentations and the lament psalms and the bits of the Bible that kind of felt a bit uncomfortable before; you're kind of like 'ooh, there's a lot of pain in that psalm! I don't really want to read that!' Actually, I now find myself very much drawn to the lament psalms. It was because I felt like oh, you get it. Like David, I understand what you're saying. It is like the psalmist, he's giving voice to what I'm feeling.

The psalms of lament provided Jane with a kind of spiritual identification and solidarity with the characters within the Bible, wherein her deep pain was recognized, and her lostness before God was at least shared by others. This shared darkness was not something that had been a part of her spiritual formation as a Christian. It was something she came to know through her experience of depression:

I have had the same experience with the book of Lamentations, although it's a very different situation, they were in exile, but I felt like I could really relate with that sense of desolation that they were having. It almost felt a bit like, well, my experience of evangelical churches. My dad was a pastor, so I've been in church since I was a baby pretty much, and I became a Christian when I was four, so I've been in church all my life. But I found that my experience of church never really looked at what the Bible says about hurting or suffering. It was kind of the difficult parts of the Bible that people never spoke about. When we looked at suffering, it sort of was talking about how God comforts those who suffer. But when I got depressed, I found paradoxes in the Bible, like where Israel doesn't understand why they're in exile and they're mourning, and their prayers aren't being answered. I hadn't noticed that before. Strangely, I found that sense of not knowing and not understanding that now seemed obvious in the Bible something I could relate to a lot more. I've been able to kind of ... I feel like I'm not shying away as much from the difficult questions that the Bible throws up. I guess it's because I have to actually live with them now.

With the coming of her depression those parts of the Bible that previously seemed strange and paradoxical emerge as points of resonance. Before, there was the fear of uncertainty; now uncertainty was central to her life experiences, something that is reflected in her spiritual experiences:

There's people in the Bible who shouted and screamed at God. But actually, they kept bringing it all to God – just keep bringing your anger to him and don't shut yourself off from God. I guess the psalms and Lamentations allowed me to bring my feelings to God. Some people might say, 'Oh! That's awful that you feel that way about God!' But actually, for me, bringing those feelings to God is exactly what got rid of them. Kind of like with Job: he's sort of crying out to God and in the end God doesn't give him any answers. He just gives him an encounter with himself, and actually that's what he needed was an encounter with God, not any answers from God. I think it's the same with me.

The pastoral hermeneutic here is quite clear. The experience of depression opens up aspects of Scripture that are closed when we assume everything is all right and presume that abundant life matches cultural expectations of happiness and freedom from pain. However, Jane's mental health hermeneutic opens up different ways of framing abundant life:

Like whenever you read a passage like a lament psalm, you think, 'my goodness, why did God allow that to happen to the psalmist?' Actually, now I'm not so kind of scared of those questions any more whereas beforehand I had to have a nice answer for everything. I am a counsellor and I think in counselling there are so many times when there are no answers. You sit with people who have had horrendous lives, and you sit in the not knowing and confusion. What can you do? So, there has been a shift in my faith. I see God differently and I think I've found as well that I've become more compassionate towards other people than I would have been before. I know what it is like to be lost and confused, and so does God.

Depression can bring out aspects of Scripture that are lost when we allow our interpretations to be guided purely by a theology of glory. If we listen differently, we can hear Scripture differently. For Jane, her encounters with Scripture within her depression journey helped her to understand her experiences differently, and even opened up a space for compassion that was not there previously. Jane discovered a positive hermeneutic in the midst of her depression. But not all ways of interpreting the Bible in the context of depression are positive.

When reading the Bible might not be wise: a suicide hermeneutic and a pain-filled reading of Mark 8.34–37

Theologian Peter Herman has lived with major depression for 25 years. His depression is deep and at times quite overwhelming. It strips the meaning out of his life and there are times when he simply sees no point in living. In his article 'Jesus Doesn't Want Me for a Sunbeam: Thoughts on Depression, Race and Theology',[11] Herman lays out his experience of depression and wrestles with the complex hermeneutical dynamics of interpreting Scripture when depressed. He notes that the gospel pushes us to think differently about power and to recognize that the strength of God is discovered in the weak and the needy – a radically different mode of power from the brute powers that drive the world. This understanding should communicate compassion and peace. However, for Peter, that is not always the case. God has a preference for the poor and the down-trodden. As a person groaning under the yoke of depression, Herman should feel comforted. But he does not. How can he find comfort in such knowledge when he is totally unable 'to feel the warmth of God's pref-erential choices':

> When I feel that my own brain is trying to kill me, that my wife cannot possibly love me, or that my son will reject me when he is old enough to realize what a nonperson I truly am, there is little comfort in … words about God's love for the lowly.[12]

The message of liberation for the poor is thus somewhat paradoxical and ambiguous in Herman's experience. This feeds back into the ways in which he interprets Scripture. He gives the example of Mark 8.34–37:

> He called the crowd with his disciples, and said to them, 'If any want to become my followers, let them deny themselves and take up their cross and follow me. For those who want to save their life will lose it, and those who lose their life for my sake, and for the sake of the gospel, will save it. For what will it profit them to gain the whole world and forfeit their life?'[13]

According to a standard hermeneutic we might interpret this passage as a call to forgo the riches of this world and follow Jesus. But when he is depressed, Herman reads this passage in quite a different way:

> The cross isn't something to be borne during my life – life is the cross. The act of being alive – breathing, eating, speaking with others – is a burden. I don't want to save my life; my life is my cross. Even though I know that there is a world of difference between martyrdom and suicide, I find myself wondering whether Mark's Jesus is letting me know that it might be OK to let go of that cross. After all, I suffer by living, and Jesus promises to end suffering, doesn't he? This question suggests a some-what unorthodox reading of these texts – a hermeneutics of suicide is not listed in theology textbooks or preached from the Sunday pulpit.[14]

The context out of which Herman interprets the text guides him towards a radical new understanding. Faithfulness to the words of Jesus leads towards a 'suicide hermeneutic':

> In the quiet hours of the day, there is an inaudible yet persistent voice that answers Jesus' suggestion that I must hate life itself with 'Yes, I do hate life. I hate it so much. Life itself is my cross. Let me lay it down, Lord. Please, let me lay it down.' I argue back against this urge. I resist. I rationalize. I take the pills. I go to the sessions. And then that internal monologue is quieter, but it's still there. I doubt it will ever be silent. When my depression is heightened and my internal struggle especially fraught, my hermeneutic of suicide dominates my encounters with Scripture.[15]

For Jane, the Bible was a source of hope; something she turned to when trying to deal with her depression. For Peter, the strange new world within the Bible brought out a strange new hermeneutic that threatened his life. In Peter's situation the advice of the seventeenth-century theologian Richard Baxter may be pertinent. In talking about how people who are melancholic can find dangers in reading the Bible, Baxter suggests that to put the Bible to one side when going through depression

> is simply to refrain from what you cannot presently do, so that by doing other things that you can, you may later do what you cannot do now. It is merely to postpone attempting what (at present) will only make you less able to do all your other duties. At present, you are able to conduct the affairs of your soul by sanctified reasoning. I am not dissuading you from repenting or believing, but rather from fixed, long, and deep meditations that will only hurt you.[16]

The Bible remains important, but there may be times and situations where it may be wise to lay it down for a season.

When reading the Bible may not be possible: hermeneutical silence

There are times when it becomes just impossible to read the Bible no matter how much one might desire to. The complexities, the symbolism, the language of the strange new world can become so dissonant that one simply can't find the energy to enter into it. For David, the Bible is important, but more retrospectively than within that moment of deep distress:

> When I get depressed, I stop engaging with the more regular routine stuff of Bible reading and things. I don't lose my faith, but I don't have the capacity to deal with the more complicated parts of the Bible. Strangely, I still pray, but I can't read. I have no concentration and no desire. It's like you are stripped away to absolutely nothing; all the onion layers have been peeled off and when you get down to it, it is just you and God. It's kind of ... [sighs] ... it's kind of like 'Ok, I can't read the Bible just now, but I don't forget what I have learned before ...'

The issue here seems to be *formation*. It is true that David can't read the Bible when he is depressed. Nevertheless, the Bible remains embedded within him:

> I don't get the sense of losing touch with God ... well, that's not true, sometimes I do, but it's more ... [sighs] ... it's more that I become

differently connected. I can't read the Bible, but it's like, I haven't forgotten what it says! Mind you, remembering what the Bible says doesn't always make much difference. So, when I'm suicidal, I know very well that the Bible says this is a sin and that if I took my own life I would go to hell, but that makes not one bit of a difference. I just want to end the pain. I know that the Bible tells me that Jesus loves me, and I do believe that, but when I am in a dark place … So I have all of these passages in my head, but I often don't feel any better for that.

The Bible has shaped and formed David's thinking in important ways. Sometimes that brings him hope, but when he is depressed he just can't read it. The Bible, however, does not leave him. It continues to function in a rather ambiguous way – sometimes for good, but sometimes not for good:

And my church is a really good church. I went and talked to the pastor once about my depression, and he prayed for me. I told him that I struggled with the Bible, partly because I couldn't really read it when I was depressed and partly because when I did read it, I found parts of it quite terrifying! He told me that whatever my issues were with understanding the canon in the church, I was welcome to participate in the church and get all the benefits of the church even if I wasn't an official member who accepted all the canon. Right now, I have the most trouble believing in the dark side of spirituality, and the enemy – or Satan – is so scary to me that I don't like thinking that that is an actual belief pattern that I should assimilate. Because, I mean, some of the things I've seen in my depressed mind I would hate to think of as demons in a real sense. Other people can live and say that they're fighting Satan by doing good and trying to follow Jesus' example, but for me if there's a Satan out there then this universe is extremely frightening. So, I don't follow some of the canon but my pastor said that doesn't matter very much. Everyone can participate fully in the church, but you need to be careful.

David struggled to read the Bible when he was depressed. When he did read it, similar to Peter Herman, he struggled with aspects of the canon that tended to exacerbate his fears rather than bring consolation and hope. The pastor's gentle, sensitive and deeply pastoral hermeneutical flexibility enabled David to remain connected to the Christian community, while at the same time being very careful about the potential impact of certain beliefs on his mental health.

Conclusion

It is clear then that the Bible has an important – if at times ambiguous – role in the experiences of Christians living with depression, and by implication those living with other forms of mental health challenges. There is a need for deeper attention to be paid to the development and exploration of a mental health hermeneutic that takes seriously the experience of people living with mental health challenges, but also remains pastorally aware of the sometimes hidden dangers of interpretations that emerge from the experience, which might actually prevent people from experiencing the kind of fullness of life that Jesus has promised us. This is a complex and sensitive task of discernment requiring at a minimum that pastors and congregations recognize and talk about the experience of mental health challenges within the ongoing liturgical life of the Church. If pastors and congregations have their consciousness raised to the hermeneutical significance of mental health issues, then the kinds of mental health hermeneutic that have been gestured to in this chapter may become a possibility. The beginning point for such consciousness-raising is liturgy and worship. As we move towards the end of this chapter, we might do well to think deeply about Dana's reflection on worship and mental health:

> I have a student who developed an entire liturgy for people with depression. He helped the church to see that many people lived with depression. However, the church had never identified it directly. And he wrote a beautiful service using Scripture, candles, anointing with oil, prayers that he wrote specifically for people with depression. And I think things like that go a long way to making people with mental illness feel welcome in a congregation, that people without mental illness become sensitive to the people around them, and need that sensitivity. I think it's always been great that churches have started to have blue Christmas services. Blue Christmas is for people who are going through grief or depression at Christmas time, and aren't putting up little Santa Clauses and having a happy pie-making time, that they're in grief or they're in sadness, that this is a worship service for the reality of those who are not somehow transcending their grief or their depression. So, I mean, I think those are really positive in-roads – naming depression in the litany of what we pray for, along with all kinds of other stigmatizing things. Just normalizing it.

As we incorporate the experience of mental health into the liturgical life of our churches, so we open up space for the introduction of a mental health hermeneutic that takes seriously – and acts faithfully towards – the mental health experiences of *all* of the members of Jesus' body. In this way, the strange new world of mental health challenges will begin to seem a little less odd as it helps us understand previously hidden dimensions of the strange new world within the Bible.

Notes

1 K. Barth, 1957, 'The Strange New World within the Bible', in *The Word of God and the Word of Man*, trans. Douglas Horton, San Francisco, CA: Harper Torchbooks, pp. 28–50.

2 S. Melcher, M. C. Parsons and A. Yong, 2018, *The Bible and Disability: A Commentary*, London: SCM Press.

3 J. M. Hull, 2001, *In the Beginning There Was Darkness: A Blind Person's Conversations with the Bible*, London: SCM Press.

4 N. L. Eiesland, 1994, *The Disabled God: Toward a Liberatory Theology of Disability*, Nashville, TN: Abingdon Press.

5 B. McKinney Fox, 2019, *Disability and the Way of Jesus: Holistic Healing in the Gospels and the Church*, Downers Grove, IL: InterVarsity Press.

6 A. Yong, 2011, *The Bible, Disability, and the Church: A New Vision of the People of God*, Grand Rapids, MI: Eerdmans.

7 L. J. Laurence, 2018, *Bible and Bedlam: Madness, Sanism, and New Testament Interpretation* (The Library of New Testament Studies Book 594), Edinburgh: T&T Clark.

8 See J. Swinton, 2020, *Finding Jesus in the Storm: Theological Reflections on the Experience of Mental Health Challenges*, Grand Rapids, MI: Eerdmans.

9 J. Wilkinson, 1998, *The Bible and Healing: A Medical and Theological Commentary*, Grand Rapids, MI: Eerdmans, chapters 1 and 2.

10 J. Swinton, 2000, *Resurrecting the Person: Friendship and the Care of People with Mental Health Problems*, Nashville, TN: Abingdon Press.

11 P. Herman, 2017, 'Jesus Doesn't Want Me for a Sunbeam: Thoughts on Depression, Race and Theology', *The Other Journal: An Intersection of Theology and Culture*, 6 April, https://theotherjournal.com/2017/04/06/jesus-doesnt-want-sunbeam-thoughts-depression-race-theology/ (accessed 4.11.19).

12 Herman, 'Jesus Doesn't Want Me for a Sunbeam'.

13 Herman, 'Jesus Doesn't Want Me for a Sunbeam'.

14 Herman, 'Jesus Doesn't Want Me for a Sunbeam'.

15 Herman, 'Jesus Doesn't Want Me for a Sunbeam'.

16 M. S. Lundy, 2018, *Depression, Anxiety, and the Christian Life: Practical Wisdom from Richard Baxter*, Wheaton, IL: Crossway Publishers, p. 86.

13

The Formation of Christian Community: Reading Scripture in the Light of Mental Health

NICK LADD

Introduction: mental health is about real people and their lives

In parish ministry, challenges and questions about people's mental health tend to come suddenly and unexpectedly in the everyday work of pastoral care. Jane[1] attended an outer estate church where I was the vicar. I remember one quiet reflective moment in a service when Jane suddenly spoke up:

> 'Nick, can I have a lift next Saturday?'
> 'Sure, Jane, that'll be fine.'
> A further pause.
> 'What time are we leaving?'

The conversation continued with gaps for further reflection; it was outside the social norms for a Sunday service, but Jane didn't notice and the congregation didn't mind.

Jane was a loved member of that congregation, sometimes regular, sometimes sporadic. When she was well, she was lively, fun, talkative and enjoyed being with others. When she was unwell, often through ceasing to take her medication, she became withdrawn, stopped caring for her appearance, and cried despairingly. The congregation had a way of accepting and embracing Jane, perhaps because they too lived close to the uncertainties and pain of life, but could do little more than be there – whether at church, or with her and her family at home, as they waited once again for the doctor to section her.

Prior to this, I had begun my ministry as a curate in an inner-city parish, just months after a severe personal bereavement. Two years in, I felt that I had nothing to offer in this unfamiliar context. In reality, I was close to a breakdown that I could not acknowledge. The congregation surrounded me with an inarticulate love that held me through some dark months and years; I needed something more, though I did not know what.

My time with these two parishes helped me as a young minister to begin to understand the breadth of mental health challenges – from diagnosed conditions to the storms that threaten to break us on the rocks of personal suffering. It drove me to ask the question about the nature of a truly supportive and healing community. How might such a community be formed? And how might Scripture inform and shape that journey?

Churches can be very supportive and caring places, where we meet people who go the extra mile in love. But they can also be blind and neglectful of the needs of others: how does this happen? It is not simply that we are all flawed human beings. There is also a tendency in any human community to gather together around shared assumptions and experiences, where identity is both formed and sustained by the stories we tell one another. It feels safer to keep the worldview simple and that can lead to categorizing, stereotyping and eventually excluding those who are different. We often talk about church as family – but families can be demanding places where new members learn in no uncertain terms what it means to 'fit in'. Churches are often uneasy with anything that challenges their practices and unsettles their convictions. However, there is also evidence that when a community opens itself up to minority voices, often the unheard and less powerful ones, that it can be transformed in profound ways.[2]

Contemporary experience of mental health has the potential both to challenge the assumptions of a church community and to lead it down new paths that will transform Christian community. But this will only happen as a community learns to be open and receptive to the voice of the 'other'.

Scripture can be used to underwrite the assumptions of the community (its ideology) and resist the challenge of the other. Or it can be the leading player in helping us to open up to the voice of the other – both the other person in our midst and also the strange otherness of Scripture itself. It is the assumption of this chapter that as we learn the two disciplines of listening openly to other people and listening openly to Scripture, we will hear God speaking to us about the way he is calling us to live. This assumption underlies the approach to Scripture in this chapter. Its authority lies not so much in offering a predetermined answer to life's questions, but as a shared narrative where people with different life experiences come together and meet God afresh as they listen to Scripture. The reading of and listening to Scripture – especially together – becomes a practice that inspires and empowers us to live afresh the story of God in today's world in the power of the Spirit.

Doing theology from experience: from doing theology *about* to doing theology *with*

Reflecting on memories of the people that I had walked with over the years and the different challenges they had faced, I decided that I did not want to write from my perspective alone, but to hear how they described and interpreted their experiences. It is always tempting to theologize about people's experience – to listen to their challenges and concerns, and then use these for our reflection. But here I want to take a step further, and let them speak for themselves, allowing them to have a voice in dialogue with me. This approach can be likened to our experience of reading the psalms – letting the other speak in their own words.

Three of my former congregants kindly agreed to be interviewed: Richard was diagnosed with schizoaffective disorder as a young adult and has been journeying with this for over 30 years; John and Liz, a married couple, experienced the heartbreak of miscarriages and childlessness, and subsequently the challenges of learning to care for adopted children with complex needs, a journey that at times has brought them both to breaking point. At various times, John and Liz have had mental health diagnoses; indeed, they comment that it was the prescribing of medication that helped them realize the extent of their mental health challenges. Their older adopted child has received extensive mental health care, initially in the community but now in a supportive residential setting with two carers assigned to him. All three have belonged to evangelical charismatic churches – though their experience has challenged the theology and spirituality in which they were formed.[3]

This chapter is not intended to be a 'how to' of approaching mental health in church life and it cannot be extrapolated from a few people's experiences or from one ministerial journey. Rather, I hope that it will point up some of the challenges and possibilities for the Church in the way in which it includes those with mental health journeys, and how listening to one another and to Scripture might shape our approach to forming Christian community in the public world, to which end I am deeply indebted to Richard, Liz and John for their openness and honesty.

Language and isolation

Language clothes our deepest thoughts and feelings. Through language we name our experiences and connect with others. Language expresses both who we are and the connection that we make with others – the way we see and are seen. God spoke the world into life (Gen. 1) and his Word became flesh for our redemption (John 1.1–14). It is perhaps unsurprising, then, that Scripture pays so much attention to our words. The letter of James alone instructs us about the importance of listening (1.19) and the dangers of lifeless or hurtful words (2.14–17; 3.1–12).

Mental illness is a disorienting experience. It takes you on a path that seems increasingly distant from other people's lives – an unfamiliar and at times frightening world that you have to come to terms with, one that most people could hardly guess at.

> Richard: Psychosis is a horrible experience, it really is. Because it causes fear – terror actually. I've known other patients go through similar emotions, screaming in terror and crying uncontrollably. It is horrible.

The first challenge lies in trying to find the words to talk about experiences that are so beyond one's expectations. For John and Liz, as one painful experience began to turn into a pattern, what they hoped for in life, and what others take for granted, looked less and less possible. Life became isolated, not just because of the experience but because of the difficulty of finding the words to speak about it.[4]

> Liz: So I think it's the isolation that's a really big deal for me, but I think it's very hard to verbalize, and when struggle becomes your normality, it's difficult to verbalize, because it's like, 'Well, isn't this just how life is?' but you know it's not.

In speaking of 'normality', Liz harks back to a different 'normal' of marriage, family and health. But perhaps also lying behind this is an evangelical story of faith in a God who blesses, 'gives good gifts' and meets the 'desires of your heart' (Matt. 7.11; Ps. 37.4). John and Liz struggled to find words to articulate their new world.

And even after gaining some understanding of what is happening, there is a profound level of risk in revealing something that causes you such confusing feelings.

> Richard: But I was deeply ashamed, I was deeply fearful, and I felt a lot of guilt. And I didn't know why. I still don't, to be honest.

Amid the struggle to understand their own experience, Richard, John and Liz encountered people's responses to their situation.

> John: The most annoying thing in the world is people give bad advice, and just feel compelled to give advice, I guess to make themselves feel

better, [because] they're having an encounter with you where things aren't positive.

Our everyday stories of faith find it hard to contain the contradictions of mental health experience and this prompts us to provide 'solutions'. This is even more striking in the next example where simplistic readings of Scripture – Jesus healed then, so he must do the same now – leads to destructive advice.

> Richard: People who offer [healing and deliverance] are, no doubt, very well-meaning but, in my experience, it just fuelled my delusions, in telling me I was possessed by a demon or that it was the devil attacking me. Or, 'Read this passage in Scripture', or 'Go to a healing service'. It just didn't help.

When we are struggling to understand what we are going through, we need a language to articulate our pain, otherwise our suffering is mute and isolating.[5] We also need a community that has a narrative that is broad enough and strong enough to encompass that pain and give the freedom to find voice and be heard. In the lament psalms, Scripture offers us the voices of troubled people who feel isolated from God and from others as a result of their experience (Ps. 13.1–2; 22.1, 6–8; 62.3–4). In the close social world of biblical culture, the communal isolation is experienced more directly through the actions of 'enemies'. In our more socially detached culture, the response is more passive, even unaware, but no less painful. The fact that such voices are heard in Scripture and are part of the liturgy of churches suggests that we should expect such experiences of alienation and learn how to respect these voices and truly see the people whose stories they represent.

So while we might expect that being part of a Christian community could be an embrace in the midst of isolation, it turns out to be complicated, because of the problems of finding voice and then a place where that voice may truly be heard. Yet the aspiration for something different remains.

> Liz: I think being in a very supportive community where it is OK to not be OK makes a significant difference to how you accept, and how you deal with, your own mental health.

Attending to the voice of the other in community

How do we form such community? I approach this with the assumption that engaging together with Scripture offers a place of encounter with God and, from that encounter, transformation. Therefore this section will address specifically how engaging with Scripture enables us to see and attend to the other in ways that are life-giving.

Scripture is unashamedly honest about the flawed nature of human community and Richard, John and Liz have suffered as a result of people trying to 'solve' their problems, telling them their feelings, or attempting empathy by assuming they have shared similar experiences.

They have learnt the importance of professional therapy and pastoral care, not just for its level of skill, but for the safe and boundaried space to process difficult stuff that they did not necessarily want or need to share in wider contexts. But this does not mean that there is no role for community that allows us, in Liz's words, 'to not be OK'.

> Liz: There's empathy and then there's understanding somebody else's mind, rather than putting your own emotions on it … kind of, 'I feel for what you're going through', and it's weird because you'd expect that would make it more isolating because it's more distanced, but actually it's more helpful, oddly.

What Liz is feeling after expressing here is 'differentiation of self'.[6] This is a relationship, a place of meeting, in which each one encourages the other to maintain their own subjectivity. Together, they then create a 'third space' in which they develop mutual understanding without obliterating each other's sense of self.[7] This allows each person, especially the one who is struggling, to be appropriately seen and heard.

The experiences Richard, John and Liz describe of people prescribing answers, imputing feelings and assuming knowledge of their predicament may be called 'fusing'. This takes place when our anxiety about what we are hearing is such that we cannot bear to encounter the emotional world of the other, and instead subsume it into our own. The result for John and Liz is the isolation that they describe as they try to free themselves from being defined by others.

Differentiation of self takes emotional wisdom and courage; how do we foster this in church communities? We are seeking what Swinton describes as 'radical friendship' that 'transcends the relational boundaries that are constructed by contemporary tendencies to associate with others on the basis of likeness, utility or social exchange'.[8] To do this we need to find ways to form community that encourages differentiated accompaniment, honesty and respect.

A scriptural shape for community

How do we form community where, on the one hand, people do not avoid or isolate those with challenging life experiences for fear of not knowing what to say, but on the other learn not to offer over-spiritualized or other unhelpful counsel? In a church context, we can seek a framework for the formation of such community in Scripture as a shared narrative of understanding for Christians in which we encounter the presence and voice of God.

There are many stories in the Gospels that illustrate Jesus' relationship to others – carefully listening and giving space for them without judgement. The Apostle Paul also picks up on these principles, and they form part of his more didactic teaching, albeit placed at times within his personal narrative. In 2 Corinthians 1.3–11, Paul talks about the kind of comfort that arises from the personal experience of God 'coming alongside' in times of trouble – the derivation of *parakaleo* (v. 4) from where the word 'Paraclete' as a designation for the Holy Spirit comes (John 14.16). By presenting pastoral care as coming alongside in the midst of shared suffering and struggle, Paul avoids the carer being an untouched giver but rather a vulnerable fellow sufferer in some shape or form; note how transparent Paul is about his own struggle and weakness (vv. 8–11). When we are alert and aware of the intractable and unpredictable nature of our own struggles, we will be more patient and less afraid of the sufferings of others. I describe this approach to relationships in community as 'alongsideness' that embodies the 'alongsideness' of God, in which there is both acceptance and appropriate vulnerability, not the kind that projects personal experience on to the sufferer.

Such accompaniment requires listening without judgement as a precursor to understanding (Matt. 7.1–5) and respect for the other which, while willing to 'bear burdens' (the word here suggests an unbearable load), allows the other the freedom to 'carry their own load' – a word that is used for a pack that one might carry for the day (Gal. 6.2–5). This is an imaginative way for describing support that respects the responsibility of the other. This in turn creates an atmosphere of genuineness and honesty in which there can be mutual learning, rather than a 'hierarchy of the healthy'[9] (Col. 3.16) and a spirit of openness and humility to learn from the wisdom of the other (James 3.17). This was the framework that guided my own leadership of church communities and I see this as the 'building bricks' of community (Figure 2).[10]

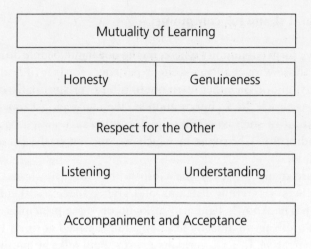

Figure 2

Richard described his experience of a church that was trying to live in this way.

> Richard: The major influence was St X Church; it was quite a community-orientated church. There was a very supportive home group, that I could open up to, and they were all aware of what was going on. I remember that as being a good time. The community aspect was very helpful. Sometimes I didn't want to join in or go along, but I always knew that it was probably good for me.

A framework is one thing; it takes shared spiritual practices to embed this vision and to form the narrative that a community lives by. So here are my suggestions.

'Dwelling in the Word'

The first suggestion revolves around how, in practice, Scripture shapes our communal narrative and especially the question of how we engage with minority or unheard voices. Traditionally in the church our communal engagement with Scripture involves listening to Scripture being read, listening to interpretations of Scripture, usually (though not necessarily) from a trained and licensed minister and discussing passages of Scripture in small groups to develop our understanding and application of it in our lives. I want to challenge the hegemony of these inherited models with a practice called 'Dwelling in the Word' (DitW) that expands our attention to the voice of the 'other'.[11]

In DitW, we listen to a passage together somewhat in the style of a communal 'lectio divina'. We ponder the passage and prayerfully wait to see where our attention is drawn. What encourages, challenges, perplexes or annoys us? What questions might we want to ask a biblical scholar? After time to reflect, we share our insight with one other person; then together, we find two others and share what we heard our partner saying. All this takes place without correcting the other or giving in to the temptation to say in response to the other's summary, 'What I really meant to say was ...' With the whole group, we take time to share and reflect together on some of the things we have heard from others. This practice inculcates the discipline of listening and articulating the voice of others, people who perhaps have never been heard before in the community. Over time, it also encourages all to wrestle with the strange voice of Scripture for themselves rather than leaving that to one interpreter in their preparation of a sermon or a small group study. This discipline prepares us for hearing voices that stand outside the usual narrative of the community and challenge the dominant story. As we will see in the next section, those who have suffered with their mental health have much to bring to the reading of Scripture in a way that will bring appropriate complexity to communal narratives, something that is consonant with the nature of Scripture.

Listening

With the second suggestion – to support 'radical friendship' that makes space for the 'other' with different experiences – the quality of listening needs to go beyond the 'listening' of everyday life. The practice of DitW raises awareness of what it means to listen deeply to others; in other words, how might this pervade the whole of life?

The Gospels tell many stories about the attentiveness of Jesus: sometimes this leads him to acts that transform people's situations (Luke 7.13; 19.5; John 4.7–9), at other times to confrontation (Mark 2.8; 3.5–6), and still others to recognize the outsider and the insignificant that others do not see (Mark 10.14, 46–52; 12.41–44). Paul encourages a factional church to be attentive to those in their midst who are socially less influential (1 Cor. 11.17–34; 12.22–26) and he teaches them to recognize the presence ('the glory') of God in one another (2 Cor. 3.18). The biblical witness suggests that attentive listening is the calling of *the whole congregation*. When it is associated only with pastoral teams the tendency is to create an ethos in which listening to the other becomes solely a response to pastoral need rather than a practice for the whole of the Church's life. I would combine this always with inculcating a practice of listening prayer in which a silent shared space is created to listen together for the word of God – through Scripture and the guidance of the Spirit.

There is a risk here of opening the door to careless counsel once again – but this can be ameliorated by attention and accountability to the biblical disciplines of community outlined in the section on pages 179–80. It is important to stress to congregations the distinctive role of professional care, but at the same time the commitment to holistic care within the Christian community is not to be abandoned; rather, it gives the opportunity to treat people – as Scripture does – as whole people and not to see the medical condition alone.

Lament

The third suggestion – attentiveness to the pain of life – is a priority in worship and in our reading of Scripture, and not in pastoral care alone. John and Liz speak about a moment when they had identified the need to lay down their hopes of having their own child and how they were drawn to a structure and a form of words, grounded in Scripture, that would be more robust than their own private prayers. So a form of liturgy was settled on and it was tentatively suggested that this might be an act of corporate prayer that was opened up to the wider congregation and not kept only for themselves.

> John: I remember when we first talked about doing it, and then we talked about opening it up to other people, I remember feeling a bit disappointed.
> Liz: Almost a bit threatened or something?
> John: Just in terms of it feeling a bit private, but it was the kind of private that maybe needed to be challenged, because as it turned out, on the day when we were doing it, I remember feeling a sense of connection with the others in the community.
> Liz: Less alone.
> John: Yes. I think that if it had just been us, it might've perhaps been less impactful, probably because I could see someone else's tears and awaken emotionally through that.

John and Liz's decision to open up the invitation to others enabled two things to happen. It allowed people who had lost children, never been able to have children, or who had not had the opportunity to have children to give voice in shared prayer to their grief and to find solidarity with others – something that John commented upon for himself. It also enabled the reality of pain and loss to be brought to the fore in the church's narrative and to make space for people who otherwise found the one-dimensional optimism of a simplistic Christian narrative an excluding experience in worship.

This is the purpose of the psalms of lament in the Psalter.[12] They allow for mute suffering to find a voice and to address God with complaint and challenge and with hope and anticipation. 'The lament as plea and petition regresses to the oldest fears, the censured questions, the deepest hates, the unknown and unadmitted venom, and a yearning, whereas the lament as praise anticipates and is open to gift. It looks ahead, consents to receive, and intends to respond in gratitude.'[13] Psalm 13 begins with a barrage of complaint focusing on the pain within and enemies outside, speaking the unspeakable fear of death – suffering that is seen as derivative of abandonment by Yahweh (1–4). This emboldens movements from victimhood to the naming of pain, from passivity to protest and from mute isolation to finding voice in the community.

Then, in verses 5–6, there is a sudden change which might be a psychological transformation through the encounter with God in prayer or an act of God's covenantal freedom in which waiting in the darkness of death is transformed by the gift of new life. Allowing pain into the narrative and liturgy of the community enables people who are suffering to bring their experience into the worship.

> Richard: Another thing I liked about the church was that you could go to a service and end up sobbing in a pew, and people not being embarrassed and avoiding you; someone would always come over and pray for you, or help you practically. And I hope I did it for other people as well, from time to time.

Richard also testifies to the transformative impact of biblical preaching.

> Richard: There was a very strong element of God's love running right the way through it. And gradually I caught on to that, that actually God loved me. I remember one sermon in particular – I can't remember the passage – but it was something about God delighting in his children.

Companionship in the ordinary

If we are used to reading the immediacy of the Gospel of Mark or the fast-paced narrative of the healing miracles, it is not hard to see how our minds turn to solving problems and our hearts to dramatic interventions; we can miss the power of the ordinary. Even in the drama of the Gospels, we find the long-term companionship of the disciples, culminating in Jesus' request that they simply be with him in his darkest hour (Mark 14.32–42). All my interviewees testify to the healing power of ordinary companionship to mental well-being – for example, the companionship of the friends of Job, *before* they turn to justifying arguments. Richard corrected my misapprehension of the place of struggle in managing mental health.

> Richard: If you struggle, you just make it worse. You have to fight it, but you fight it by, in a sense, relaxing and doing the mundane and keeping an ordinary life and trying to meet people and talk to people, not isolate yourself.

He valued highly the fact that he could call up members of the home group when he was under pressure and be welcomed into their homes and spend time doing something mundane.

> Liz: When [our son] was an in-patient, there were people bringing us meals, and actually that had a massive impact on the other families that were there, because they saw that there was a Christian community looking after us. I guess that's one of those things that's often reserved for new babies and people in, kind of, good difficult situations, rather than bad difficult situations.

Notice the prophetic aspect of this simple act of care as it draws them into a social exchange that is normally reserved for the happy challenges of childbirth. For a couple who first struggled to have children and now care for troubled adopted children, the validation of their place in the community and the presence of God in this simple act is palpable. This is the integrity of life in community where the substance of faith is action (James 2.14–26).

Learning from people with mental health challenges

Beyond caring

We have explored some of the practices that help communities open up to unheard voices of struggle in their midst. We saw how the lament psalms offer a language and a spirituality in which this can be expressed both personally and in community. But can we take a step further and ask whether these voices and the experiences they represent can be integrated into the narrative and life of the community? If not, the danger is that the meaningful care described in the previous section becomes one-directional and we do not move beyond the illness to see the person.[14]

> Richard: I got a sense of, 'Oh, Richard is ill again, this is what helps, this is what doesn't help, this is what we'll try and do, we'll give him support.' And they are very good at that. But whether they consider they could learn something from it, I didn't get that sense at all, actually.

Challenging assumptions, growing in God

In addition to offering a language of prayer to speak pain to God, the lament psalms also contain a challenge directed towards the community, particularly when its narrative excludes uncomfortable experience. Lament psalms confront an ideology of praise within Old Testament worship by speaking the pain and bringing it into the public arena.[15]

> Liz: I think also, in charismatic circles, there's a little bit of a 'Oh, the overcomers.' You know, there isn't much of walking through stuff. Of course you wouldn't say you have to be healed, but I still think there's an underlying tone.
> John: People have a certain picture of what [healing] looks like, and that sometimes conflicts with walking with people on the journey.
> Interviewer: So, an ability to walk with the long-term unresolvedness of this, is that it?
> Liz: And to be OK with people having mental health difficulties.
> Interviewer: You don't think the Church is OK with it, deep down?
> Liz: Not really, no.

What ideology might the Church be protecting? A vision that the goodness of God is always directed towards our comfort and healing – something perhaps that owes more to a culture of the consumption of health rather than a scriptural vision of God?[16] John and Liz have gone through the excruciatingly painful realization that their adopted son needed specialist residential care that their home life could not provide. This has shaken them to the core because they believed that God's call to them was to provide a home and family for their adopted children. And so where did they find God in this?

> Liz: I think it's been a process of realizing that God has a much bigger picture than we do, which is a good thing because we couldn't cope with the big picture all at once, and God gives us little bits of the picture. There was a question in your email about verses that have been unhelpful, and I remember when we were struggling with childlessness. The verse that I really, really struggled with was [the one] about hope never disappoints. I was like, 'No, it's the hope that's the problem. If I didn't have the hope month after month after month after month, this wouldn't be so hard.' I think what we've come to realize over the years is that it's not hoping for something. It's hoping in God. It's about God's character and God's faithfulness. It's not about what he does or doesn't do, or what we perceive him doing or not doing.

I find this a deeply moving and challenging perspective. Bernard of Clairvaux in his stages of contemplation suggested that people grow from loving God for their own sakes to loving God for God's sake.[17] John and Liz have travelled this road by refusing to deny or spiritualize their experience and thus have faced the full force of their grief. In doing this they have found not a false and brittle confidence but a hope born of meeting God in the darkness.

This experience of dislocation lies at the heart of the Old Testament story of exile. So, in Psalm 39.1–3, the writer breaks out of the mute world that ideology imposes, to finally express pain and distress. The honest owning of pain leads the psalmist to hope, and so to appeal to God to break out of passivity (vv. 7 and 12–13). But note how it is placed within a critique of wealth and the presumptuousness it engenders (vv. 4–6 and 10–11). John and Liz's journey with this biblical reality has so much to bring to a church community that can become myopic about the fulfilment of its own needs and the assumptions of its own comfort.

Richard, too, witnesses to a profound journey with God in the midst of more than 30 years of challenge to his mental health. In the illness, he remembers dark delusions of himself as the Antichrist, doomed to judgement, but he also recollects moments of 'utter beauty and transcendence'.[18] In his journey, he learnt how to distinguish the two and reflected deeply on Scripture along the way. He wrestled with Revelation, trying to come to terms with it and its involvement in his delusions; he thought deeply about the humanity of Jesus in John's Gospel – touched in particular by Jesus' courage, something I believe Richard has exhibited in his life; he faced up to the healings in Jesus' ministry of those we might consider to be psychologically ill, and explored ways of integrating theology and psychology in their interpretation.

A learning Church?

John and Liz are struck by the fact that their non-religious therapists constantly ask them where God is in their experience, but the church leadership never does. So why has the church community not sought out their insights on life with God? Perhaps because they still see the illness rather than the person? Or perhaps because integrating the reality of suffering and struggle and the absence of answers would undermine the narrative of comfort and healing that the Church espouses? What practical steps might the Church take to integrate people like Richard, John and Liz into the community and draw more fully on all that they have learnt about life with God? One possibility seems to offer itself from John and Liz's experience.

The complexity of their family life has meant that participation in 'normal' church life has been extremely difficult and they describe themselves as 'cynical and disillusioned'. The model of church that they are used to is very driven, with high expectations of participation and involvement in leadership; like a 'hospital without patients' is how they describe it. And 'there isn't much room for mental health in that'. Any expression of dissatisfaction draws the response, 'Well, you do something about it' – but they haven't the energy within their highly stressed lives. This is presented as 'bottom up' leadership, but it feels more like abrogation.

However, John and Liz have extensive experience of supportive informal community beyond the church, especially among those who share their challenge with adopted children, and when asked about the potential gift of their experience to the church they were extremely responsive and the energy in the room increased noticeably.

Interviewer: So could you imagine your experience being a gift to the church?
Liz: Definitely. I think there's a huge amount of people going through all sorts of stuff.

So here is my suggestion: what if instead of leaving it to them to forge their own place in a church whose structures preclude this, the leadership said to them, 'How about if a few folk from church partnered with you and some of the people you've been getting to know in forming community together and seeing where it takes us?' Instead of expecting John and Liz to make what they can of church on the church's terms, what would happen if the church sought to learn from the people with whom John and Liz have built informal community and be welcomed into their world? How might they meet God together?

In Scripture, God consistently calls us out of familiar territory, and expects us to learn from those who seem to be unexpected teachers – younger sons, women, the poor, foreigners. What if instead of fearing the experience of Richard, John and Liz as a failure of the happy vision of God's blessing, the Church could commit to learning from them and seeing God at work in more diverse and complex ways in uncharted territory with unexpected partners? In a world where 1 in 4 adults and 1 in 10 children are affected by mental health issues, what might a partnership like this mean for flourishing life in God's world?

Conclusion

Richard has been in remission for many years now. He attributes this to a number of things – medication, therapy and, most of all, to the relationship with his wife and young son. But he also believes that a significant role has been played by the Christian community. John and Liz continue to face the challenges of their children's struggles with fortitude – drawing strength from the informal communities beyond church boundaries they have formed along the way. At the time of writing, organized church was not working for them.

The vocation of the Church is tied to its maturity – and maturation involves openness to the other, both personally and communally. As we noted at the beginning, social groups tend towards a monochrome identity, as like gathers with like and unconsciously exclude the one who is different – community is easier this way. But we can see from the experience of Richard, John and Liz what potential there is for people to grow when they face up to the realities of suffering and struggle, and the way this complexifies our faith, and by contrast what is lost to the Church when difference is avoided.

The biblical narrative is no stranger to complexity and struggle. But church congregations do not tend to start with Scripture and ask how it applies to an issue like mental health. Communities grow and change through their response to disruptive experience and this happens most creatively as they reflect on their experience in the light of Scripture – something that changes both them and their reading of Scripture.

This can be encouraged in a number of ways. First, by supporting people like Richard in their in-depth reflection on Scripture in the light of experience – Richard should not have had to journey alone with this. Second, we can shape the structure of the Church's practices through Scripture and, third, let it guide the content of our reflection. Dwelling in the Word is ideal for this as it allows people to dialogue with one another and with Scripture in a way that encourages reflective questioning about our experience. Finally, if we have courage, Scripture can help us encounter the experience of people on the margins and challenge the comfortable assumptions of our community, encouraging us into an adventure in discipleship beyond what we have so far discovered in our Christian community.

While we would not wish the challenges of mental illness on anyone, it is also true that Richard, John and Liz are a gift to the Church, just as the Church could be to them (and sometimes is); together they might participate not just in the flourishing of the Church but of the wider world as they make room and partner with people who live with challenges to their mental health. Scripture can both inform and guide this journey in ways that continue to open our lives to God in our midst and in the other.

Taking action

Things you could consider:

Church community

- Inform yourself:
  (a) Read Matt Haig's book about his experience of depression (see note 4).
  (b) Check out mental health websites like MIND, or new initiatives like 'Britain Get Talking'.
- Volunteer with a mental health charity
- Try Dwelling in the Word with church and non-church people – especially those whose life experience is different from yours.

Church leadership

- Ensure that listening skills training is on offer in your church or across a group of churches. Can you combine this with training in listening prayer?
- Introduce Dwelling in the Word or other Scripture-based practices to your congregation.
- Reflect with your congregation on how far Scripture informs the structure and content of your church's practices.
- Ask yourself whether people with different life experiences are expected to fit in with the culture of your church or whether their experience might instead be a springboard into your wider community.

Notes

1 Names have been changed to preserve anonymity.

2 See S. Savage and E. Boyd-Macmillan, 2007, *The Human Face of the Church*, Norwich: Canterbury Press, for a more detailed explanation and for pointers to the grounding of this in social psychology.

3 For those who would like to explore this way of doing theology further, I offer three resources from different traditions: K. A. Cahalan and G. S. Mikoski (eds), 2014, *Opening the Field of Practical Theology: An Introduction*, Lanham, MD: Rowman and Littlefield; B. J. Miller-McLemore (ed.), 2012, *The Wiley Blackwell Companion to Practical Theology*, Chichester: Blackwell Publishing Limited; and A. Root, 2014, *Christopraxis: A Practical Theology of the Cross*, Minneapolis, MN: Fortress Press.

4 See also N. Hussein, 2019, *Anxiety and Me*, BBC One, 15 October; M. Haig, 2015, *Reasons to Stay Alive*, Edinburgh: Canongate, pp. 63, 68, 116.

5 See D. Soelle, 1975, *Suffering*, London: Darton, Longman and Todd.

6 F. L. Shults and Steven J. Sandage, 2006, *Transforming Spirituality: Integrating Theology and Psychology*, Grand Rapids, MI: Baker Academic, pp. 187–270.

7 L. Irigaray, 2000, *To Be Two*, London: Athlone Press, pp. 62–67.

8 J. Swinton, 2000, *Resurrecting the Person: Friendship and the Care of People with Mental Health Problems*, Nashville, TN: Abingdon Press, p. 39.

9 Swinton, *Resurrecting*, p. 123.

10 I have preached at length on each of these passages over the years, but there is not room to include more here.

11 This is an approach to Scripture reading that has been developed in missional practice by Partnership for Missional Church, www.churchinnovations.org (accessed 9.10.19). See P. Keifert, 2006, *We Are Here Now: A New Missional Era*, St Paul, MN: Church Innovations Institute; P. Taylor Ellison and P. Keifert, 2011, *Dwelling in the Word: A Pocket Handbook*, Robbinsdale, MN: Church Innovations; P. Keifert and N. Rooms, 2014, *Forming a Missional Church: Creating Deep Cultural Change in Congregations*, Grove Pastoral Series 139, Cambridge: Grove Books.

12 W. Brueggemann, 2002, *Spirituality of the Psalms*, Minneapolis, MN: Fortress Press, pp. 25–45.

13 W. Brueggemann, 1995, *The Psalms and the Life of Faith*, Minneapolis, MN: Augsburg Fortress Press, p. 24.

14 Swinton, *Resurrecting*, p. 137. See also his strategy for community formation, pp. 145–91.

15 W. Brueggemann, 1988, *Israel's Praise: Doxology against Idolatry and Ideology*, Philadelphia, PA: Fortress Press, pp. 55–121.

16 '... the importance we put on avoiding suffering ... seems to be unique among higher civilisations' (C. Taylor, 1989, *Sources of the Self: The Making of Modern Identity*, Cambridge, MA: Harvard University Press, p. 12).

17 St Bernard of Clairvaux, 1970, *Sermo 5: On the Words of Habakkuk 2.1*, pp. 4–5. Opera Omnia, ed. Cisterc, 6.1, pp. 103–4. https://catholicgnosis.word press.com/2008/09/10/on-the-stages-of-contemplation-st-bernard-of-clairvaux/ (accessed 23.1.20).

18 See C. C. H. Cook, 2013, 'Transcendence, Immanence and Mental Health', in C. C. H. Cook (ed.), *Spirituality, Theology and Mental Health*, London: SCM Press, pp. 141–59, for an argument for the place of transcendence in psychiatry based upon Charles Taylor's critique of an over-dependence on immanence in secular culture.

14

Bible and Trauma

MEGAN WARNER

The burgeoning of interest in reader-response approaches to interpretation of the Scriptures has created a ready platform for exploring aspects of disability and mental health as interpretive tools. In particular, the impact of traumatic experience, upon both readers and authors/editors, has attracted the interest of biblical scholars in recent years. A rapid explosion in the incorporation of trauma theory, itself developing at a great rate, by scholars from an extremely wide range of disciplines, has helped to stimulate this interest.[1] It might perhaps be not inappropriate to describe the application of trauma theory to biblical exegesis as one of the 'hottest' areas of biblical scholarship at present.[2]

This chapter offers an introduction to the use of trauma as a lens for reading biblical texts. It sets out, first, reasons why the historical background to the writing of those texts makes trauma theory a helpful and appropriate lens, before exploring the difference that reading through the lens of trauma makes when reading the Scriptures with those who have experienced trauma in their own lives. Finally, it poses some questions about the therapeutic value, and good pastoral practice, of reading the Bible with the traumatized.

How lonely sits the city[3]

One of the more helpful ways for twentieth-century Christians to begin to understand the impact upon the ancient Israelites of the violent destruction of Jerusalem, its temple and monarchy by Babylonian forces in the early sixth century BC is to meditate upon the impact of the attack on the Twin Towers in New York on 11 September 2001. We sensed pretty quickly, I think, that the impact was going to be significant, even if we couldn't predict the ways in which that impact would manifest itself. As I write, it has been 18 years since the attack and the world seems to have changed dramatically in that time. It would not be too great a stretch, I suspect, to count 9/11 as a contributing factor to the Trump/Johnson/

Brexit phenomenon. The only thing we can be sure of is that the impact of 9/11 has not yet fully played itself out in our world.

One of the reasons why 9/11 has had such an impact – greater by far than the impact of similar attacks in other places with greater loss of life – is that New York had always been presumed inviolable. Other places, other cities, might succumb to attack, but New York – capital of God's supposedly modern-day 'chosen nation' – was thought immune. A successful attack on the iconic city at the centre of the free world was 'unthinkable' – until it happened. New Yorkers, Americans, first-worlders, all had to readjust their understandings of vulnerability and the USA's place in the world. It may not be being too dramatic to suggest that the history of the modern West will come to be classified as pre- or post-9/11.

Hebrew Bible texts, meanwhile, are routinely classified as either pre- or post-'exile' (the mass removal of higher status and literate Israelites to Babylon that followed the destruction of Jerusalem) – while recognizing that some texts were probably composed in Babylon during the period of the exile itself. The compound crisis of the destruction of Jerusalem and the exile was, of course, only one of the disasters that struck Israel during the Old Testament period, but it was the most significant. Others include enslavement and exodus from Egypt (to the extent that these two things occurred as reported in Exodus), the Maccabean Revolt, and any number of other minor military encounters. The Ancient Near East was a violent place. The period immediately following the destruction of Jerusalem was, however, uniquely generative of literary output, and most Hebrew Bible scholars now recognize that much, if not most, of the Hebrew Bible was written, or substantially edited, following Jerusalem's fall (with a very substantial amount of that work being done following the return of the exiles to Jerusalem in the late sixth century).[4] Rainer Albertz wrote of this:

> It is common knowledge that times of crisis and radical historical change have often led writers to record the history of the preceding period to prevent its being forgotten. Israel's extraordinary will to survive is evidenced by its refusal to turn its back on its history even under circumstances so extreme that most nations would have disintegrated, even though that history seemed to be at a dead end: instead, they wrote it down.[5]

There are a number of parallels between the 9/11 attack and the destruction of Jerusalem, which could be likened to '9/11 on speed'. Stunned by an attack by forces from the east, Jerusalem – like New York with 9/11 – considered herself to be inviolable. The peoples of the southern kingdom,

Judah, had watched (slightly smugly, I like to think) while the northern kingdom, Israel, had succumbed to the superior might of the Assyrians, thinking something along the lines of 'we always knew those northerners would come to a bad end'. They also 'knew' that Judah would never suffer a similar fate – YHWH would continue to go out with their armies and would continue to ensure military victory for YHWH's chosen people and city. That Jerusalem should be taken shook every certainty that the Judahites held dear. How could this have happened, and what did it portend about the power and authority of YHWH and about Judah's status as the chosen nation? The shock of military defeat was compounded by the forced removal of the upper echelons of Judahite society to exile in Babylon and, then again, by the profound disappointment engendered by the longed-for eventual return to Jerusalem, permitted by Persian King Cyrus roughly 50 years later. Instead of the 'land of milk and honey' of the returners' memories, the returning exiles found a relatively small, dusty Jerusalem, still lacking walls, temple and a Davidic king. Worse still, the poorer and lower-skilled Jerusalemites, who had been left behind by the Babylonians, had colonized the returners' homes, land and businesses. In addition, disillusioned returnees were forced to face not only the indignities of Persian occupation, but a protracted and bitter identity struggle with the 'remainers' to be recognized as the 'true' Israel and children of Abraham.

It was against this bleak background that much of what we know as the Old Testament was composed. The flurry of composition catalysed by this situation was the locus in which the returned exiles worked out their new identity and theology, and forged a way forward for the chosen people of YHWH.

Unfortunately, much of this history was to be repeated shortly after the turn of the century. The year AD 70 saw Jerusalem sacked and the temple destroyed once again – this time at the hands of the Romans. Once again, disaster proved generative. New Testament scholars have reached something of a consensus that three of the Gospels, Matthew, Luke and John, were written in the aftermath of AD 70. Mark, meanwhile, is thought to have been written sometime in the previous decade, but none the less in the context of a period of protracted violence and (this time) impending doom.

The Gospels, unlike many of the post-destruction Hebrew Bible books, don't tell the story of the disaster. Whereas many of the prophetic books, the (so-called) Deuteronomistic History, Ezra and Nehemiah, and some of the wisdom books, explicitly narrate the disaster, attributing to it causes and meanings, the Gospels recount the words and deeds of Jesus of Nazareth and only very, very rarely give any hint of the historic context against which they were written. It is true, of course, that a large portion of the Gospels (like other forms of ancient biography)[6] recounts the violent and incomprehensible events of Jesus' death, and perhaps, in that recounting, outlets were found for the evangelists' emotions, stirred up by their own context, but neither those emotions – nor contemporary events – are reflected on the surface of the texts of the Gospels.

This is the case also for a number of Old Testament books. Genesis, for example, was very significantly edited following the return from exile,[7] but tells the story of a time long before, and only very rarely allows explicit reference to the conditions and religion of later times, including the times of the scribes who carried out the editing.[8] The mood of Genesis, for the most part, and certainly when compared to the other books of the Pentateuch, is eirenic,[9] yet under the surface of the text (in what Jonathan Sacks calls the 'counter-text')[10] the book responds to the events of the exile and resists both the Persian occupation and the dominant ideology and theology of the period.[11]

What all of this historical background points to is that very large amounts of our Scriptures, perhaps even most of them, were written in the context of, and as a consequence of, trauma. Sometimes, as in the prophetic books of Jeremiah and Ezekiel, for example, violence and trauma are readily apparent on the face of the text, while at other times and in other texts the impact of trauma upon the authors is veiled, and apparent only in subtle ways.

Trauma as lens

Elizabeth Boase and Christopher Frechette write, in the introduction to their landmark collection of essays on the use of trauma as a hermeneutical lens in biblical studies,[12] that three dominant disciplinary strands currently inform biblical trauma hermeneutics: psychology, sociology, and literary and cultural studies:

> Psychology contributes to our understanding of the effects of trauma on individuals and on those processes that facilitate survival, recovery and resilience. Sociology provides insights into collective dimensions of traumatic experience. Literary and cultural studies open pathways for exploring the role of texts as they encode and give witness to traumatic suffering and construct discursive and aesthetic spaces for fostering recovery and resilience.[13]

Perhaps inevitably, given the influence of these discrete bodies of scholarship, it is not possible to point to a single method of trauma hermeneutics; rather, Boase and Frechette identify a 'framework' for using trauma as a focus for the reading of biblical text, in which the insights from each of these disciplines inform one another. This 'framework' allows today's readers to gain fresh insights into the background of the text, and, in turn, to make new or richer meaning of the text itself. Some examples may serve to illustrate this. So, for example, an insight into the tendency of traumatic experience to overwhelm the psychological capacities of individuals, which might cause a traumatic event to fail to be integrated into an individual's memory but to be stored instead as jagged fragments in the body,[14] helps to explain why some of the more violent prophetic material, for example, lacks coherent narrative but is instead characterized by gaps. Boase and Frechette argue that an appreciation of the impact of trauma can help the reader to fill in some of these gaps.[15] On another front, an appreciation of the impact of collective trauma can assist the reader to identify, in the text, how the adoption of a 'chosen trauma' influences both further events and the manner of their reporting.[16] Alternatively, the same background knowledge may assist the reader to identify those features of the text that point to literary strategies of survival, resilience and meaning making.[17]

The employment of trauma theory as lens, then, can enrich understanding of the world behind the text, and of the world of the text itself, but what of the world in front of the text – the world that the reader herself brings to her reading? An appreciation of the impact of trauma upon the history of our Scriptures may impact both how a trauma survivor reads biblical texts, and how ministers of religion, pastoral carers, therapists, spiritual directors, family and friends approach biblical texts with survivors of trauma. When it is recognized that nearly all of us are survivors of trauma to one degree or another, this means that using trauma as a lens can unlock gifts, and help to avoid traps, in the reading of biblical texts in a quite significant manner.

Elsewhere, writing for a volume about trauma and practical theology that I edited with other members of the 'Tragedy and Congregations' project, Christopher Southgate, Carla Grosch-Miller and Hilary Ison,[18] I have asked the question 'What difference does it make to recognize that our Scriptures are informed by trauma?' I suggested four specific differences for readers. First, I suggested that it means that readers can have confidence that biblical stories are robust:

> The biblical books are not in any sense trite or fragile. They come out of
> the experience of individuals and communities who have gone through

the most painful and violent experiences that life can throw at human beings. They are written against a background of famines, wars, enslavement, political power struggles, natural disasters, forced migrations and apparent betrayal and desertion by God. The irreverent tags that we sometimes attach to the Bible – 'nice', 'conservative', 'boring' and 'irrelevant' – even when we don't mean to ... are mostly unwarranted and inaccurate. When understood against its own contexts the Bible is none of these things. It has street cred. It understands suffering. And that means that the biblical stories, letters, poetry etc. that make up the Bible are resources for ministering in the context of trauma in which we can have confidence. When read, sung, enacted, performed or prayed with sensitivity and imagination these biblical writings can be the most profound resource for ministry with traumatised people and congregations. They meet traumatised people where they are.[19]

Second, I argued that reading the Bible through the lens of trauma lets us know that we are not alone:

When we read biblical stories we know that ... our trials and tribulations are not unique. As unimaginable as some of today's disasters may seem, God's people lived through comparable experiences during the biblical period and we have their stories. We can therefore read for the 'company' of others who understand the depth of the pain of our experience. We find this 'company' not only with the biblical characters whose stories are told in the text, but also with the generations of Jews and Christians who have read and studied and taken solace from those stories over two millennia or more. Even if we may be physically, emotionally or spiritually isolated in our own lives, reading these stories tells us that we are not unique, but that our individual story can be situated within a rich and thick history of the experience of God's people, all of whom are 'with' us through relationship with the text.[20]

Third, I suggested that the Bible offers us what I called 'a language and a literature of suffering':

First, the Bible offers language to those who have no words. British OT scholar John Goldingay describes the psalms as '150 things that God doesn't mind having said to him'.[21] When there are no words the psalms can step in and fill the gap.[22] ... Secondly, the Bible offers a literature to those who have no stories. I suggested above that trying to live without stories can be excruciating, and that trauma can make story-telling difficult or impossible. Here is a set of stories (robust, pre-loved and

authorized) that can become our own stories and function as a foundation for our identity building, even after the most disorienting and
destructive experiences.[23]

Finally, I suggested that the Bible models resilience:

Story-telling is an important element of building resilience. Specifically,
what is important for resilience is preparedness to be flexible in the
telling of one's story, allowing it to shift and develop with changing
experiences. If you've lived through an experience of suffering, ...
you may have found that the story you told about yourself before the
experience was not one you could tell afterwards. Perhaps the story
didn't allow space to acknowledge the reality or pain of the experience
of suffering, or you might have felt that you were a completely different
person afterwards, so that your early stories no longer fit you ... Hospital
chaplains tell me that their ministry is all about encouraging and helping people to tell their story in a new way – a way that takes account of
illness and suffering as well as wellness, but that also sees a way ahead
to some form of peacefulness and acceptance of what the present is and
what the future may or may not bring.[24] This re-telling of one's story
needn't involve dramatic change. It is best when the resulting story
resembles a tapestry or carpet, into which new experiences are woven,
influencing the colour and pattern of the whole, but without making
it an entirely new carpet ... One of the ironies of Christian attempts
today to 'follow the Bible' and to do what 'it' says, is a tendency to
overlook the Bible's own inner-processes of development and revision,
which ensured that the revelation of YHWH to the Israelites continued
to speak to successive generations. The Bible is profitably understood as
modelling, across its various books and genres, a practice of re-telling
that has proven remarkably resilient.[25]

Reading with survivors of trauma

This book is focused on the Scriptures and mental illness, and so it may
be helpful to explore more closely some of the particular gifts of reading
the Scriptures through the lens of trauma with trauma survivors, as well
as some of the pitfalls to be avoided.

In addition to the gifts of the Scriptures already outlined (very) briefly
above, trauma survivors may benefit particularly from exposure to the
tradition of 'lament' that underlies a good deal of the Old Testament
'writings' in particular, and that has been largely lost by Western socie-

ties and even by Western churches. Notable texts in this regard are the lament psalms (which comprise the largest single genre group among the psalms) and Lamentations itself. Scholars of the impact of trauma on congregations argue that the sign of a congregation that has recovered (to the extent that recovery is possible) from the trauma caused by a disaster that it has suffered is the ability to say 'this happened to us – *and* there is still good in the world'. Both elements of this sentiment are important.

'This happened to us'

One of the features of trauma response is an inability to comprehend the disastrous event that caused it, or to incorporate the disaster into one's senses of reality and identity, or even to acknowledge it at all. This is the body's self-preservation response to the 'overwhelm' caused by the disaster, and it comes into play in both individuals and groups. This element of trauma response tends to be magnified in cultures that frown upon what they deem to be excessive displays of emotion – as in England, for example, where the pressure to 'carry on' and keep a 'stiff upper lip' has the effect of discouraging public, and even private, displays of anger, rage and grief. Acknowledgement of disaster, and full expression of its associated emotions, is necessary – but often difficult in a country such as England. Further, writers about lament routinely lament (sorry!) that churches are often very bad at acknowledging painful events.[26] In some Anglo-Saxon church traditions, in particular,[27] it is common to choose not to 'interrupt' liturgy by alluding either to internal or external disasters, but instead to paper over the awkwardness with praise songs and inspirational preaching. Similarly, most of us have been to excruciating funerals at which any mention of the less edifying elements of the deceased's life, or manner of death, is resolutely avoided. This tendency is beautifully summed up by Kathleen Norris in a short poem in which she observes that our response to Jesus having nails pounded into his hands has been to wear hats to church.[28]

One of the real needs of the trauma survivor is authenticity – in their own speech, in their actions, and in their surroundings. Trauma survivors need (to get to) a place where they can know and speak their own truths, however difficult. Lament is a way of combining authentic speech with resistance against the system or circumstances that caused the injury.[29]

'... and there is still good in the world'

Recovery from trauma tends to be characterized by an ability to hold together the disastrous experience and hope for the future. During the worst periods following a disaster, survivors may be so consumed by their reaction that they may be entirely unable to countenance or picture a future that includes elements of joy or hopefulness. Ironically, in the first few days after a major disaster, the period that scholars term 'the heroic phase', survivors may be supernaturally buoyed up by a combination of adrenaline, shock and thankfulness to those who rally round to offer comfort and support. This period cannot be maintained for long, however, and after a major disaster disillusionment inevitably sets in, for a period of weeks, months or years. During this period there may be flashes of joy or hopefulness, but not in a sustainable way. The survivors of a major trauma know that they are reaching the end of this 'disillusionment phase' when they can begin to hold the reality of what has happened together with a sense that life can also contain goodness.

Although survivors can be assisted in their recovery by the support of warm, compassionate, 'less-anxious' others, there is nothing that anybody can do to 'speed up' the process. Recovery is an organic process, and a person, or group, cannot be cajoled or managed into recovery, and any attempt to do so will be counterproductive. Laurie Kraus, David Holyan and Bruce Widmer write that in a congregational context the disillusionment period can usefully be termed 'the valley of the shadow of death'.[30] The only way through the valley, they maintain, is *through* it. As frustrating as it might be for well-meaning others, the best physician for a traumatized person is the traumatized person themselves.

The gifts and the dangers of biblical lament

In the light of all of this, the gifts of the psalms, and other biblical laments including those in Lamentations, are remarkable. The practice of lament offers to the traumatized person (or group) agency, outlet, witness and escape from the identity of victimhood. The biblical laments, found particularly in the psalms, offer still more. Here is a collection of 150 unexpurgated, often satisfyingly unedifying, *authorized* things with which God doesn't mind being door-stepped. The psalms assure us that letting our upper lip droop, or curl, and letting God *have it* is not like failing to wear a hat to church – rather, it is quintessentially faithful because it proceeds from the understanding that God is *the* place where such anguish should be taken, *and* that God can take it.

For the trauma survivor lacking the language or the narrative to tell their own story and speak their own emotions, what's more, the psalms (which have a tendency to be helpfully vague)[31] provide the language, the story and the emotions that may be needed in order to express the inexpressible.[32] They also provide the other thing most needed by the survivor of trauma – a witness to their suffering. Gabor Maté suggests that '[t]rauma is not what happens to us, but what we hold inside in the absence of an empathetic witness'.[33] This need is expressed clearly in Lamentations 5, in which the men of the city plead with God to 'see' them and to witness their predicament.[34] For the individual, railing at God in the privacy of their room, the witness is God. For those who lament in the context of congregations, or in small groups, the witnesses include those others present. A number of writers on lament recommend small group practice in particular, suggesting that a small number of group members provides the ideal balance between being witnessed and being able to build and develop strong relationships through the practice.[35]

One further element of biblical laments further fits them for use with and by traumatized people. Biblical laments typically hold together acknowledgement of injury (and its accompanying emotions) with a sense of hope, trust or praise. Very often lament psalms, for example, move towards expressions of these – usually, although not always, at their end.[36] Sometimes these movements from despair to hopefulness happen quite abruptly (Psalm 13 is a good example), so that scholars have long puzzled over the general pattern by which lament psalms move towards hopefulness, or expressions of faith or trust in God, and have suggested possible explanations for the phenomenon. There have been many such explanations, but those currently attracting the most support offer a psychological explanation for the shift: the very act of praying the words of the psalm, before witnesses, these explanations suggest, causes an emotional shift in the pray-er, so that by the end of the psalm the person has genuinely moved to a place in which hopefulness, trust or praise feel right.[37] Certainly, people today who pray with the psalms report experiencing shifts of this kind, or suggest that the sometimes jumbled presence of hope and despair in many of the psalms matches their own inner state, as well as helping to reshape it. Similarly, those who undertake the exercise of composing their own psalms according to the pattern of the biblical laments sometimes report the experience to be life-changing.[38]

The gifts of the biblical laments, then, are rich indeed for the person who has undergone a traumatic experience.[39] However, the gifts do not come without the need for caution. The presence within most of the lament psalms of elements of joy and hopefulness (Psalm 88 being a gloriously and relentlessly miserable exception) means that use of the lament psalms with traumatized people should be undertaken with care. Just as a person cannot be cajoled from the 'disillusionment stage' too early without suffering further damage, so a traumatized person should not be expected to speak words of hopefulness or trust in God before he or she is ready. To push somebody too quickly into expressions of positivity and well-being could be the cause of re-traumatization.[40] Once again, the traumatized person themselves will be the best judge of their own readiness. A helpful practice might perhaps be to work with a single lament psalm, encouraging the person to engage with only as much of the psalm as seems appropriate at any given time, and working up to an expression of all the elements of the psalm only when to do so feels right.

A similar note of caution may be sounded with respect to the subject matter of the various psalmists' complaints. Some of the more violent or bleak psalms may in fact be unhelpful, and cause further traumatization. As always, the traumatized person – unpressured – will be their own best guide in this.

Finally, it is to be hoped that it goes without saying that 'pastoral' approaches should, wherever possible, avoid commending to the traumatized person biblical passages that highlight theologies of punishment, so as to suggest that the person brought the disaster upon themselves. If it is the case that the traumatized person themselves has a personal theology of divine punishment and retribution for human wrongdoing, this should be respected where possible and gently challenged only when the person clearly has the capacity for this. One of the effects of trauma is the shattering of previously held assumptions and certainties. A traumatized person will not be helped by the well-intentioned dismantling of yet more aspects of their world, even if those aspects might be judged to be less than ideal by others.

Conclusion

Our world, of course, is not unique in being prone to disasters small and large, and nor was the world of the biblical writers. Recent scholarship has shown us the extent to which disaster, and the responses of trauma caused by it, has shaped our Scriptures. This new understanding of the background to biblical texts makes them especially rich for readers today who live with some degree of trauma response – that is, all of us. For those ministering with, or caring for, the survivors of traumatic events the Scriptures are a valuable resource, albeit one that is best approached with care.

Notes

1 Some identify a 1974 essay about the lament tradition in the Old Testament by Claus Westermann as the beginning of the scholarship in this field: 'The Role of Lament in the Theology of the Old Testament', *Interpretation*, 28, pp. 20–38.

2 The scholarly literature on this topic is growing at an impressive rate. See, in particular, E. Boase and C. Frechette, 2016, *Bible through the Lens of Trauma*, Semeia Studies 86, Atlanta, GA: SBL Press; D. M. Carr, 2014, *Holy Resilience: The Bible's Traumatic Origins*, New Haven, CT: Yale University Press; M. G. Brett, 2016, *Political Trauma and Healing: Biblical Ethics for a Postcolonial World*, Grand Rapids, MI: Eerdmans; K. Erikson, 1994, *A New Species of Trouble: Explorations in Disaster, Trauma, and Community*, New York: Norton; J. Kauffman (ed.), 2002, *Loss of the Assumptive World: A Theory of Traumatic Loss*, New York: Brunner-Routledge. This work is essentially inter-disciplinary in nature, and although the application of trauma theory to biblical interpretation owes its greatest debts to the fields of psychology, sociology and literary theory, other fields of study have also been influential.

3 Lam. 1.1.

4 See, for example, the schemas of K. Schmid, 2012, *The Old Testament: A Literary History*, Minneapolis, MN: Fortress Press; D. M. Carr, 2011, *The Formation of the Hebrew Bible: A New Construction*, New York: Oxford University Press.

5 R. Albertz, 2004, *Israel in Exile: the History and Literature of the Sixth Century B.C.E.*, Leiden/Boston, MA: Brill, p. 273.

6 R. A. Burridge, 2018, *What Are the Gospels?*, 3rd edn, Waco, TX: Baylor University.

7 M. Warner, 2018, *Re-Imagining Abraham: A Re-Assessment of the Influence of Deuteronomism in Genesis*, Old Testament Studies 72; Leiden/Boston: Brill.

8 Genesis 26.5 is a parade example of a rare case in which the language and forms of a later time are permitted to enter the text. The description of Abraham as Torah-observant, at a time (in the story world) before the Torah had been handed down to Moses is a famous crux. See my discussion in Warner, *Re-Imagining Abraham*, pp. 65–76.

9 N. Habel, 1995, *The Land is Mine: Six Biblical Land Ideologies*, Minneapolis, MN: Fortress Press, pp. 115–33, 146.

10 J. Sacks, 2015, *Not in God's Name: Confronting Religious Violence*, London: Hodder and Stoughton.

11 M. G. Brett, 2000, *Genesis: Procreation and the Politics of Identity*, London: Routledge; Warner, *Re-Imagining Abraham*.

12 Boase and Frechette, *Bible through the Lens of Trauma*.

13 Boase and Frechette, *Bible through the Lens of Trauma*, p. 4.

14 See, generally, on the effects of trauma in the individual, B. Van der Kolk, 2014, *The Body Keeps the Score: Brain, Mind and Body in the Healing of Trauma*, New York: Viking; P. A. Levine, 1997, *Waking the Tiger: Healing Trauma*, Berkeley, CA: North Atlantic; P. A. Levine, 2010, *In an Unspoken Voice: How the Body Releases Trauma and Restores Goodness*, Berkeley, CA: North Atlantic.

15 Boase and Frechette, *Bible through the Lens of Trauma*, p. 11.

16 See, for example, Erikson, *A New Species*; V. Volkan, 2004, *Blind Trust: Large Groups and their Leaders in Times of Crisis and Terror*, Charlottesville, VA: Pitchstone; V. Volkan, 1998, *Bloodlines: From Ethnic Pride to Ethnic Terrorism*, Boulder, CO: Westview.

17 See, for example, Kauffman, *Loss of the Assumptive World*; C. L. Park, 2010, 'Making Sense of the Meaning Literature: An Integrative Review of Meaning Making and its Effects on Adjustment to Stressful Life Events', *Psychological Bulletin*, 136, pp. 257–301; M. Warner, 2019, *Joseph: A Story of Resilience*, London: SPCK.

18 M. Warner, 2020, 'Trauma through the Lens of the Bible', in Megan Warner and colleagues (eds), *Tragedies and Christian Congregations: The Practical Theology of Trauma*, London/New York: Routledge, pp. 81–91. The project website can be found at http://tragedyandcongregations.org.uk. It contains details and news about the project, an occasional blog and helpful links, as well as an extensive bibliography of trauma resources.

19 Warner, 'Trauma through the Lens', pp. 83–4.

20 Warner, 'Trauma through the Lens', pp. 85.

21 Goldingay reportedly does not recall having said this. Generations of his students, however, witness to the fact that he did. For an account of Goldingay's personal and academic journey with the psalms, see J. Goldingay, 1996, *After Eating the Apricot: (Inside Out Meditation)*, Carlisle: Solway.

22 According to Westermann, in 'Role of Lament', p. 31, 'The lament is the language of suffering; in it suffering is given the dignity of language: it will not stay silent!'

23 Warner, 'Trauma through the Lens', pp. 87–8.

24 Helpful in this regard is the work of gerontologist, W. L. Randall concerning the therapeutic application of narrative in ageing. See, for example, W. L. Randall, 2013, 'The Importance of Being Ironic: Narrative Openness and Personal Resilience in Later Life', *The Gerontologist*, 53, pp. 9–16, 14.

25 Warner, 'Trauma through the Lens, pp. 89–91.

26 See the examples recounted in my essay, 'Teach to Your Daughters a Dirge: Revisiting the Practice of Lament in the Light of Trauma Theory', in Warner and colleagues, *Tragedies*, pp. 167–81; and especially J. Swinton, 2007, *Raging With Compassion: Pastoral Responses to the Problem of Evil*, Grand Rapids, MI: Eerdmans, pp. 90–129; D. E. Saliers, 'Psalms in Our Lamentable World', *Yale Journal of Music and Religion*, 1(1), Art. 7, p. 104, https://doi.org/10.17132/2377-231X.1013; D. M. Ackermann, 2003, *After the Locusts: Letters from a Landscape of Faith*, Grand Rapids, MI: Eerdmans, p. 108; K. D. Billman and D. L. Migliore, 1999, *Rachel's Cry: Prayer of Lament and Rebirth of Hope*, Eugene, OR: Wipf & Stock.

27 See the exploration of responses to trauma in black-led congregations in Britain by D. Garner, in 'Responding to Disaster in an Afro-Caribbean Congregation' in Warner and colleagues, *Tragedies*, pp. 134–46, for a different outlook.

28 K. Norris, 1996, *The Cloister Walk*, New York: Riverhead, p. 107.

29 Swinton, *Raging*, pp. 90–129.

30 L. Krause, D. Holyan and B. Widmer, 2017, 'Post-Traumatic Ministry: Pastoral Responses in the Aftermath of Violence', *Christian Century*, 29 March, pp. 22–5, 23. See also the discussion in Warner, 'Teach to Your Daughters', pp. 176–8.

31 H. G. M. Williamson, for example, writes, 'the language is such that it is capable of serving to articulate an almost infinite number of such experiences, and this no doubt accounts for the enduring value that is set upon them' (see H. G. M. Williamson, 2003, 'Reading the Lament Psalms Backwards', in B. A. Strawn and

N. R. Bowen (eds), *A God So Near: Essays on Old Testament Theology in Honor of Patrick D. Miller*, Winona Lake, IN: Eisenbrauns, pp. 3–16, 4).

32 Brent Strawn, 'Trauma, Psalmic Disclosure, and Authentic Happiness', in Boase and Frechette, *Bible Through the Lens of Trauma*, pp. 143–60, 144–9, argues strongly that disclosure (of whatever kind) of traumatic experience acts to counterbalance and redress the negative health impacts of non-verbalization or inhibition of traumatic experience. Note, however, that the emphasis on verbal expression of traumatic experience that used to be apparent in earlier writing about trauma recovery has now been discredited to some degree, with the focus on the corporeal nature of trauma response now suggesting that approaches to recovery that begin with attention to the body are more likely to be successful, with less danger of re-traumatization. See, for example, K. O'Donnell, 'Eucharist and Trauma: Healing in the Body', in Warner and colleagues, *Tragedies*, pp. 182–93.

33 G. Maté, Foreword, in Levine, *Unspoken Voice*, p. xii; S. Rambo, 2010, *Spirit and Trauma: A Theology of Remaining*, Louisville, KY: Westminster John Knox; S. Rambo, 2017, *Resurrecting Wounds: Living in the Afterlife of Trauma*, Waco, TX: Baylor University Press, Rambo also writes of the therapeutic importance of witnesses to the expression of trauma-related emotions. For example, in the discussion of the power of the 'healing circle', she writes, 'It is not just that one's "hurt" recognizes the hurt in another, but that the collective attunement to pain forges routes of healing that did not previously exist' (*Resurrecting Wounds*, p. 130).

34 See, for example, the discussion in K. M. O'Connor, 2002, *Lamentations and the Tears of the World*, Maryknoll, NY: Orbis Books, pp. 70–82.

35 Swinton, *Raging with Compassion*, pp. 121–8, esp. pp. 122–5; D. M. Ackermann, 1998, '"A Voice Was Heard in Ramah": A Feminist Theology of Praxis for Healing in South Africa', in D. M. Ackermann and M. Bons-Storm (eds), 1998, *Liberating Faith Practices: Feminist Practical Theologies in Context*, Leuven: Peeters.

36 Many scholars consider a final expression of praise of God and/or hope that God will answer the petition to be an essential, or universal, element of psalms of lament (both individual and corporate). Walter Brueggemann, 1985, in *The Message of the Psalms: A Theological Commentary*, Minneapolis, MN: Fortress Press, pp. 54–6, takes the view that lament always turns to praise. J. Swinton, in *Raging*, pp. 105 and 122, shares this view: 'Lament provides us with a language of outrage that speaks against the way things are, but always in the hope that the way things are just now is not the way they will always be. Lament is thus profoundly hopeful.' He goes on to assert that '[s]uch a return to God in faith and hope is really the only resolution that Scripture gives to the problem of evil'. However, Frederico G. Villanueva, 2008, in *The Uncertainty of a Hearing: A Study of the Sudden Change of Mood in the Psalms of Lament*, Vetus Testamentum, Supplement 121; Leiden: Brill, puts the case strongly that the movement towards hope is not found uniformly in the lament psalms.

37 See, for example, E. S. Gerstenberger, 1980, 'Der bittende Mensch', *Wissenschaftliche Monographien zum Alten und Neuen Testament*, 51, Neukirchen-Vluyn: Neukirchener, pp. 163–9.

38 Swinton, in *Raging*, pp. 128–9, sets out some guidelines for undertaking this exercise.

39 See generally, Strawn, 'Trauma, "Psalmic Disclosure and Authentic Happiness"'.

40 See, particularly, Krause and colleagues, 'Post-Traumatic Ministry', pp. 22–5.

15

Christian Scripture as a Pastoral Resource for Promoting Resilience

NATHAN WHITE

Introduction

Before recounting the narratives of seminal scriptural exemplars the author of Hebrews introduces their stories with the iconic description, 'Now faith is the assurance of things hoped for, the conviction of things not seen' (11.1). He concludes this survey with the summary, 'Yet all these, though they were commended for their faith, did not receive what was promised' (11.39). These phrases bracket the author's depiction of victorious (and faithful) service to God, but how should the author's assessment be regarded? From an earthly perspective, these individuals were anything but successful; they died 'in-between' promise and fulfilment. From another perspective, however, these individuals might be described as 'resilient' in their faith – those who remained faithful despite significant adversity.

Certainly, a degree of resilience must characterize current Christian existence in this world. This 'resilience' entails holding the tension between present hope and future glory; in other words, the realm of faith is the realm of resilience.[1] It encompasses the struggle to remain faithful to God despite the deceits of the world, the flesh, and the devil (Eph. 2.1–3). But any consideration of resilience in relation to Christian faith also raises questions such as, 'How do Christians remain faithful in this quest and help others to do so as well?' and 'What does it mean to be successful in faith?' These are not merely theoretical considerations but rather are of vital pastoral import, especially given many recent societal trends[2] and the continuing challenge of remaining faithful to Christ in new and changing contexts. Moreover, these are all the more important given that research indicates that spirituality and religion can have a significant effect upon mental health resilience outcomes.[3]

Still, it is not always clear why religious resources, such as the Christian Scriptures, may prove beneficial for promoting human resilience to adversity. Further examination is therefore needed to assess why the Scriptures may be considered as engendering resilience rather than detracting from it.

Defining resilience

The beginnings of the term lie in the antecedent Latin term, *resilire*, but contemporary use largely derives from the scientific description of the capacity of physical materials to bear heavy loads without breaking.[4] By metaphorical extension, scholars, practitioners and the public have increasingly utilized the term 'resilience' to describe the ability of individuals, systems and materials (among many other things) to 'bounce back' from stressors.[5] The breadth of this transdisciplinary shift is evident in the exponential growth of the term in published academic literature – increasing eightfold in 20 years.[6] Such wide use makes denoting the contours of the concept difficult.

Many definitions of resilience exist, displaying a variety of emphases with distinct applications in particular fields and/or distinct understandings of the concept. For our purposes, resilience may be understood as the 'process of harnessing biological, psychosocial, structural and cultural resources to sustain well-being'.[7] We may identify several key elements of the concept, including: '(i) confrontation of significant adversity or risk; (ii) use of internal and external resources to adapt despite adversity; and (iii) a positive outcome'.[8] Particular conceptions of each of these aspects delimit and shape understandings of the concept in ways significant for praxis, but also in ways pointedly influenced by cultural currents.

Research indicates that human resilience is influenced about equally by genetic and environmental factors.[9] This suggests that resilience outcomes may be affected by interventions focused on changeable personal, environmental and societal factors. As one such category of factors, a growing body of research indicates that religion and spirituality (including resources from these sources such as Scripture) may aid in promoting resilience, as well as in engendering health more broadly.[10]

How might Scripture and 'resilience' intersect, then? The answer is not straightforward. The word 'resilience' does not appear in major English language translations of the Bible. This is not surprising since the term is quite new in broad usage, especially in relation to human action. There are, however, conceptual and linguistic parallels to the term in the original Greek and Hebrew biblical texts.[11] Full analysis of these lie beyond the scope of the present chapter, but it must be noted that there is no one-to-one correspondence of the modern concept of 'resilience' to any specific term or concept in the biblical canon. Metaphorical and linguistic reasoning is therefore necessary to relate biblical texts to modern conceptions of resilience.

Scripture, resilience and mental health

That the word 'resilience' does not appear in the Bible does not mean that Scripture has no relevance to discussions regarding human resilience to adversity. By affording insight into human beings – including their origin, purpose and worth – the Bible implicitly informs how we should understand resilience and mental health more generally. Some scholars and practitioners have begun to assess the Scriptures through the lens of trauma and of resilience.[12] More reflection is needed, however, regarding the pastoral possibilities of the Bible to shape resilience outcomes.

Encouragement to persevere

Many encouragements found within the pages of Scripture could be regarded as exhortations to resilience.[13] While these encouragements were addressed to specific individuals or communities within a particular context, many people throughout the centuries have found comfort and support through these words as the Holy Spirit applies the truth of Scripture in new contexts. Significant for a proper understanding of resilience, rather than being a call to 'pull oneself up by your bootstraps', these exhortations are predicated upon divine empowerment.[14]

Many biblical encouragements are to groups of believers and not simply to individuals. This highlights the importance of communal encouragement in supporting resilient adaptation. In view of this, the communal reading of Scripture in corporate worship can be a powerful tool to support both individual and corporate resilience, especially in the wake of a significant event such as a community tragedy or disaster.

Testimony of struggle

Parts of Scripture are also a testament to the complexity of human trauma and attempts at recovery – a kind of repository of sacred memory from the lives of past believers. These scriptural records do not allow, in the end, easy 'pat' answers to the intractable problem of human suffering, but rather suggest possible approaches to healing that preserve the mystery of human free will, evil and divine goodness.

Many Scriptures are records of the struggle of the faithful amid adversity.[15] At times these could be regarded as testimonies of resilience, and at others chronicles during struggle. These Scriptures can offer words to those whose painful experiences lead them to feel that they have none to give voice to their experiences. They may frame and provide a scaffolding for expressing – and, in some measure, understanding – experiences of adversity. These 'snapshots' of resilient adaptation found in Scripture are vital to a Christian vision of resilience because they display that resilience is not simply an *outcome*, but rather is inherently a *process*. Throughout most of life we do not live 'on the mountaintop', but rather somewhere on the journey between the mountaintop and the valley. When too much focus is placed on resilience as an outcome, individuals can begin to believe that they are not resilient if they do not immediately achieve a hoped-for outcome. Yet, as Hebrews 11 portrays, most of the faithful in Scripture did not see the hoped-for outcome of their faith; instead they died, still believing (resiliently) without fully experiencing the *outcome* of resilience. This ought to suggest a reshaping of who is considered 'resilient' or 'un-resilient'. Resilience may not always look like resilience (as popularly conceived), but rather may look more like the process of struggle along the path to a finally positive outcome in the context of eternity.

The psalms, in particular, can serve as a catalyst for understanding the *process* of resilience that often may include lament over loss, processing expectations and hopes with God in prayer, and giving thanks amid pain and loss.[16]

Depiction of exemplars

Scripture provides a range of exemplars who help clarify conceptions of resilience, both through positive and negative example. These exemplars can encourage resilient adaption in readers of Scripture today through opening realms of possibility beyond the reader's present vision.[17] Think, for instance, of Abraham and his belief in the faithfulness of God despite not having an heir; of Jacob and his wily but ultimately futile schemes; of Moses and his early political success turning into years of waiting in the desert; of Ruth and her faithfulness to family even when it cost her everything; of David and his later years dealing with the consequences of his sin; of Jeremiah and the hope of the exilic community; of Daniel's faithfulness to God despite persecution; of Mary seeing her son tortured and crucified; of Paul's preaching despite persecution; of the resilient growth of the early Church; of Jesus and the counterintuitive resilience of the cross.[18]

Some care is needed in the use of exemplars since God is not obligated to work in the lives of any two people in the same way, and there are also the unique contexts and callings of biblical characters. Still, the stories of exemplars can reveal the character of the God who is the 'same yesterday and today and forever' (Heb. 13.8), encouraging readers to respond in appropriate and faith-filled ways to the work of God in their lives by providing a vision of others who have also traversed difficulty.[19] The Scriptures invite readers, for instance, to believe that the God who was faithful to Moses during his 40 years in the desert will be faithful to them in their times of distress, though the particular circumstances and outcomes will invariably be different.

Vision of hope

Further, the Bible projects a vision wherein individuals may view their lives, including suffering, as part of a larger story that provides meaning and hope that go far beyond temporary circumstances. The Scriptures raise the reader's sights above time-bound contingent circumstances to heavenly realities and the larger narrative of God's salvation history which situate our smaller narratives within the framework of God's work in the world.

Significant in this respect, Scripture presents God's unfailing love[20] not as an abstract concept, but rather as an ever-present reality that has continuing implications for particular human lives. The promises of God in Scripture elicit hope that the current broken world is not the ultimate reality; adversity will occur but it does not have the final word.[21] Thus, readers of Scripture are challenged to believe the promises of God on their behalf, displaying a new horizon of possibility in their lives and in the world.[22] As they do so, they find that this shapes their core identities.

Invitation to a new identity

Scripture – as an exhortation to perseverance, a repository of individual and communal religious memory, a storehouse of exemplars, and a vision of hope – shapes Christian self-identity in fundamental ways. In particular, a source of resilience may be found in the encouragement within Scripture towards a new identity in relation to God as those redeemed in Christ. In this view, Scripture as a whole suggests a vision of redeemed humanity in which the Christian is formed in relation to God as one who is 'in Christ' (ἐν Χριστός)[23] with an identity rooted in the permanence of heavenly realities.[24] This identity is described in a number of different ways including the Christian as a 'new creation'(2 Cor. 5.17), as the beloved of God (Col. 3.12), as a child of God (1 John 3.1), as a recipient of every heavenly blessing (Eph. 1.3), as one who overcomes evil (1 John 5.4), and more. Each of these truths shapes individual and communal identity in particular ways that may be significant for resilient adaptation.

Prophetic reshaping

By viewing one's life in relation to the identity and narrative projected by Scripture, a new type of 'storytelling' reframes one's self-understanding of personal history in ways significant for resilience.[25] A part of this reframing requires deeper engagement with Scripture's prophetic challenge to conceptions of human flourishing, including the *telos* of resilience. Any engagement with the God of the Christian Scriptures, who is a consuming fire (Heb. 12.29), might mean that shallow conceptions of human happiness, well-being or good may be challenged in order to make way for the in-breaking of God's kingdom which constitutes the true *telos* of human existence.[26] The stream of revelatory, prophetic and wisdom literature in Scripture often challenges human visions that are too limited and shortsighted.

Significantly, such prophetic engagement showcases that resilience ultimately (in terms of the true *telos* of human flourishing in the kingdom of God) is secured by God alone. Further, this re-imagined resilience is not at odds with, and indeed must coexist with, human suffering. Such assumptions should shape implicit expectations regarding resilience to acknowledge that trials and difficulty are an inherent part of fallen human existence rather than an aberration.[27] Yet because God is the author and guarantor of ultimate human flourishing (and therefore also of resilience towards this *telos*), earthly flourishing and resources are not the final standard by which to judge resilience.[28]

Case study

The pastoral use of the Scriptures in the promotion of resilience may seem beneficial in the abstract, but the practical utility of such an approach remains to be demonstrated. More study is necessary to determine the extent of the benefit of this approach, but some initial suggestions are possible. To this end, I offer here a reflection on my own experiences. I provide it not as a type of prooftext but rather as an exploration of one individual's experience and, further, as a means of describing the genesis of many of the above reflections.

My own exploration of resilience stems in large part from my experience of being wounded in combat while serving as a chaplain for US Army personnel on deployment in Afghanistan. In the multi-year recovery from the wounds that I sustained, I found Scripture to be a guide, a comfort and a challenge. Beyond particular instances of inspiration or comfort afforded by reading the Scriptures, I discovered that my recovery and outlook upon life were shaped by an identity formed through Scripture. The Bible did not always provide a 'quick fix' or 'silver bullet' for my, at times, discouragement or perceived lack of 'resilience', though there were certainly instances when God seemed to bring the right Scripture to mind at the right time. More often than not, however, what I needed was not a scriptural 'soundbite' of encouragement, but rather to get on with the work of recovery – doing the next thing in front of me, assured of God's continued goodness to me even amid circumstances that could lead me to believe otherwise. This 'resilience' was undergirded by the secure identity already formed in me through years of studying and 'putting myself under' the Scriptures and the God to whom they attest.

Similarly, pastoral use of Scriptures for the sake of promoting resilience should be utilized in a holistic manner with consideration for long-term formation. This use should not be limited to 'crisis Scripture interventions', but rather more fundamentally should shape individuals and communities to view the world and live in it in renewed and resilience-enhancing ways. Further, the pastoral use of Scripture must not reductionistically devolve into a utilitarian input/output strategy. Scripture cannot be merely a means to an end – even a beneficial end such as health.[29]

A renewed vision

The Scriptures challenge modern understandings of resilience that regard the concept primarily as an encouragement towards human self-actualization. Instead, a biblical view of resilience suggests that the concept should be grounded in a dialectical tension between the realities of human finitude/frailty and well-being/strength.[30] This dialectic is implicit within one of Scripture's most enigmatic descriptions of the Christian life: what Paul describes as 'this mystery, which is Christ in you, the hope of glory' (Col. 1.27). Here the dialectic between present experience and future fulfilment is rightly described as a mystery – one that is at the heart of the 'already but not yet' kingdom of God.[31] The present reality of life in a broken and sinful world is none the less, for the believer, a reality that is indwelt by God – 'Christ in you' – yet this reality is not the fullness of the promise, thus hope is needed. Glory awaits the Christian as the *telos* of human existence, but this end will not be reached in this life. Human existence, therefore, is necessarily one characterized by 'restless resilience'[32] that ultimately, for the Christian, is aimed not primarily at temporal flourishing, but rather at a resilience judged in the context of eternity whose outcome is guaranteed by God alone.

The time 'in-between' the inauguration of the kingdom of God and its complete fulfilment is the realm of resilience – a resilience that would be impossible apart from God's sustaining of this good but fallen world, but that will be unnecessary when the full instantiation of God's grace occurs. It is to these, at times paradoxical, truths that Scripture bears witness; discarding either results in a diminished view of human resilience.

In the 'here and now', then, we can acknowledge that resilience may serve as a useful interpretive category for understanding human responses to adversity, but we must also recognize its limitations and its situatedness within a particular hermeneutical framework. Care should be taken, then, not unnaturally to impose interpretive categories (including 'resilience') upon the Scriptures, but rather to allow the truths of Scripture to 'exegete' its readers, engaging with particular situations in meaningful and relevant ways. In this way, the divine Word may meet human need; divine strength may transform human suffering; ancient texts may inform contemporary application.

Conclusion

The Scriptures may be regarded as a significant repository of resources that can aid in the promotion of resilience. In particular, individuals of faith ought to find the Bible reshaping their visions of human life and flourishing, further eliciting hope that their lives can become places of flourishing amid, not despite, difficulty. In these ways and many more, Scripture prompts its readers to believe that the God of the universe – who still speaks through the Bible – will be to us, as for so many before us, the 'pioneer and perfecter of our faith' (Heb. 12.2).

Notes

1 For example, 1 Cor. 13.12; 1 John 3.2–3.

2 Trends towards greater incidences of maladaptive behaviours and worsened mental health are alarming in their consistency, especially among youth. See, for

example, J. M. Twenge and colleagues, 2019, 'Age, Period, and Cohort Trends in Mood Disorder Indicators and Suicide-related Outcomes in a Nationally Representative Dataset, 2005–2017', *Journal of Abnormal Psychology*, 128, pp. 185–99.

3 Indeed, the Church of England has included resilience in its definition of mental health, also describing resilience as a positive characteristic associated with mental health (The Church of England Archbishops' Council, 2004, *Promoting Mental Health: A Resource for Spiritual and Pastoral Care*. Available at: www. salisbury.anglican.org/resources-library/learning/ministry/lpa-resources/promoting-mental-health-a-resource-for-spirituality-and-pastoral-care, pp. 29, 31). See also C. C. H. Cook and N. H. White, 2018, 'Resilience and the Role of Spirituality', in D. Bhugra and colleagues (eds), *Oxford Textbook of Public Mental Health*, Oxford: Oxford University Press, pp. 513–20; and K. Pargament and J. Cummings, 2010, 'Anchored by Faith: Religion as a Resilience Factor', in J. W. Reich, A. J. Zautra and J. S. Hall (eds), *Handbook of Adult Resilience*, New York: Guilford Press, pp. 193–210.

4 D. E. Alexander, 2013, 'Resilience and Disaster Risk Reduction: An Etymological Journey', *National Hazards and Earth System Science*, 1, pp. 1257–84.

5 In relation to human beings, this reflects a movement away from pathogen-centric models of health (especially mental health) towards a focus on holistic well-being. Cf. A. Antonovsky, 1980, *Health, Stress, and Coping*, San Francisco, CA: Jossey-Bass. This, arguably, is a model of health that is more in line with biblical conceptions of human well-being than a pathogen-centric model that 'parcels out' particular issues rather than seeing a person as a whole in need of salvific healing. Cf. P. S. Fiddes, 2007, 'Salvation', in K. Tanner, J. Webster and I. Torrance (eds), *The Oxford Handbook of Systematic Theology*, Oxford: Oxford University Press. Further, because resilience describes 'bouncing back' to a desired point of health, an understood goal (*telos*) is vital to making sense of the construct. This has significant implications for definitions of 'health' and is critical for understanding resilience since this determines the implicit *telos* of the construct. Cf. A. M. Almedom and D. Glandon, 2007, 'Resilience is Not the Absence of PTSD Any More than Health is the Absence of Disease', *Journal of Loss and Trauma*, 12, pp. 127–43.

6 C. Panter-Brick and J. F. Leckman, 2013, 'Editorial Commentary: Resilience in Child Development – Interconnected Pathways to Well-being', *Journal of Child Psychology and Psychiatry*, 54, p. 335.

7 Panter-Brick and Leckman, 'Editorial Commentary', p. 333.

8 Cook and White, 'Resilience', p. 513. See also G. Windle, 2011, 'What is Resilience? A Review and Concept Analysis', *Review in Clinical Gerontology*, 21, pp. 152–69.

9 B. Amstadter, J. M. Myers and K. S. Kendler, 2014, 'Psychiatric Resilience: Longitudinal Twin Study', *British Journal of Psychiatry*, 205, pp. 275–80.

10 Cook and White, 'Resilience', pp. 513–20; H. G. Koenig, D. E. King and V. B. Carson, 2012, *Handbook of Religion and Health*, 2nd edn, Oxford: Oxford University Press. It must also be noted that religion, in general, and Scripture, more specifically, can be utilized in a negative manner so as to elicit negative outcomes. This is an unfortunate reality, but one that must both be acknowledged and regarded as not being in line with the overall thrust of Christian Scripture.

11 See Collicutt and Kraftchick's respective contributions in N. H. White and C. C. H. Cook (eds), 2020, *Biblical and Theological Visions of Resilience: Pastoral and Clinical Insights*, London: Routledge, for an extensive discussion of the variety of conceptual and linguistic parallels of terminology for resilience within Scripture.

12 R. J. Schreiter, 2016, 'Reading Biblical Texts through the Lens of Resilience', in *Bible through the Lens of Trauma*, Atlanta, GA: SBL, pp. 193–208. See also White and Cook (eds), *Biblical and Theological Visions of Resilience*.

13 For example, Josh. 1.9; Isa. 41.10; Luke 18.1–8; Gal. 6.9; 2 Tim. 1.7; 1 Pet. 2.19.

14 See, for instance, John 15.4; Rom. 15.5; 2 Cor. 3.4–18; Col. 1.28b–29.

15 Cf. Ps. 22; Lamentations; Jer. 20.7–9; 2 Cor. 11.23–33; Phil. 3.12.

16 E.g. Pss. 17; 42—43; 73; 76; 88; 137. See W. Brueggemann, 2001, *Spirituality of the Psalms*, Minneapolis, MN: Fortress Press.

17 Research supports the use of exemplars for promoting resilience (S. M. Southwick and D. S. Charney, 2018, *Resilience: The Science of Mastering Life's Greatest Challenges*, 2nd edn, Cambridge: Cambridge University Press, pp. 158–74).

18 Cf. Job 13.15; 19.25–27; Isa. 53.11.

19 Providing an expansive vision of potential responses to adversity can broaden the vision of what is possible, thereby creating new potentialities for different action where only cycles of dysfunction existed before.

20 As just one example, Psalm 136 repeats the refrain 'His steadfast love endures for ever' because the affirmation of God's unfailing covenantal love is central to Scripture's portrayal of God's character. See also John 3.16; 1 John 4.8.

21 Cf. John 16.33.

22 Cf. P. Ricoeur, 1995, 'Intellectual Autobiography', in L. E. Hahn (ed.), *The Philosophy of Paul Ricoeur, The Library of Living Philosophers* (trans. K. Blamey), Chicago, IL: Open Court Publishing, p. 47.

23 See C. Campbell, K. J. Vanhoozer and M. J. Thate (eds), 2018, *In Christ in Paul: Explorations in Paul's Theology of Union and Participation*, Grand Rapid, MI: Eerdmans.

24 Cf. Heb. 6.17–20; 1 Pet. 1.3–5.

25 J. D. Whitehead and E. E. Whitehead, 2016, *The Virtue of Resilience*, Maryknoll, NY: Orbis Books, p. 3.

26 So also in the earthly ministry of Jesus, who saw his mission as bringing a sword that pierces through shallow claims to temporal peace in order to reveal true flourishing. Cf. Matt. 10.39.

27 Cf. James 1.2–4; 1 Pet. 1.6–7; 4.1, 12.

28 Earthly flourishing and the human resources utilized to achieve it are what Dietrich Bonhoeffer (D. Bonhoeffer, 1993, *Ethics*, London: SCM Press, pp. 110, 118) termed 'penultimate goods', meaning that they are inherently good and worthwhile of being pursued but fall short of the ultimate purpose of humankind. Penultimate and ultimate flourishing, however, are both undergirded by God's sustaining grace (e.g. Col. 1.15–18).

29 J. J. Shuman and K. G. Meador, 2002, *Heal Thyself: Spirituality, Medicine, and the Distortion of Christianity*, Oxford: Oxford University Press.

30 Thus Paul's statement: 'So we do not lose heart. Even though our outward nature is wasting away, our inner nature is being renewed day by day' (2 Cor. 4.16). Note both that Paul considers internal (spiritual) flourishing as central to human flourishing, and that this inward flourishing is dependent upon the continual reception of God's strength (e.g. the present passive indicative 'being renewed' (ἀνακαινοῦται). Cf. John 15; Rom. 8.37; 2 Cor. 12.9–10; Phil. 4.13.

31 For the Christian, this tension is embodied in the reality of the indwelling Christ. Note the implications of the present reality ('Christ in you') for the present

(hope) as well as for the future (glory). These realities are embodied in the person of Christ, though the future fullness of this reality is yet to be unveiled. In this way, the Christian becomes an embodiment of the dialectic of the kingdom of God, holding in herself the reality that unites past, present and future in Christ, yet working out this reality within time by means of the tangible effect of the indwelling Christ – hope.

32 See A. Powell's contribution in White and Cook, *Biblical and Theological Visions of Resilience*.

Conclusion: Towards a Biblical Theology of Mental Health

CHRISTOPHER C. H. COOK

AND ISABELLE HAMLEY

In the introduction to this book we indicated that it was our intention to bring together two worlds. In the one, conversations about mental health take place using the language of science, and people needing help receive this from health professionals. In the other, conversations about sin and human flourishing take place using the language of theology, and people needing help seek this from their priest or pastor. Sometimes conversations are had in the borderlands, where scientists and theologians, health professionals and clergy engage in serious attempts to understand one another, but these are few and far between and are frequently mediated by an academic vocabulary that is unfamiliar to lay people. Often, ordinary pilgrims find themselves wandering in uncharted territory, without any aids to interpretation of the unfamiliar languages and cultures that they encounter in the foreign lands in which they find themselves. If men are from Mars and women are from Venus, then mental health and Christian faith must sometimes seem as though they are in different galaxies.

Despite this alienation of Christian faith and mental health from each other, they do in fact share many concerns in common. Professor Bill Fulford, a psychiatrist and philosopher, even went so far as to suggest in 1996 that, 'Religion and psychiatry occupy the same country, a landscape of meaning, significance, guilt, belief, values, visions, suffering and healing.' Different worlds, different galaxies, but perhaps not so very far away from each other after all?

Narrative

A key device that might enable better mutual understanding within the shared landscape of Christian faith and mental health is that of narrative. As Jocelyn Bryan demonstrated in Chapter 1 of this work, narrative is psychologically important in support of meaning making and personal identity; meaning and identity are – in turn – important to mental well-being. Narrative is an important tool in clinical practice in psychiatry.[1] Enabling people to tell their stories well has healing value in itself, but it is also foundational to the therapeutic relationship that enables the clinician to use the resources of medicine to bring healing. Without narrative, psychology and psychiatry would be deeply impoverished. However, narrative is also important in the Bible and in theology.[2] For Christians the narrative of the life, death and resurrection of Jesus is central to life and faith. Christianity would not exist without this narrative. As Bryan says:

> The narrative of Scripture is not before us to be read or listened to like other stories; rather, it is a story that we are called to perform. It is a story that takes its place deep within us and shapes our own story fed by the living word that satisfies our need for life purpose and identity.

It is therefore not surprising that narrative has re-emerged in successive chapters of the book as an important theme. Centrally, the narratives about Jesus (as in the chapters by Joanna Collicut (Chapter 3) and Christopher Cook (Chapter 11)), but also the theological narrative constructed by Stephen Barton in Chapter 4, the narrative of Job's suffering (Isabelle Hamley), Esther's distress (David Firth), Jeremiah's distress (Jill Firth), and of the trauma experienced by God's people (Megan Warner), all play their part in presenting an account of what mental health might look like within the lives of Jewish and Christian people and their community of faith. In the chapters by John Swinton and Nick Ladd (Chapters 12 and 13), we are able to read fragments of narrative from the lives of Christians living with their own experiences of mental ill health and/ or other challenges to emotional well-being. Finally, in Nathan White's chapter (Chapter 15), we are able to glimpse some of the ways in which the narrative might enable hope and foster resilience.

The Bible is important for mental health – in part because it facilitates the embedding of our narratives within the meta-narrative of faith. It correspondingly embeds the gospel narrative within our individual narratives. Narrative is thus, at the same time, both theologically and psychologically profoundly significant. It is the medium within which Christian mental health may be fostered, understood, and – when wounded – healed. It is for this reason, if no other, that mental health professionals need to listen well to the stories that their clients tell about their faith, and not just the stories that they tell about their illness. Equally, pastors need to be attentive to the dual stories of Scripture and those of parishioners and friends who come to them. There is a tendency, in certain quarters of the Church, to focus on the sayings and teaching of Jesus, and Paul. Soundbites and sound advice. While the more didactic material has its place in shaping the moral imagination of a community of faith, story and narrative open up different possibilities: they offer a place of encounter between reader and text. Narratives are often less tidy, yet the frayed edges of narrative are precisely where those who struggle can find themselves, wrestle or even argue with the text – and the God who reaches out to them within it.

One problem with narratives is that none of us can presume to be the sole narrator. Even with my own story – the story of my life, which I know better than anyone else – I may not be best placed to tell the story well. I am far from objective. My subjectivity as narrator of my own story is both a strength and a weakness. This is why mental health professionals often like to speak to families, from whom they gain additional insights into the strengths and weaknesses of their client. It is why the Bible is important, because it challenges our avoidant, convenient and all too self-flattering (or too self-critical) narratives with the narratives of the Hebrew people and the early Church. Most importantly, our personal narratives are brought into conversation with the Gospel narratives, with the narratives of the life, death and resurrection of Jesus. However, with multiple narrators, the cacophony of voices can become difficult to disentangle. Whose account of the story carries most weight? The doctor's, or the priest's? The patient's, or her husband's? As Christians, we might say that it is God's account that matters most, but we don't have direct access to that in any specific or objective sense. Even the biblical narratives have to be interpreted. Am I depressed because I am guilty, or do I feel guilty because I am depressed? I may be deeply convinced that the former account is the true one, but my psychiatrist may be equally convinced that the latter account is correct. The theologian may well point out that we are all sinful, and thus guilty, so why are we not all depressed?!

If narrative facilitates conversation, it thus also potentially obstructs it, or at least renders it conflictual. Psychiatry has increasingly recognized the importance of not using medical power to suppress the narrative of the patient. Psychiatry therefore seeks (even if it often still fails) to be person centred.[3] Clergy are taught to listen well to those to whom they provide pastoral care, and Nick Ladd emphasizes the importance of this in Chapter 13, but often the urge to 'fix' things over-rides the wise imperative to listen well. There is also a further complexity. The patient or congregant may need to adjust their narrative as a means to recovery; they may need to take on board at least a part of the medical narrative (for example, as to the efficacy of antidepressants) or the biblical narrative (for example, as to the importance of repentance) even if they do not feel fully convinced by it. Equally, one person's interpretation of the narrative of faith may also be distorted in destructive ways. For instance, they may overplay narratives of guilt and rejection in Scripture, and believe themselves to be incapable of being loved by God – despite the wealth of narrative and non-narrative evidence to the offer of divine love throughout Scripture. If the clinical/pastoral encounter is to be therapeutic it cannot simply or uncritically adopt the perspective of the person seeking help. There is a need for at least some negotiation over the narrative.

Relationships

Social psychiatry recognizes the importance of taking into account not just the relationship between patient and doctor (and their respective narratives), but the whole web of social relationships within which a patient is located. Family, friends, workplace, community and the wider cultural/religious context all have a part to play in the full understanding of health and illness. This expanding vista of narratives and relationships within which mental health may be understood to flourish (or fail) brings us to another point of common ground between the worlds of Christian faith and mental health. Over recent decades there has been an increasing trend within psychiatry to recognize that spirituality and/or religious faith are important to mental well-being. While there are still controversies, the body of empirical research evidence in support of this contention is now huge.[4] Mental health is to be understood not only in relation to individual narratives, or social networks, but also in relation to the transcendent. As Gordon McConville articulates in Chapter 2: 'the conditions for human wholeness consist in relationships, between human persons, between humans and the non-human creation, and between humans and God.'

For secular psychiatry this is a real challenge. Psychiatrists are more likely to be atheist or agnostic than are their patients. Psychiatry has a history of antipathy towards religion, which has its origins both in the views of Freud, who saw religion as wish fulfilment, and in a more deterministic view of the human condition derived from behaviourist and materialist scientific paradigms. It now operates within a pluralistic context in which people of all faiths and none seek help, and some would argue that religion is best kept out of the consulting room. However, the transcendent can be articulated in diverse ways, among which the notion of 'God' is certainly the most popular worldwide. Christian theological articulations of the transcendent still have their legacy within the ways of thought of the Western world, and for Christians the revelation of God in Christ is central to understanding the human condition. Human well-being, including mental health, can only be understood in relationship to God. Furthermore, an anthropology based on Scripture drives towards a holistic understanding of the human person, as the chapters by McConville, Barton and Gooder exemplify. There is a unity between body and soul/psyche, so that to be human is to be understood within a nexus of relationships between the embodied self, their social networks, their situation in time and place, the world they inhabit, and the God who breathes life into being. Biblical anthropology suggests that the immanent and the transcendent inherently belong together, and that spiritual, psychological and physical well-being are closely interdependent.

Stephen Barton, in his study of Paul and mental health in Chapter 4, points to an ambiguity of relationship that is fundamental to Christian conceptions of well-being. Within Paul's writings, Barton identifies a 'christological de-centring' of the self that challenges social norms. Individual persons matter deeply to Paul, but not in the way that they do to us in our very individualistic twenty-first-century Western culture. Barton's reading of Paul is deeply relational, but also highly paradoxical. God's wisdom is revealed in the foolishness of the crucifixion, and in human weakness and humility. The Pauline narrative reinterprets emotions such as grief and joy within an apocalyptic context so that 'his sights are set, not on personal advantage in a competition for glory, but on the fulfilment that comes in service of his risen Lord'. This would certainly not be a helpful thing to say to a depressed person, but equally, within this narrative, our conceptions of mental well-being are more or less turned upside-down.

Theological anthropology

Within the web of relationships in which mental health may flourish or flounder, the human being is a complex unity. Drawing on the theological understandings of human unity and wholeness evident within the Hebrew Scriptures, Gordon McConville argues in Chapter 2 against reductive dualisms and affirms the unity of the person – body, mind and spirit – in relationship with God. Both breakdown and recovery of mental well-being are best understood in this context.

Paula Gooder, in Chapter 5 on Paul and the mind of Christ, demonstrates that the vocabulary that we use when reading Paul is deeply problematic. When Paul talks about the 'mind' and when we talk about the mind, we are talking about completely different things. Paul's vocabulary, in many ways, reflects more truly the understanding of the human heart and mind that is found in Hebrew Scripture (as explored by McConville) than it does our dualistic understanding of mind over and against the body. It is also (as already argued by Barton) much less individualistic. However, Gooder also explores the possibility that Paul may (according to our understanding of things) have suffered from depression. In this context, we might read Paul differently. She concludes that 'Paul learns to live with his frailty'. It is in this context – the context of (what we would call) mental suffering – that Christ's power is revealed in him.

Coming from a different angle, in Chapter 5 Nick Ladd stresses the centrality of communal formation in responding to mental health challenges. Biblical anthropology presents human beings as inescapably communal. The story of Israel is the story of a people, and the New Testament relates the story of the formation of a new community of faith. The stories of Jesus' engagement with ill-health almost always include an element of social reintegration. Ladd's chapter draws our attention to the need to think about Scripture therefore shaping not just the narrative and ethos of individual believers, but of the entire faith community, so that their understanding of self and other can yield a better context for flourishing.

Research and clinical practice are just beginning to catch up with these insights as work on spiritually integrated psychotherapies recognizes the value of incorporating biblical texts (such as those drawn by McConville from the psalms) into treatment.[5] However, when it does so, psychotherapy does not show much discrimination in the use of these texts. They are more or less slotted into standard approaches to treatment, such as those offered by cognitive behavioural therapy, regardless of the broader religious traditions from which they originate. Psychology becomes the unifying paradigm. Ladd, in his spiritual practice of 'Dwelling in the Word', offers something coming from the other direction. Here, mental health concerns are (we might say) 'slotted into' spiritual practice. The theological question at stake here is one of perspective. Do we see the human condition in the context of our understanding of God, or do we see God in the context of the human condition? Such questions are not merely academic; they have significant implications for practice.

Strange worlds

The worlds of mental health and Christian faith have something further in common. They both offer a landscape that can seem strange to outsiders. Visions and voices, and ecstatic states – as narrated in the Bible and attested to by religious experience – are deeply significant for those who have had them, but hard to understand for those who haven't.

Christians (and those of other religions) also believe things that are hard (or impossible) to prove according to the usual standards of what is socially accepted as 'true'. Notoriously, Richard Dawkins has argued that such beliefs are delusional, thus equating them with the kinds of false beliefs that arise within the context of major mental disorders such as schizophrenia. Psychiatrists are more cautious, and recognize that there are important differences, but it is actually much harder to distinguish between normal religious beliefs and the delusions of psychosis than most lay people realize.[6]

Getting to the theological and social-scientific heart of the matter, Joanna Collicutt provides in Chapter 3 an in-depth study of Jesus and madness. She points out that the 'odd, the weird, and the strange' are often difficult to interpret. They can be signs of madness, or of religious wisdom. Using insights drawn from anthropology, she distinguishes between behaviour that is culturally sanctioned (including religious behaviour) and that which is not (including 'madness'). As she points out, people with mental health problems (because of the loss of social sanction) suffer loss of the social support and affirmation that would be beneficial to their recovery. Mental well-being and recovery are relational and social concerns. However, she also draws attention to vocabulary. Where some Christians, taking on board the New Testament worldview, might understand demons as the cause of strange behaviour, others might use the medical language of psychosis and its appeal to causes such as disharmonious social relationships or early trauma and abuse. Yet, 'all agree that people are demonized by the largely invisible operation of malign forces' (page 42).

Trauma, suffering and resilience

The case studies in Part 2 of this book illustrate a number of the themes already identified in Part 1. They also all address, in different ways, the universal human struggle with suffering, trauma and pain.

In her study of Job, Isabelle Hamley, taking a narrative approach, demonstrates in Chapter 6 that faith (and the community of faith) and our understandings of God can themselves contribute to distress. Yet, the book of Job legitimizes our theological discourses of distress and, as such, offers an untapped resource for helping people struggling with trauma. Turning to the vocabulary of anxiety in the Old Testament, David Firth argues in Chapter 7 that anxiety does not contradict faith, but rather it provides something to pray about.[7] Anxiety is contextualized by recalling the broader framework (or, we might say, narrative) of life and faith within which 'God has helped'. Walter Brueggemann, in a study of the lament psalms in Chapter 8, generalizes the affirmation of the importance of honesty before God about the realities of our emotional state and our mental goings-on. 'Truth-telling', before God, might be understood as the road to 'well-making' (although, we might note, that for Job this strategy might have felt like it was making things worse before they got better!). Jill Firth, in her study of Jeremiah in Chapter 9, similarly explores the importance of honesty with God about the depth of psychological and spiritual pain in providing the starting point for finding hope. Making links with later Christian tradition, she shows that John of the Cross, Bonhoeffer, Moltmann and others all drew from Jeremiah in their respective theological and spiritual reflections on suffering. Jeremiah offers resources for working with victims of trauma, such as those suffering from the 'moral injury' sometimes associated with post-traumatic stress disorder.

In two case studies that take examples from the teaching and works of Jesus, respectively, Christopher Cook argues in Chapter 10 that mental health was a much more central concern in the life and ministry of Jesus than we usually imagine. Of course, had different passages been chosen, then things might have looked different, but the Sermon on the Mount is hardly an inconsequential example of Jesus' teaching in Matthew's Gospel. All four Gospels raise questions over the sanity of Jesus (as explored by Collicutt in Chapter 3). In the passion narratives, Jesus personally faces trauma and mental anguish of the most horrific kind – thus mental health issues are not peripheral to the gospel of Christ.

While trauma, in its diverse forms, is not the only cause of human suffering, it is a significant one. It is also another common feature of the landscape that is universal to the worlds of Christian faith and mental health. In a chapter focusing specifically on trauma, in Part 3 of the book, Megan Warner demonstrates (Chapter 14) that trauma, and trauma theory, provide a 'lens' for reading biblical texts. This lens shows that the Bible is robust. It arises from the experiences of people who have been traumatized in the most profound ways. It shows us that we are not alone in our experiences of trauma. It provides us with ways of talking about suffering and trauma in the context of our faith, and it models resilience.

Resilience is taken up again by Nathan White in the final chapter of the book, Chapter 15. He proposes that the Bible offers encouragement to perseverance in the face of adversity. It provides testimony to the complexity of trauma, and diverse examples of resilience and recovery from trauma. It offers a vision of hope that places our experiences of adversity within the context of the 'larger narrative of God's salvation history'. It shapes, and reshapes, Christian identity. It challenges simplistic and popular conceptions of human flourishing and resilience, offering a vision of something 'guaranteed by God alone'. In this, it takes us back to the Pauline dynamic (also identified by Barton in Chapter 14) of a 'dialectical tension between the realities of human finitude/frailty and well-being/strength'.

The Bible and mental health

Contributors to this book were all encouraged to think about what the Bible has to say about mental health. As editors, we asked them to focus on different topics, and we expected them to undertake their task in different ways. We hope that you, the reader, will agree with us that they have opened up a vista of possibilities that are largely under-exploited within the Christian Church, let alone in wider society. They have dispelled some important myths, by refusing to see anxiety, depression or suffering as failures of faith, but rather as opportunities for prayer and Christian growth. They have complexified some understandings that are all too easily reduced to over-simplification. The role of the demonic, for example, is not best served either by radical demythologization or resorting to a crude literalism. However, in showing us the value of Christian Scripture for a richer understanding of mental health, they have also set us some challenges.

We are aware that the Bible has much more to say about mental health than we were able to include in this volume. Notably, we did not include a case study on suicide (although we would like to have done this). Depending upon how the counting is done, the Bible includes accounts of somewhere between three and eleven suicides.[8] Pastoral responses to suicide and self-harm have changed considerably over the last century, at least in part as a result of our greater understanding of the mental health issues involved. Nor have we given any detailed attention to anything that the Bible might have to say about child and adolescent mental health, eating disorders, addiction, personality disorders, or the mental health of older people. Some of these topics have already been considered elsewhere, but there is much more to be done.

The Bible is not a feature of Professor Bill Fulford's shared landscape of faith and psychiatry. It firmly belongs within the world of Christian faith and it is not understood, or even widely read, within secular society. As Christopher indicated in the introduction, it is not something that can be brought into the consulting room. Both mental health services and Christian clergy need to be much more imaginative, creative and energetic in attempting to bridge this gulf.

For its part, the Church needs to be much more critical in its use of Scripture in relation to the pastoral care of people facing mental health challenges. Scripture aids us in the struggle of reconciling faith with adversity, trauma and suffering. It does not avoid the struggle. It must therefore be used sensitively and wisely. John Swinton explores this process helpfully in his chapter on the Bible and pastoral care. Reading the Bible can be helpful when we adopt a positive mental health hermeneutic that reads Scripture *with*, and alongside, people who have experienced mental health problems. Swinton states, in Chapter 12:

> A [positive mental health] hermeneutic strives to bring the experience of people living with mental health challenges into critical conversation with the interpretation and usage of Scripture, with a view to more accurately understanding the meaning and the scope of the text and enabling the recipients of our interpretations to live well even in the midst of difficult experiences.

Experiences of mental ill health open up new, and potentially life-giving, interpretations of biblical texts. However, there are also pitfalls. As Swinton argues, there are times when 'reading the Bible might not be wise'. Read within the context of a severe mental disorder such as depression, Scripture can deny hope and even feed suicidal thoughts. Swinton also identifies a hermeneutic of silence, when it is simply not possible to read the Bible. It is interesting that the examples given by Swinton for both hermeneutics – of silence and of suicide – are of depression. Many other mental health disorders may adversely influence biblical interpretation, and some passages are particularly problematic (see, for example, Cook's case study of the Sermon on the Mount in Chapter 10). Equally, Scripture itself opens up a space for grace in our relation to faith in difficult times, whether it is in Job's long silence and struggles, in some of the psalms' expressions of anger and despair (notably Psalm 88), or in Ecclesiastes' contemplation of the futility of life. Allowing the breadth of Scripture to shape the community of faith would enable healthier, more diverse and creative responses to those who struggle.

Ladd's practice of 'Dwelling in the Word' in Chapter 13 offers an imaginative approach to bringing Scripture and mental health together in a local church setting. The group dynamics may well offset some of the potential hermeneutical problems identified by Swinton in Chapter 12. However, one can also imagine circumstances within which they could be quite complex. How would such a group react if one of its members adopted a hermeneutic of suicide? The safeguarding implications of such initiatives are not insignificant.

Towards a biblical theology of mental health

The chapters included in this volume are only a beginning, and we hope that readers will find within them food for further theological thought. We believe that they do, however, demonstrate that Christian faith and mental health are not worlds apart. They share a common landscape, albeit one described very differently according to the worldview adopted. The Bible, seen perhaps by some as being another world apart, actually offers a robust and realistic view of this landscape. It does not employ the medical or scientific language of contemporary mental healthcare, but it does address some of the lacunae of meaning, transcendence and purpose that research shows to be beneficial to mental health. Moreover, it provides the basis for a biblical theology that is realistic about the human condition. This theology should be, we would argue, firmly Christocentric. This does not mean that we do not need to read the Old Testament, but it does mean that we read it in the light of the revelation of God in Jesus. This reading will not always be easy. Job, the psalmist, Jeremiah, and others all grapple with the suffering that is an inescapable feature of the human condition. They are honest with God about their struggles. Paul, and the authors of the canonical Gospels, do not lack either enthusiasm or honesty in their attempts to convey the full height, breadth and depth of what God has done in Christ. They invert our understandings of what mental flourishing really looks like. It is not all about avoiding suffering, or feeling always at peace. As Swinton argues, mental health may well not be best conceived of as a biomedical category at all. It is a theological concept. It is not an end in itself, for the end of the human being is to be found in God. For Christians, mental health is a relational matter; to be explored with God in prayer. It is a vocation to life in the kingdom of God.

Notes

1 C. C. H. Cook, A. Powell and A. Sims (eds), 2016, *Spirituality and Narrative in Psychiatric Practice: Stories of Mind and Soul*, London: Royal College of Psychiatrists.

2 This is explored further in C. C. H. Cook, 2016, 'Narrative in Psychiatry, Theology and Spirituality', in *Spirituality and Narrative in Psychiatric Practice: Stories of Mind and Soul*, C. C. H. Cook, A. Powell and A. Sims (eds), London: Royal College of Psychiatrists, pp. 1–13.

3 Royal College of Psychiatrists, 2018, *Person-centred Care: Implications for Training in Psychiatry*, London: Royal College of Psychiatrists.

4 See, for example, C. C. H. Cook, 2013, 'Controversies on the Place of Spirituality and Religion in Psychiatric Practice', in C. C. H. Cook, *Spirituality, Theology and Mental Health*, London: SCM Press, pp. 1–19; H. G. Koenig, 2018, *Religion and Mental Health: Research and Clinical Applications*, London: Academic Press; R. J. Cullinan and C. C. H. Cook, 2019, 'Spirituality and Mental Health', in L. Zsolnai and B. Flanagan (eds), *The Routledge International Handbook of Spirituality in Society and the Professions*, London: Routledge, pp. 213–22.

5 K. I. Pargament, 2011, *Spiritually Integrated Psychotherapy*, New York: Guilford; H. G. Koenig and colleagues, 2015, 'Religious vs. Conventional Cognitive Behavioral Therapy for Major Depression in Persons with Chronic Medical Illness: A Pilot Randomized Trial', *The Journal of Nervous and Mental Disease*, 203, pp. 243–51.

6 For a helpful, in-depth account of what distinguishes delusional thought, see P. McKenna, 2017, *Delusions: Understanding the Un-understandable*, Cambridge: Cambridge University Press.

7 For a similar argument in relation to New Testament texts on anxiety, and particularly to the teaching of Jesus, see C. C. H. Cook, 2021, 'Worry and Prayer: Some Reflections on the Psychology and Spirituality of Jesus's Teaching on Worry', in R. Re Manning (ed.), *Mutual Enrichment between Psychology and Theology: Essays In Honour of Fraser Watts*, London: Routledge.

8 B. M. Barraclough, 1992, 'The Bible Suicides', *Acta Psychiatrica Scandinavica*, 86, pp. 64–69; H. J. Koch, 2005, 'Suicides and Suicide Ideation in the Bible: An Empirical Survey', *Acta Psychiatrica Scandinavica*, 112(3), pp. 167–72.

Select Bibliography

Ackermann, D. M., 2003, *After the Locusts: Letters from a Landscape of Faith*, Grand Rapids, MI: Eerdmans.

Barraclough, B. M., 1992, 'The Bible Suicides', *Acta Psychiatrica Scandinavica*, 86, pp. 64–9.

Beck, J. R., 2002, *The Psychology of Paul: A Fresh Look at his Life and Teaching*, Grand Rapids, MI: Kregel Academic and Professional.

Billman, K. D. and Migliore, D. L., 1999, *Rachel's Cry: Prayer of Lament and Rebirth of Hope*, Eugene, OR: Wipf & Stock.

Black, D. A., 2012, *Paul Apostle of Weakness*, Eugene, OR: Pickwick Publications.

Boase, E. and Frechette, C. G. (eds), 2016, *Bible through the Lens of Trauma* (Semeia Studies), Atlanta, GA: SBL Press.

Brueggemann, W., 1995, *The Psalms and the Life of Faith*, Minneapolis, MN: Fortress Press.

Brueggemann, W., 1997, *Theology of the Old Testament: Testimony, Dispute, Advocacy*, Minneapolis, MN: Fortress Press.

Brueggemann, W., 2002, *Spirituality of the Psalms*, Minneapolis, MN: Fortress Press.

Brueggemann, W., 2002, 'Meditation upon the Abyss: The Book of Jeremiah,' *Word & World*, 22, pp. 340–50.

Brueggemann, W., 2014 (ed. Brent A. Strawn), *From Whom No Secrets are Hid: Introducing the Psalms*, Louisville, KY: Westminster John Knox Press.

Bryan, J., 2016, *Human Being: Insights from Psychology and the Christian Faith*, London: SCM Press.

Capps, D., 2008, *Jesus the Village Psychiatrist*, Louisville, KY: Westminster John Knox Press.

Carasik, M., 2006, *Theologies of the Mind in Biblical Israel*, Studies in Biblical Literature, 85, New York: Peter Lang.

Carr, D. M., 2014, *Holy Resilience: The Bible's Traumatic Origins*, New Haven, CT: Yale University Press.

Collicutt, J., 2009, *Jesus and the Gospel Women*, London: SPCK.

Collicutt, J., 2012, 'Bringing the Academic Discipline of Psychology to Bear on the Study of the Bible', *The Journal of Theological Studies*, 63(1), pp. 1–48.

Cook, C. C. H., 2006, *Alcohol, Addiction and Christian Ethics*, Cambridge: Cambridge University Press.

Cook, C. C. H., 2012, 'Psychiatry in Scripture: Sacred Texts and Psychopathology', *The Psychiatrist*, 36, pp. 225–9.

Cook, C. C. H., 2013, *Spirituality, Theology and Mental Health: Multidisciplinary Perspectives*, London: SCM Press.

Cook, C. C. H., 2016, 'Narrative in Psychiatry, Theology and Spirituality', in

Spirituality and Narrative in Psychiatric Practice: Stories of Mind and Soul, C. C. H. Cook, A. Powell and A. Sims (eds), London: Royal College of Psychiatrists, pp. 1–13.

Cook, C.C.H. and N. H. White, 2018, 'Resilience and the Role of Spirituality', in D. Bhugra, K. Bhui, S. Wong and S. Gilman (eds), *The Oxford Textbook of Public Mental Health*, Oxford: Oxford University Press, pp. 513–20.

Cook, C. C. H., 2018, *Hearing Voices, Demonic and Divine: Scientific and Theological Perspectives*, London: Routledge.

Cook, C. C. H., 2021, 'Worry and Prayer: Some Reflections on the Psychology and Spirituality of Jesus's Teaching on Worry', in R. Re Manning, *Mutual Enrichment between Psychology and Theology*, London: Routledge.

Cook, C. C. H., 2020, *Christians Hearing Voices: Affirming Experience and Finding Meaning*, London: Jessica Kingsley.

Crenshaw, J. L., 2011, *Reading Job: A Literary and Theological Commentary*, Macon, GA: Smyth & Helwys.

Davies, S. L., 1995, *Jesus the Healer: Possession, Trance, and the Origins of Christianity*, New York: Continuum.

Davis, R. H., 1997, 'Calling a Divine Summons: Biblical and Depth Psychological Perspectives', *Union Seminary Quarterly Review*, 51, pp. 136–7.

Dodd, C. H., 1934, 'The Mind of Paul: A Psychological Approach', *Bulletin of the John Rylands Library* 18, pp. 69–110.

Eisland, N., 1994, *The Disabled God: Towards a Liberatory Theology of Disability*, Nashville, TN: Abingdon.

Gooder, P., 2016, *Body: Biblical Spirituality for the Whole Person*, London: SPCK.

Greene-McCreight, K., 2015, *Darkness Is My Only Companion: A Christian Response to Mental Illness*, Grand Rapids, MI: Brazos Press.

Harris, W., 2013, *Mental Disorders in the Classical World*, Leiden: Brill.

Hastings, S., 2020, *Wrestling With My Thoughts*, Nottingham: IVP.

Hull, J. M., 2001, *In the Beginning there was Darkness: A Blind Person's Conversations with the Bible*, London: SCM Press.

Janzen, J. G., 2009, *At the Scent of Water: The Ground of Hope in the Book of Job*, Grand Rapids, MI: Eerdmans.

Keener, C. S., 2016, *The Mind of the Spirit. Paul's Approach to Transformed Thinking*, Grand Rapids, MI: Baker Academic.

Kille, D. A. and Rollins, W. G. (eds), 2007, *Psychological Insight into the Bible: Texts and Readings*, Grand Rapids, MI: Eerdmans.

Koch, H. J., 2005, 'Suicides and Suicide Ideation in the Bible: An Empirical Survey', *Acta Psychiatrica Scandinavica*, 112(3), pp. 167–72.

Koenig, H. G., D. E. King and V. B. Carson, 2012, *Handbook of Religion and Health*, 2nd edn, Oxford: Oxford University Press.

Lawrence, L., 2018, *Bible and Bedlam: Madness, Sanism, and New Testament Interpretation*, London: T&T Clark.

Lindstrom, F., 1994, *Suffering and Sin: Interpretations of Illness in the Individual Complaint Psalms*, Stockholm: Almqvist and Wiksell.

McGann, D., 1985, *The Journeying Self: The Gospel of Mark through a Jungian Perspective*, New York: Paulist Press.

Meggitt, J., 2007, 'The madness of King Jesus: Why was Jesus Put to Death, but His Followers Were Not?', *Journal for the Study of the New Testament*, 29, pp. 379–413.

Melcher, S. , Parsons, M.C. and Yong, A., 2018, *The Bible and Disability: A Commentary*, London: SCM Press.

Olyan, S. M., 2008, *Disability in the Hebrew Bible: Interpreting Mental and Physical Differences*, Cambridge, MA: Cambridge University Press.

Pennington, J. T., 2017, *The Sermon on the Mount and Human Flourishing*, Grand Rapids, MI: Baker Academic.

Pennington, J. T. and Hackney, C. H., 2016, 'Resourcing a Christian Positive Psychology from the Sermon on the Mount', *The Journal of Positive Psychology*, 12(5), pp. 427–35.

Rollins, W. G., 1999, *Soul and Psyche: The Bible in Psychological Perspective*, Minneapolis, MN: Fortress Press.

Shuman, J. J., and Meador, K. G., 2002, *Heal Thyself: Spirituality, Medicine, and the Distortion of Christianity*, Oxford: Oxford University Press.

Schweitzer, A., 1913 [1948], *The Psychiatric Study of Jesus* (trans. C. J. Joy), Boston, MS: Beacon Press.

Schwerkoske, J. P., Caplan, J. P. and Benford D. M., 2012, 'Self-Mutilation and Biblical Delusions: A Review', *Psychosomatics*, 53, pp. 327–33.

Sharp, C. J., 2015, 'Wrestling the Word: Submission and Resistance as Holy Hermeneutical Acts', *Anglican Theological Review*, 97, pp. 5–18.

Shults, F. L. and Sandage, S. J., 2006, *Transforming Spirituality: Integrating Theology and Psychology*, Grand Rapids, MI: Baker Academic.

Smith, W. J., 2004, 'Soul and Psyche: The Bible in Psychological Perspective', *HTS Teologiese Studies* 60(1 & 2), pp. 431–40.

Southgate, S., Grosch-Miller, C., Ison, H. and Warner, M. (eds), 2020, *Tragedies and Christian Congregations: The Practical Theology of Trauma*, New York: Routledge.

Strawn, B. A. (ed.), 2012, *The Bible and the Pursuit of Happiness*, Oxford: Oxford University Press.

Stuckenbruck, L. T., 2013, 'The Human Being and Demonic Invasion: Therapeutic Models in Ancient Jewish and Christian Texts', in C. C. H. Cook (ed.), *Spirituality, Theology & Mental Health*, London: SCM Press, pp. 94–123.

Swinton, J., 2000, *Resurrecting the Person: Friendship and the Care of People with Mental Health Problems*, Nashville, TN: Abingdon Press.

Swinton, J., 2007, *Raging With Compassion: Pastoral Responses to the Problem of Evil*, Grand Rapids, MI: Eerdmans.

Swinton, J., 2012, *Dementia: Living in the Memories of God*, London: SCM Press.

Swinton, J. (forthcoming), *Finding Jesus in the Storm: Theological Reflections on the Experience of Mental Health Challenges*, Grand Rapids MI: Eerdmans.

Theissen, G., 1983 (trans. J. P. Galvin), *Psychological Aspects of Pauline Theology*, Edinburgh: T&T Clark.

Warner, M., 2020, 'Trauma through the Lens of the Bible', in M. Warner and colleagues (eds), *Tragedies and Christian Congregations: The Practical Theology of Trauma*, London/New York: Routledge, pp. 81–91.

Warner, M. (forthcoming), *Joseph: A Story of Resilience*, London: SPCK.

Watts, F., 2018, 'Theology and Science of Mental Health and Well-Being', *Zygon*, 53(2), pp. 336–55.

Welborn, L. L., 2011, 'Paul and Pain: Paul's Emotional Therapy in 2 Corinthians 1:1–2:13; 7:5–16 in the Context of Ancient Psychagogic Literature', *New Testament Studies*, 57/4, pp. 547–70.

White, N. H. and Cook, C. C. H. (eds), 2020, *Biblical and Theological Visions of Resilience: Pastoral and Clinical Insights*, London: Routledge.

Wilkinson, J., 1998, *The Bible and Healing: A Medical and Theological Commentary*, Grand Rapids, MI: Eerdmans.

Witmer, A., 2012, *Jesus, the Galilean Exorcist: His Exorcisms in Social and Political Context*, London: T&T Clark.

Index of Biblical References

Old Testament

New Testament

Index of Names and Subjects